The Complete Book of Freezer Cooking

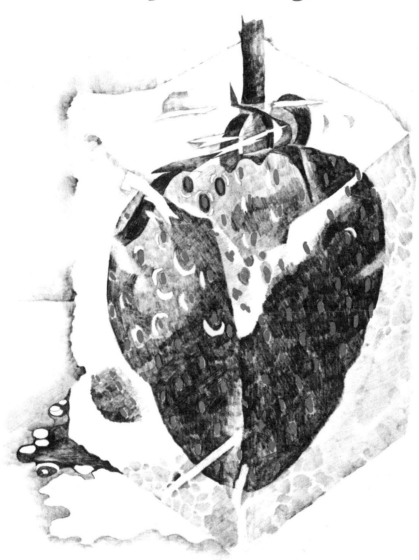

The Complete Book of Freezer Cooking

by Mary Berry

Cathay Books

This edition published 1978 by
Cathay Books
59 Grosvenor Street
London W1

© 1975 Hennerwood Publications Limited

ISBN 0 904644 53 7

Produced by Mandarin Publishers Limited
22a Westlands Road
Quarry Bay, Hong Kong

Printed in Hong Kong

Contents

Owning a freezer

If you enjoy good food but would like to cut down on cooking time and fuel bills, you are, like me, a freezer person! Contrary to popular belief, home freezers are not only for big families in out-of-the-way-places. They are for everyone who wants better food, more conveniently. This is why freezer sales are increasing in the biggest kitchen revolution of our time.

It is a revolution in shopping habits, in menu planning . . . and in increased leisure. You shop now when you want to, when you have the time. There need be no more last-minute trips to buy something you have forgotten in a crowded store, with nowhere to park the car. And it's the same with cooking. You can cook when *you* are in the mood to do it.

If you are the mother of a young family, you can have a grand cook-in and stock up for the school holiday invasion, or just make an extra portion or two during normal cooking of favourite dishes, to be frozen and used when needed. You can bake and freeze a month's supply of cakes and scones in one afternoon. You can be prepared for impromptu picnics with ready-cut sandwiches and other portable foods stored in the freezer.

The men of your family, if they are left on their own, can reach into the freezer to find a dish to reheat — and eat as well as if you were there at home cooking for them. That means you'll have more freedom to pursue your own interests, whether they be art classes, visits to the seaside or a game of badminton one evening a week.

If you're a busy career woman, living on your own, a freezer is for you, too, because your time is precious and you don't want to spend it fighting your way round busy shops during your lunch hour or after work. And you can eliminate the boredom of eating the same thing two or three days running, of finishing up a dish just because it is there. On the contrary, it is worthwhile making, say, a goulash or a curry in larger quantities than you need and leaving one or two portions in the freezer to eat later in the month.

If you do a lot of entertaining, the freezer will ensure you enjoy it. You will have more time to spend with your guests and less to do in the kitchen; you will have a stock of ready-prepared dishes and a supply of sauces, herbs and flavourings, so that you need never be taken by surprise when guests turn up unexpectedly — whether they are old friends who drop in unannounced for a meal, business acquaintances of your husband, or a crowd of hungry children brought home by your youngsters after school.

Those of you who live in the country will want to freeze the fruit and vegetables from your own gardens when these are at their best; town dwellers can make expeditions to buy produce in bulk when it is at its cheapest and freshest.

There are benefits for older people, too. You can make fewer visits to the shops — no need to go out when the weather is bad — and you can save money, which is very important when you are living on a fixed income.

A word about money saving: this is where bulk buying comes in. By sensible planning and buying the same commodities as you did before but in greater quantities at a time, you can save from 10 to 25 per cent on retail prices. Also, buying foods in season when prices are lower and taking advantage of special offers cuts down expenditure.

Even if you actively dislike cooking, there are all sorts of gourmet foods that can be bought and stored in the freezer, then cooked in half an hour or so.

Then there are the special treats that cost less. Fresh raspberries at Christmas used to be the prerogative of millionaires. Now you don't have to have them flown in by special plane; you can have them from your own freezer at any time of year.

— What type of freezer —

Principles of freezing

Freezing, that is reducing food to a temperature at which bacteria become inactive, is the simplest and most natural method of preserving food. It is the one that most closely maintains the quality and texture and keeps food closest to its original state.

Freezing food has been known since the 18th century when 'ice houses' were built in the grounds of country houses. Natural ice, collected in winter from a lake or river, was stored here and used later for preserving food in the kitchen. The discovery of mechanical refrigeration made ice available all the year round. Thus the first refrigerators were born and the whole thing started from there.

It is important to understand just what is meant by food freezing. Food is frozen either commercially or domestically at very low temperatures. The major component of most foods is water. If the food is frozen quickly, the water content forms small crystals which do not damage the cell walls. Slower freezing means larger crystals, which can impair the quality and the structure of the food. Therefore, one of the main essentials of successful freezing is speed. And just as there are degrees of heat in cooking, so there are degrees of cold in freezing.

It is also important to understand the difference between a refrigerator, a frozen food storage compartment and a food freezer. They are not interchangeable. A refrigerator keeps perishable foods fresh, clean and safe for relatively short periods and, in the frozen food storage compartment, stores frozen food bought from a shop.

A food freezer freezes and preserves for long periods fresh produce and foods prepared and cooked at home. It will, of course, also store bought food for periods up to one year, depending on the type of food. But to perform its main function, that is to bring a specified quantity of food in 24 hours to a temperature of $-18°C$, $0°F$, without reducing the quality of the food already stored, the temperature must be capable of being reduced considerably below $-18°C$, $0°F$ for a certain period. This is what distinguishes the freezer from the ordinary food storage compartment.

The amount of food which can be frozen at a time, usually in 24 hours, in each cabinet without lowering the quality of that already frozen is shown on the rating plate and in the manufacturer's instructions.

Freezers have a dial which can be set to give lower temperatures; there is also a fast-freezing switch. These are operated to give internal temperatures in the range of $-24°C$ to $-30°C$, $-12°F$ to $-22°F$.

The manufacturer's instruction book will always give details of control settings on your particular model, and suppliers will also be able to advise you. Different systems do apply internationally. In North America there is no standard distinguishing symbol for food freezers. In Britain a special symbol — a large six-pointed star in a rectangular frame — is used together with the three star symbol (used to indicate the length of time food can be kept in a frozen food storage compartment: one star *, one week; 2 stars ** one month; 3 stars ***, up to 3 months) to distinguish between those appliances designed for the storage of frozen foods and those designed to freeze as well as store.

Choosing your freezer

There is a wide range of freezers available today and the one you pick is, of course, up to you, but do buy one by a well-known manufacturer and do go to an electricity board or reputable dealer who can offer an efficient after-sales service. This is important. Freezers do not often go wrong, but when they do you need help quickly if the food inside is not to be spoiled.

What size do you need? Sizes range from a capacity of about 113 litres (4 cubic feet) up to about 566 litres (20 cubic feet). Makers used to recommend about 57 litres (2 cubic feet) per person in the family. This figure has now been revised upwards to 85 or even 113 litres(3 or 4 cubic feet) per person. It is probably safe to say that you need a bigger freezer than you think, so buy the biggest that you have room for and that you can afford.

This is not an extravagance. A lot of new freezer owners have told me that if only they had realised its possibilities they would have bought a bigger freezer to start with and that they would have considered the money well spent.

There are three basic types to choose from: the chest, the upright and the combined refrigerator-freezer. Each has its own characteristics and advantages and much will depend on the space available and where the freezer is to be kept. A tiny kitchen, for example, is obviously not the place for a large chest type cabinet, but a tall, narrow refrigerator-freezer could fit in very well.

Upright type: this has a front-opening door, adjustable shelves and often provision for storage of small items in compartments on the inside of the door. Packing of food and selection of packages is much easier than with the chest type and it occupies a much smaller floor space — particularly important if it is to be installed in the kitchen. When the door is opened some cold air, being heavier than the surrounding air, escapes, but this does not greatly affect the temperature of the air inside, although slightly more frequent defrosting is needed with the upright model. Do not open the door any more often than you have to, and do not leave it open. Many of the larger uprights are fitted with two doors which reduces the loss of cold air.

Some small upright models are designed to stand on top of a refrigerator, and some have a top which makes a useful work surface.

Chest type: this has the maximum storage space per cubic foot; it makes for easy storage of large and awkwardly-shaped packages; it also occupies the greatest floor space. If it is too big for your kitchen, consider putting it in the garage, or an outhouse, or in a well-ventilated dry pantry that could accommodate it.

The chest type has a top-opening lid and it is marginally cheaper to buy than the upright. The coldest part is at the bottom and as cold air falls and warm air rises there is slightly smaller loss of cold when the lid is opened. If you are keeping the chest in the garage, buy a freezer with its own light, or keep a torch — flashlight — always handy. A lock is useful when you are keeping valuable contents outside the house. And do make sure that you can reach right down to the bottom of the cabinet — packing and cleaning can be difficult if you are small.

Removable baskets or trays are usually supplied, to make packing and selection of food easier. It must be said that access to packages in the depths of a chest is not as easy as it is in an upright model.

Refrigerator-freezer: this is ideal where kitchen floor space is at a premium. It is a combination of an upright freezer and a refrigerator, usually of about the same cubic capacity. The two are housed in the same cabinet, with two doors, usually with the freezer underneath. Big advantages here are that you have freezer and refrigerator occupying no more floor space than did your old fridge, and that you have your chilled and your frozen foods stored in one place — a big saving in time and effort when you are busy.

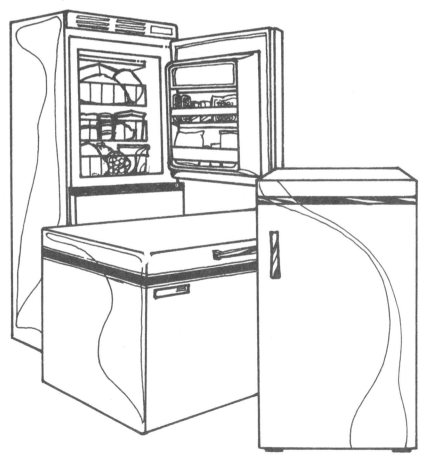

A meal packaged ready for freezing
(right) The same meal, ready for serving

—Where to put your freezer—

There is, as we have seen, not always much choice about this. A big chest freezer won't go into a small kitchen. But it might live very happily in the garage — although this does not make it very accessible. On the other hand, a warm kitchen, convenient as it may be, is not always the best place for your freezer; a pantry, or even a corridor, might be better. Of course, there are no hard and fast rules, and the layout of most houses effectively dictates the position. So let us say that any cool, well-ventilated, dry place will bring good performance and low running costs. You can, indeed, put your freezer anywhere that suits you where there is an earthed electrical outlet.

Finally, do take care that the mains switch is not accidentally turned off — you can cover it with adhesive tape as an extra precaution. And remember that with a freezer in the house you do not switch off the electricity supply when you go on holiday.

—Running costs—

These can be calculated approximately by allowing between one and a half and two units of electricity for each 28 litres (one cubic foot) capacity per week. There is little difference in cost for the three types of freezer, although the upright tends to cost a little more as a certain amount of cold air drops out every time the door is opened. Actual running expense depends much more on the situation of the freezer (preferably not next to the hot water boiler in the kitchen, for example), the number of batches of food put in for freezing, and the number of times the door is opened.

—How to look after your freezer—

Freezers are available in a variety of finishes as well as white and you can have one to suit your kitchen colour scheme. Keep the outside clean and shining by wiping it down regularly; an occasional polish with white furniture cream will keep it looking as good as new.

The first thing to do with a new freezer is to wash out the inside with warm (not hot) water and dry it thoroughly before switching on. Check with the instruction book and make sure that the temperature control is properly set and that you understand fully the system of controls and warning lights. (There is nothing difficult about these; they are arranged for your convenience.) Leave the freezer closed and running for at least 12 hours before putting in any food.

Defrosting
This is necessary when a certain amount of frost or ice has formed on interior walls and shelves. Here again, consult the manufacturer's instructions.

With an upright model defrosting should not be necessary more than twice a year, and with a chest type once. If the build-up of frost is making defrosting necessary more often than this, check that the magnetic seal on the door is working properly. Some freezers now have an automatic defrosting device, which is particularly useful in the case of upright models, but as yet this is expensive. In any case, I find defrosting a good opportunity for removing all the packs from the cabinet, if only to sort them out.

Incidentally, one friend of mine, who has a chest-type freezer, when defrosting puts into one basket all the foods that ought to be used up in the next month. When she opens the freezer she can see them at a glance and nothing is overlooked. I recommend this idea. It does away with worrying about that odd pair of pig's trotters you know you have somewhere in the cabinet, but haven't seen for a long time.

It is wise to arrange to do your defrosting at a time when the freezer's contents are low — after the children have gone back to school at the end of the holidays, perhaps, or when one year's supply of home-grown produce has been used up and the next is almost ready to be harvested.

Switch off the freezer and make sure it is disconnected from the power supply, then remove all the food. This must be well protected. Small items can go temporarily into the refrigerator. For the rest, pack the parcels together into as solid and compact a block as possible, putting ice cream in the centre, and wrap the whole lot in aluminium foil or in five or six sheets of newspaper. Finally, wrap a blanket — which perfectionists will have already chilled in the freezer — around everything and leave in a cool place. Protected like this the food will retain its quality for at least two hours.

As soon as the freezer is empty put bowls or buckets of very hot water inside and shut the lid or door. Leave for 15 minutes. This loosens the ice. Then with a plastic scraper start removing the ice from the walls and the shelves of the freezer. Never use metal which would damage the interior of the cabinet. Put in a plastic tray to catch the drips if you have an upright freezer. Use a dustpan to scoop up the ice from the bottom of a chest freezer.

When the cabinet is clear of ice and frost, wipe out the interior with a solution of 1 tablespoon bicarbonate of soda dissolved in a quart of hot water. Then dry really thoroughly with an absorbent cloth. Close the lid or door and switch on again, to fast freeze. You can either replace the food at once or leave the freezer running empty for an hour. In any case, the whole operation should not take more than two hours altogether.

Emergencies

These won't seem so bad if you are ready for them. Have the name, address and telephone number of the maintenance engineer ready where you can lay hands on them immediately; you will then be less inclined to panic if the freezer suddenly stops working. Here I should emphasise that freezers are extraordinarily reliable pieces of

Open freeze small whole fish suspended from inverted freezer basket
(right) Cook's aids, see page 33

equipment – but something can go wrong, and it is better to be prepared.

If the freezer should suddenly and mysteriously stop working, don't assume the worst. Check first of all that it has not been accidentally switched off. Then check the plug; a replacement of the fuse may be all that is needed. If things are more serious than this and you have to call the maintenance engineer, while you are waiting for him to arrive, resist the temptation to open the door or lid and look at the contents of the freezer.

There are various estimates of the length of time food will remain frozen in a fully-loaded freezer. This ranges from 12 to 24 hours, depending on outside temperature and on whether or not the door or lid has been opened. Unhappily, today the possibility of power cuts cannot be overlooked. But so far the electricity authorities have managed to arrange that these seldom last more than about three hours at a time, not long enough to have any adverse effect on a store of frozen food.

A word about moving house. It is only wise to reduce the contents of the freezer before you move. Assuming that your move takes place in one day, arrange with the removal men that the freezer is the last item to be disconnected and taken out of the old house, and the first to be unloaded and installed in the new (detail someone to have the responsibility for switching it on at the first possible opportunity – you have, naturally, already checked that the plug will fit).

However, if the move is to occupy more than one day and you cannot conveniently arrange for the food to be stored, then it is best to use it up before you move, and give away the rest. Or you could, perhaps, sell the freezer along with the house, and buy a bigger one for the new.

How to insure your freezer

Most manufacturers give a one year guarantee on a new freezer. This covers its mechanical and refrigerating operation, but not the contents. Also your existing household policy may well cover you for all likely kinds of damage to the freezer itself – but, again, not the contents. You need special insurance to protect you against damage to or deterioration of food because the freezer is not working, for whatever reason.

A chest freezer kept in a garage might be damaged if someone accidentally backed the car into it and your household policy should cover you for this, and probably for the actual damage to the food inside. But it would not cover subsequent deterioration of the food while the freezer was not working. Nor is it likely that the ordinary household policy would cover deterioration of food caused by a power cut or other electricity failure.

Special insurance to cover such eventualities as these can be added to your household policy or it can be a separate negotiation. Your insurance broker can arrange it for you. This cover is for unavoidable accidents such as mechanical failure and power cuts not due to industrial action (power failure caused by strikes is not usually covered). And remember that the policy will not cover accidents such as forgetting to plug in the freezer.

There are block insurance schemes operated by insurance companies in conjunction with selected stores and other approved retailers. This means that when you buy you may be offered a package deal of freezer and insurance together.

Obviously, as freezers grow older, claims are likely to increase and the premium you are asked to pay may well depend on the age of your appliance and whether it is still under maker's guarantee or warranty.

You have bought an expensive piece of equipment; you have spent precious time and money stocking it with food. So the proportionately small extra amount a year to protect your investment is well worthwhile. The time to make inquiries and decide on your insurance policy is when you buy your freezer.

Stocking the freezer

There it is, that expensive piece of equipment standing in your kitchen. You know how it works, how to look after it, how to switch it on. You have even put a packet of frozen food inside it for luck.

The question now is — how do you make it earn its keep? There are three returns that the new freezer owner can expect from the investment: to save money, to live better and to have time to enjoy life. The big savings that you can hope to make lie in growing your own produce for freezing, and in buying carefully and wisely, often in bulk. I shall come to these in a minute.

The first thing that probably strikes you is that there is an awful lot of space to fill. This feeling doesn't last long. Once you have started building up a store of your family's favourite foods, when you have discovered the pleasure and practicality of cooking for your freezer, and when you have begun to plan your vegetable garden with a view to freezing next year's harvest, then you are well on your way and your days have taken on a new dimension.

But don't be a slave to your freezer. It is there to serve you, not the other way round. So fill it with foods that you and your family enjoy. They may be conservative in their likes and dislikes; introduce them gradually to a wider variety of food. Try out some of the dishes you have enjoyed abroad. Cook in quantity and divide and freeze the food in meal-sized portions. Use some now; keep the rest for another time. Save time and money by making one ingredient serve for a number of different dishes. Minced (ground) beef, for instance, is relatively inexpensive and it can become the basis of many dishes — a meatloaf, savoury meatballs, a spiced beef mixture, fillings for pasties and pies and for vegetables like peppers and tomatoes. You will freeze food cooked and uncooked. Stews and casseroles and other 'made-up' dishes can be cooked in bulk, frozen in individual or family-meal containers, to be thawed and heated as required, with the minimum of trouble. A supply of basic sauce, white or brown, will be ready when needed to be flavoured for the particular recipes you are using. You will also have different kinds of sauce available in small containers.

Uncooked food — meat, fish and poultry — will be there as you want it. Ice cream and desserts of all kinds are ready for eating. You need never be short of bread. A sliced loaf can be frozen and the bread toasted straight from the freezer. All kinds of rolls, scones and cakes freeze well.

Having explored these possibilities, you will soon want to go on to something even more exciting — producing your own raw materials from the garden.

⸻ Growing for your freezer ⸻

This aspect of freezing — preserving the fruit and vegetables you have grown in your own garden — is the one above all that seems to give the greatest pleasure. New freezer owners have told me of the enormous satisfaction they have got from the first batch that goes into the cabinet of their own runner (string) beans, their own apples.

It is surely not too fanciful to say that the freezer has become the modern equivalent of the old-fashioned kitchen with its ropes of onions, its whole smoked hams hanging from the ceiling, its shelves filled with jars of home-made preserves, pickles and chutneys. With the freezer today we can recapture something of that feeling of plenty.

If you have no garden, you can still share something of this very real pleasure. In towns there are markets where fresh country produce can be bought — and buying it in season means buying it as cheaply as possible. Fruit and vegetable growers on farms and market gardens are glad in these days when labour is hard to come by, to let visitors driving out from towns at weekends to pick their own produce, pay for it on the spot and take it home with them. In summer there are plenty of fruit and vegetable stalls at the roadside to tempt motorists.

But let us assume for the moment that you have your own garden, however small. It is always possible to find room for some vegetables — a row of Brussels sprouts among the gladioli, a planting of sweetcorn among the sweet peas.

When you are growing your own vegetables and fruit for freezing, planning is essential. You should know the time to plant and the time to pick. And you don't want to find that, through lack of forethought, you have not enough space in your freezer to accommodate the glut of your favourite vegetable that is just asking to be picked. So think ahead.

Vegetables can soon lose their pristine quality, so be prepared to pick them young for freezing. Until you have enjoyed tiny new carrots, little sweet turnips, new broad (lima) beans straight from the garden, you don't know what flavour is. Try them and be glad that now you can enjoy them all the year round.

What should you grow? The average garden is small, so devote your space to varieties which are easy to grow and which crop abundantly. Take the advice of your nursery or garden centre who will recommend something suitable.

Pick fruit just before or when fully ripe. Discard any fruit that is damaged or over-ripe. Sort out firm unblemished fruit for freezing. The remainder can be cooked and eaten at once, or it can be puréed and frozen.

⸻ Buying for your freezer ⸻

One of the first things the new freezer owner discovers is that she must change her shopping habits. Today housewives who seldom bought further ahead than the meal after next are filling their freezers with enough food to keep their families eating happily for a month. You may at first miss your daily visit to the shops, but when you realise the scope that your freezer gives you for planning in advance, for thinking big, you will soon begin to enjoy the game of large scale shopping.

One of the objects of bulk buying is to save money. You won't save much if you fill your freezer with an indiscriminate collection of foods your family does not enjoy and which do not fit in with your way of life. No one can lay down hard and fast rules for you, but it is obvious that, for instance, the family which likes to eat a lot of meat will want to devote much of its freezer space to carcass meat. The grow-your-own addict will concentrate on freezing fresh produce, both fruit and vegetables, and the country dweller will also bulk buy fish and the more interesting items of food not available in the local shop. The working mother and mothers of large families will prefer to concentrate on prepared dishes because of their convenience.

The object of bulk buying is to obtain goods at a reduced rate because you have bought them in quantity, because they are economically packed without too much outlay on wrappings, expensive printing of labels and on labour costs. Distribution costs, which are high on small units, have been lowered and in return you accept the loss of some of the refinements of individual shopping, such as personal service, delivery, credit accounts.

Where to buy

Shop around and decide what method of buying suits you best. Decide whether it suits you to bring home your own goods from a freezer centre, or whether, where possible, you prefer to have them delivered. Study the brochures of different suppliers and compare prices. Also compare their prices with those for the same amount of food bought in small quantities at frequent intervals. You may not have noticed how much prices varied from one retailer to another, but when you are buying 5 to 10 kg. (10 to 20 lb.) of food at a time, you will see how those odd pennies mount up.

Quality is important. It is not necessarily an economy to buy, say, poor quality frozen peas which you do not enjoy. It is usually worth paying a little more to get the best. Discover which suppliers specialise in the type of food you want. Keep an eye on your local supermarket for the bargains of the week.

Butcher: a bulk purchase of meat is one of the most important and the most expensive freezer investments you are likely to make. You can buy a whole, half or quarter carcass and have the butcher cut it to your own requirements, or you can buy packs of beef, lamb or pork made up by the butcher. Do remember that, in both cases, you will have to accept some cuts of meat which are always cheaper — stewing beef, breast of lamb, belly of pork. Some of these may cause problems if yours is a family that likes only roasts or grills (broils), but all are excellent and make delicious dishes — so look out for appropriate recipes. With only 1½ kg. (about 3 lb.) of fillet steak in up to 150 kg. (300 lb.) of beef, steak must obviously be an expensive buy at any time, and in these days almost prohibitive.

It is wise, therefore, to consider whether you have a use for offal (variety meats) and the cheaper cuts, which take longer to prepare and are not always convenient for the housewife with a job, or whether you would do better to buy better cuts prepared by a specialist butcher and use them for gala meals. Some firms will supply mixed packs of meat to the customer's choice.

So while bulk buying of meat can make real savings, perhaps more than in the case of other commodities, you are not saving so much unless you are buying meat that you can use to best advantage — and enjoy using it.

Freezer Centres: the best and biggest of these offer an outstanding service — from buying your freezer and insuring it, to a budget account for your purchases of frozen food and free advice from their own home economists. These multiple firms have branches all over the country and are expanding as home freezing increases in popularity. If there is one within driving distance of your home and if you have your own transport, it is well worth patronising. They usually make a point of providing good parking facilities for customers.

The good freezer centre specialising in foods for the freezer offer a bewildering variety, set out in display cabinets, from which you fill your trolley. Goods are then packed in an insulated container or sack to keep the food cold until you get it home. Some centres supply containers; in others you bring your own. Insulated boxes made of expanded polystyrene can be purchased, or you can make yours by lining a cardboard box with polystyrene offcuts.

Freezer centres cut down on the price of their goods by employing the minimum of staff necessary to run them, so do not buy more than you can transport yourself; there may be no one to carry purchases to your car.

One final point: check the loading line on display freezers and make sure goods are packed below that line.

Home delivery service: go to a home freezer specialist in your area, one with a well-established local trade and a quick turnover, so that you can be sure of getting food that has been in store for the minimum time. Choose a supplier who really understands frozen food and home freezing and who is willing to discuss your problems with you. But do not become involved in any schemes which tie you to one particular supplier; you must be free to buy where you choose.

Home-delivered food probably costs a little more than that from the freezer centre. The supplier must charge something to make his delivery service pay. The convenience to you may well be worth the extra price.

Some firms in this category specialise in particular lines — seafood, perhaps, game, or gourmet dishes. This is the top end of the market where you will be paying more money for quality foods by firms who are household names, rather than buying huge packs at big savings. There is room for both in anybody's freezer.

When you first order from your supplier, make sure that your purchases will be delivered in a refrigerated van, so that if you are at the end of the delivery round your goods will arrive in the same condition as if you were at the beginning. Make a note of the day and time when the delivery will be made and clear an appropriate space in the freezer. There should be no time wasted in receiving the goods and packing them in.

Above all, be there when the van arrives. Delivery rounds are carefully timed and costed and the price of petrol (gasoline) these days allows no scope for return visits.

If delivery is free, it is better to get into the habit of giving a small order monthly rather than a larger one quarterly. In this way the contents of the freezer are turned over more frequently. And with regular deliveries you can keep a closer check on what you have in store.

Supermarket: look out for the so-called loss leaders. These are items offered at reduced prices and they are usually changed every week. They are good buys and the freezer owner is in a position to take full advantage of them. Best value is often in the meat and poultry departments where there are sometimes spectacular price reductions over a short period. You won't miss them; they will be well-advertised in the windows of the supermarket — after all, the object is to attract customers. The supermarket is also good for large freezer packs of frozen food.
Market stalls: these can be useful for fresh fruit and vegetables, sometimes for poultry and dairy produce. Do be sure that fruit and vegetables are really young and fresh and worth freezing.

What to buy

The variety of commercially frozen products is now enormous, and new ones are coming on the market all the time. Here is a general guide to purchases you can make.

Meat and poultry: meat comes in packs of selected cuts, or as portions of steaks, chops and so on. Minced (ground) beef, steak and kidney and diced beef are available in ½ kg. (1 lb.) bags. Pork (link) sausages, skinned and skinless, come as chipolatas or full size. Hamburgers are a considerable saving in packs of 24.

There is a huge choice of prepared meat and poultry dishes, ranging from meat pies to boeuf stroganoff and duck à l'orange. These may be expensive, but they are quick to serve and it may be that time is more important than money when you are entertaining. There are chickens, whole or in pieces; there are turkeys large and small. Duck and game can be enjoyed throughout the year.

You will find, at a very economical price, packs of raw or cooked meat for your dog or cat, too.

Vegetables: buy them in free-flow packs so that you can remove the quantity you want and return the rest of the pack to the freezer. Peas, beans and Brussels sprouts are the standbys, but think, too, of sweetcorn, asparagus and broccoli. Think of tiny onions, mushrooms, ratatouille, green and red sweet peppers, and the more and more exciting mixtures of vegetables that can be bought.

Fruit: Many fruits are obtainable in free-flow packs of ½ kg., 1 kg. and 2½ kg. (1 lb., 2 lb. and 5 lb.). Fruit salad and melon balls are usually sold packed in syrup in 1 kg. (2 lb.) bags. You can also buy apples, peaches and pineapple slices. Concentrated orange and grapefruit juices are an excellent buy; they have all the flavour and goodness of the fresh fruit.

Fish: almost every kind can be bought frozen. You can have cod, haddock, kippers, sole, trout, salmon; you can have fish smoked, or in breadcrumbs or batter ready for frying; and you can have ready-prepared dishes from fish fingers to sole mornay. Shellfish — lobster, crab, scallops, prawns and shrimps — is available in all its forms, and not at an unreasonable cost.

Dairy produce: In the United States frozen dairy product is sold as a cream substitute to be used in emergencies. Where this is unavailable, the best kinds of cream to buy are whipping cream and clotted cream. It is essential to thaw the whipping cream in the refrigerator for one or two days before whipping straight from the fridge with a whisk or rotary or electric beater. (If the cream is not cold when whisked you get no volume and in the end it separates!) Clotted cream is delicious — thaw it in the refrigerator for eight hours before serving. Storage time is three months.

Ice cream in all sorts of flavours is available in the ordinary retail packs or in half or 1 gallon packs. It should keep for up to three months in the freezer. Mousses, strawberry, chocolate or lemon, are popular in family or individual sizes. Yogurt is now becoming available in most of the popular flavours. Dairy cream products, such as cream sandwich cakes, thaw quickly and are a useful standby, especially as the basis of party dishes. You can buy chocolate eclairs filled with dairy cream individually wrapped in boxes of 36, and trifles in small or large sizes.

Pastry: both shortcrust and puff pastry is available in 200 g., 350 g. and 1½ kg. (7½ oz., 13½ oz. and 3 lb.) blocks, ready to thaw, roll out and bake. Vol-au-vent cases are frozen, ready to use. And there are ready-to-bake sausage rolls, meat, poultry and fruit pies, and puddings.

Cakes: you can buy frozen Danish pastries which need only to be thawed. Sponge cakes of various sizes, usually filled with dairy cream, are well worth storing for unexpected guests.

This is a brief list of the more usual frozen foods. New varieties are appearing all the time. Keep looking out for them. Stocking your freezer is a fascinating game.

The freezer at work

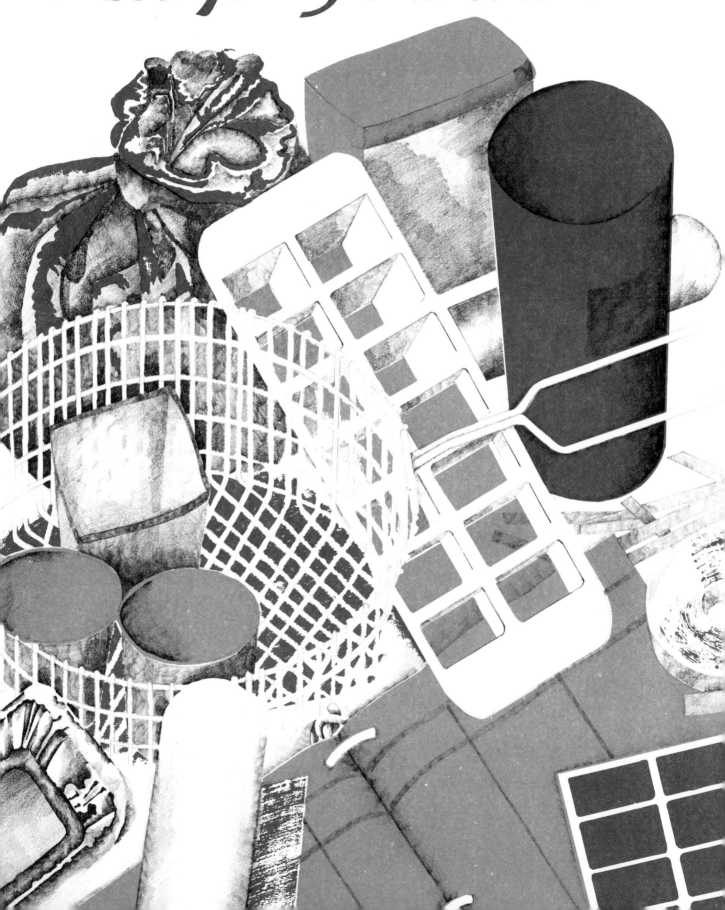

The really efficient freezer owner should know what her freezer contains at all times. That statement is easy to make, but extremely difficult to live up to. In chest freezers in particular, small items have a habit of dropping to the bottom of the cabinet where they remain, out of sight and out of mind, until the next defrosting time comes round. If you are not very careful, some food may have dried out so much that it becomes inedible.

Proper organisation is the only way to overcome this. No doubt, you will evolve your own method, but if it is any help here is my own scheme which, after a great deal of trial and error, seems to me as nearly perfect as I can make it.

The secret lies in colour-coding. Red is meat; blue is fish; yellow is fruit; green is vegetables; and black is prepared dishes. Whatever item I am freezing, each one is put into the most suitable packaging and placed in a large polythene or string bag of the appropriate colour. At the same time it is entered in my record book, where I keep all the details which will be of help to me later on. As long as I keep my record book up to date, I can tell at once what my freezer contains and take steps to correct the imbalance of foodstuffs which is bound to occur.

As well as coloured bags, I also use cardboard boxes — the kind that contained canned foods. These boxes fit the floor of the freezer and are fitted with string handles so that they can be removed easily. Bulky items, identified by their coloured bags, fit into the boxes. Smaller items, and packs which are used most often, also colour-coded, go into the freezer baskets at the top. A layer of newspaper on the freezer floor catches the frost that has been scraped off the walls. Coloured labels and twist ties, used with transparent polythene bags or on rigid cartons, are a further aid to instant identification. Chinagraph pencils, which will write directly on polythene bags or boxes and will wash off later, are another handy means of labelling the contents of a freezer.

—Packaging—

You might wonder why it is necessary to bother with packaging some items, since wrapping them only adds to their bulk and the amount of storage room they take up. The answer lies in the principle of freezing.

Water within the cell structure of the food is converted into ice and must remain in this state. Without a suitable covering, from which as much air as possible has been extracted, the food will draw moisture from other foods or from the freezer and may eventually become dehydrated and lose some of its nutritional value. The longer food is kept in the freezer the more likelihood there is of this happening, which is why there is a recommended storage time for each item. In cases of careless packaging freezer burn can occur, especially on meat, fish or poultry, which causes the surface to become dry and tough and is indicated by the appearance of greyish-white marks. Packaging is also necessary to prevent strongly flavoured food from affecting other foods with its taste or smell. So, however tedious it may be, proper packaging is a chore you cannot escape.

There are, of course, many different kinds of packaging, not all of which are available in every country. Most people tend to settle for two or three types and it is for you to decide which ones you like best, of the types available to you.

Aluminium foil: the thicker the better is the general rule and heavy-duty freezer foil is the most suitable. If thin foil is used it must be doubled so that it will not tear when packets are being moved about in the freezer. Foil should also be doubled over when used for lids or for lining casserole dishes or for protecting sharp bones on meat and poultry.

Foil bags: these are suitable for liquids or for foods containing liquid, like stews. They are expensive, but can, with care, be washed and used again.

Foil dishes and plates: handy for pies, flans, etc. Once frozen, the contents should be covered and sealed. Their advantage is that they can be used to heat the food without removing it from its container.

Freezer tape: a special adhesive tape which is unaffected by frost, this is like the masking tape used by decorators and is an efficient means of sealing a package.

Polythene bags or heavy-duty plastic bags: without doubt, the most popular packaging medium because of their versatility, they are used as a wrapping for most vegetables, pastries, cakes, meat, fish, poultry, etc. They come in a variety of sizes and colours, are cheap to buy, easy to use and unless they have been accidentally torn they can be used again and again. It is best to use the thickest, heavy-duty, type for freezing; thinner bags should only be used for short term storage.

Polythene film or wax paper: small sheets of polythene or wax paper are designed to make the separation of items packed in one bag as easy as possible. Chops, steaks, fillets of fish, hamburgers, etc., should be interleaved with polythene film or wax paper so that any number of helpings can be taken from the bag without difficulty.

Boil-in bags: these polythene bags are specially treated so that you can take them from the freezer and put them in boiling water to thaw and reheat. They are, of course, more expensive.

Auto-seal seamless plastic: this usually comes in a 12 m. (40 ft.) roll, 25 cm. (10 in.) wide and has an electrically operated heat-sealer.

Rigid containers: these are waxed or made of polythene and are used for storing liquids, fruit, vegetables and some prepared dishes. If waxed containers are selected, the food must be cooled before being poured into them or the wax surface will melt. Always leave a space at the top of the container to allow for expansion.

Stockinette or mutton cloth: often used to wrap joints to protect an inner wrapping of aluminium foil, the cloth is not in itself suitable as a freezer wrap and should never be used alone.

Freezer wrap: this is a thick waxed paper, sold in rolls so that you tear off the quantity you need. It is not so versatile as polythene bags or foil but it is moisture- and vapour-proof and useful for wrapping meat. It has to be sealed with freezer tape.

Plastic containers with airtight lids: the best known of these is Tupperware, which is, of course, expensive to buy initially but lasts for many years. The airtight lids make the containers convenient to use and they are excellent for storing fragile items.

Clear wrap: self-clinging polythene film, this is useful for small parcels of sandwiches and individual foods. Use with an overwrap of a polythene bag or seal with freezer tape. It comes in small rolls but also in 1000 foot rolls which is the best way to buy it.

Glass jars: before using glass jars, test them in the freezer to make certain they can withstand the temperature. Fill them with water to within an inch of the top and as a precaution put them in polythene bags — you do not want to spend an afternoon picking glass fragments out of the rest of the food. But once you have established their strength, they are perfect for packing small items — baby foods, grated cheese, breadcrumbs, etc. Use jars with screw-tops to ensure an airtight seal.

Yogurt, cream and cottage cheese cartons: these are useful standbys which can be used in the same way as glass jars.

— Basic freezing methods —

The freezer is capable of freezing 10 per cent of its loading capacity in 24 hours. To calculate the loading capacity, multiply the net capacity by the amount of food which can be contained in 28 litres (one cubic foot). In chest freezers this amount is reckoned to be 10 kg. (20 lb.), in upright freezers, $7\frac{1}{2}$ kg. (15 lb.). Thus a 12 cubic foot chest freezer has storage space for 120 kg. (240 lb.) of food and the ability to freeze at any one time 12 kg. (24 lb.). An upright freezer of similar size can store 90 kg. (180 lb.) and freeze 9 kg. (18 lb.).

Fast freezing

It is important to freeze food quickly and this is where the fast freeze compartment comes into its own. Food frozen slowly loses its nutrients when it is defrosted or cooked and is also poor in texture and flavour. Operating the fast freeze switch overrides the thermostat, which in normal use maintains a temperature of −18°C (0°F), and brings the temperature down to between −28°C (−18°F) and −30°C (−22°F).

The temperature, of course, is lowered throughout the whole of the freezer, so that the freezing process will take place wherever you put the food. But a fast freeze compartment, which is a feature of the larger chest cabinets, enables the unfrozen food to be kept separate from the rest of the contents. When it is not actually being used for freezing it is an additional storage area. In upright cabinets, where there is no special fast freeze compartment, it is wise to keep either the top or bottom shelf for this purpose. Or your model may have a special fast freeze shelf.

Must you fast freeze? When putting 250 ml. ($\frac{1}{2}$ pint) or 1$\frac{1}{4}$ cups of gravy or $\frac{1}{2}$ kg. (1 lb.) of meat in only, no as long as the food is absolutely cold. A simple rule I make is to fast freeze when I have over 1 kg. (2 lb.) weight of food to freeze.

How long to fast freeze for? This depends on how much food you are freezing at any one time, the size and make of freezer. The idea is to fast freeze until the food is frozen solid all the way through. As a rough guide I suggest two hours per $\frac{1}{2}$ kg. (1 lb.) for meat, poultry, fish, pies and prepared meals. One hour per $\frac{1}{2}$ kg. (1 lb.) for vegetables, fruit, liquids, bread and cakes.

Preparing for freezing

Blanching: this is the process whereby vegetables are plunged into boiling water and, after the water has been brought back to the boil, allowed to boil for a short period of time. They are then rapidly cooled in iced water before being quick frozen.

Not all vegetables have to be blanched. Mushrooms, for example, can be frozen raw or sautéed in butter before freezing. Potatoes should be almost cooked. There is a school of thought that includes French (green) and runner (string) beans among those vegetables for which blanching is unnecessary, but before you make up your own mind you should consider the following facts.

Storing food in the frozen state – that is, at a temperature not exceeding −18°C (0°F) – causes bacterial activity to become dormant and thus prevents the food from going bad. But the chemical substances known as enzymes continue to be active even at very low temperatures and, as they govern the colour, flavour and texture of the food, it is important that their activity should be kept to the minimum.

Blanching inactivates the enzymes and helps to retain Vitamin C. Blanched vegetables can be stored in the freezer for a year or more. Unblanched vegetables will keep well for only a quarter of that time. The section on freezing vegetables which starts on page 39 shows the blanching time for each variety.

If you want to you could spend a lot of money on blanching equipment and still achieve no better results than you could with the tools you already have in your kitchen. For example, a blanching basket is useful but nylon or muslin wine-straining bags bought from wine-making specialists shops would do instead. Blanch only small quantities at a time and cool as rapidly as possible as soon as the blanching is finished. One lot of water can be used for blanching several batches of vegetables.

Cool by plunging the basket or bag of vegetables into a bowl of iced water. Keep plenty of ice cubes handy for topping up. The cooling can also be done by holding the basket or colander under cold running water. Pack in quantities most suitable for your family's needs, unless you are open freezing, in which case one large bag can be used.

Open freezing

This method is ideal for such things as chips (French fries), peas, beans, raspberries, etc. Put items to be frozen on plastic trays or baking sheets lined with foil. In the case of small items such as sprouts, place as close together as possible without touching. If you have a lot of sprouts to open freeze at a time it can be done in two layers with two trays, one on top of the other, separated by an upturned cake tin. Freeze in the fast freeze compartment or quick freezing shelf until absolutely solid. The time will vary according to the item being frozen but it can take from 1 to 8 hours. Once solid, the vegetables or fruit can be tipped into a polythene bag or rigid container.

The aim is to freeze the food before it is packed into bags so that it remains in separate pieces and only a small amount or a few need be taken from the freezer at any one time. This free-flow method has obvious advantages from the storage point of view, since one large bag of peas, for example, will take up less room in the freezer than the same quantity packed into several small bags. Small cakes also freeze well by this method and for decorated cakes it is essential if the decoration is not to be spoiled.

For freezing fish see picture on page 14.

How to pack for the freezer

Remember firstly that all liquids and solids plus liquids, for example stews, casseroles and fruit salad expand with freezing. I remember as a child, when we didn't know about freezers, opening the refrigerator door after the fridge had been set on the lowest setting for ice cream making. All the milk was frozen and there was an inch or more of cream frozen solid on top of the bottles with the foil cap sitting on top! Well this is just what happens in the freezer if room is not left for the liquid to expand in the container. When filling, say, a ½ l. (1 pint) container leave 2 cm. (¾ in.) headspace at the top of the container before sealing the lid.

Casseroles and Stews

When freezing there are various ways of packing for the freezer.

In original dishes I find it best to freeze in the dish until frozen solid. The frozen food can then be removed from the dish by standing it in hand-hot water. This unmoulds the casserole like a jelly leaving the dish free to use for other casseroles. Wrap the block of casserole in foil or put in a polythene bag and label. Return the package to the freezer.

In blocks when cooking in bulk make, say, four times the usual amount of your favourite casserole or stew. When cooked, turn into a clean roasting tin, cool and freeze until almost firmly frozen. Remove from the freezer, cut into four with a knife, dipping the tin if necessary into water to free the food from the tin. Wrap each block of meat separately in foil or in a polythene bag, seal and label. Return the blocks to the freezer and stack one on top of the other.

In blocks when cooking for one meal freeze as for original dishes, but use a square polythene container lined with a polythene bag instead of the dish. When frozen solid slip the food out by standing the container in hot water. Then seal the bag, label and return to the freezer. In this way you don't need a vast amount of polythene boxes all being stored in the freezer. You have them in the cupboard for further uses.

In foil dishes and waxed containers these are expensive but handy. Remember to cool food before putting in waxed containers and cartons, otherwise the wax will melt and lose its shape and also be porous.

Packing in bags

It is important for the sake of the quality of the food to remove as much air from the bag which it is packed in as possible. To do this, press the bag on all sides with your hands and push the air out, then seal. Or insert a straw into the neck of the bag and suck the air out before closing the bag and sealing with a tie twist. Or lower the bag slowly into a bowl of water so that the air inside is forced up and out through the neck, then close and tie as before. Care must be taken, of course, to see that water does not get into the bag.

The unfreezables

How nice it would be if all food could be frozen and emerge from the freezer as appetizing as when it went in. Unfortunately, there are a few items whose quality is affected by being deep frozen. Some of these are touched on in the next chapter but here is a check list.

Cream and cream cheese: containing less than 40 per cent butter fat: both separate.
Green salad: such as cucumbers or lettuce: goes limp and mushy on thawing.
Eggs: whole ones break; hard-boiled ones go rubbery; yolks harden when yolks and whites unmixed are stored together. See page 46 for methods by which eggs can be stored in the freezer.
Potatoes, boiled whole, and spaghetti: tend to go mushy.
Previously frozen food: since thawed food deteriorates rather more quickly than fresh food, it is not a good idea to re-freeze raw food. However, cooking alters its state, so dishes made out of frozen ingredients may themselves be frozen with no ill effects.
Mayonnaise: curdles.
Yogurt: separates unless it is commercially frozen yogurt which contains a stabilizer.

Storage times for frozen food

The times given apply both to food which you have frozen yourself and to food bought from a freezer centre. Commercial freezing and storage are carried out at temperatures far lower than a domestic freezer is capable of, and enzyme activity is nil. Careful checks are carried out at freezer centres to ensure that the food is not kept in the retail cabinets for longer than a few weeks at the most.

	Jan	Feb	Mar	Apr	May	June	July	Aug	Sept	Oct	Nov	Dec
BREAD AND BAKED FOODS												
12 Danish pastries	━	━	━	━								
2 Victoria sponges (plain)	━	━	━	━	━	━	━					
4 wheatmeal loaves	━	━	━	━	━	━	━					
DAIRY PRODUCE												
1kg./2lb. butter (unsalted)	━	━	━	━	━	━	━					
1kg./2lb. butter (salted)	━	━	━	━	━	━						
2½kg./5lb. Cheddar cheese	━	━	━	━	━	━						
FISH												
8 fishcakes	━	━	━	━								
4 trout	━	━	━	━	━	━	━					
FRUIT												
2kg./4lb. strawberries	━	━	━	━	━	━	━	━	━	━	━	━
3kg./6lb. peaches	━	━	━	━	━	━	━	━	━	━	━	━
MAIN DISHES												
moussaka (2 meals)	━	━	━	━	━							
lasagne (1 meal)	━	━	━	━	━							
8 pizzas (bought)	━	━	━	━								
MEAT												
1½kg./3lb. leg of lamb	━	━	━	━	━	━	━	━	━	━	━	━
8 rump steaks	━	━	━	━	━	━	━					
4 x ½kg./1lb. minced (ground) beef	━	━	━									
POULTRY												
2 x 2kg./4lb. chicken	━	━	━	━	━	━	━	━	━	━	━	━
1½kg./3lb. pheasant	━	━	━	━	━	━	━	━	━	━	━	━
VEGETABLES												
2½kg./5lb. asparagus	━	━	━	━	━	━	━	━	━	━	━	━
2½kg./5lb. courgettes (zucchini)	━	━	━	━	━	━	━	━	━	━	━	━
5kg./10lb. peas (bought)	━	━	━	━	━	━	━	━	━	━	━	━

Bread and Baked foods	Bread, brown and white *6 months*
	enriched rolls *4 months*
	crusted loaves and rolls *1 week*
	Bread dough, risen *4 months*
	unrisen *6 months*
	Cakes, undecorated *6 months*
	decorated *3 months*
	Pastries *4 months*
	Sandwiches *3 months*
	Breadcrumbs *6 months*
	Yeast (fresh) *1 year*
Dairy produce	Butter, salted *6 months*
	Butter, unsalted *12 months*
	Cheese, hard *6 months*
	Cheese, soft *3 months*
	Cream *8 months*
	Eggs *6 months*
	Ice cream *4 months*
	Margarine, lard, cooking fat *5 months*
	Milk, homogenized *1 month*
	Yogurt, commercially frozen *6 months*
Fish	Shellfish and cooked fish *3 months*
	All other fish *6 months*
Fruit and vegetables	Most (for exceptions, see A–Z fruit and vegetables, pages 34–45) *12 months*
Home cooked dishes	All *3 months*
Ready-prepared food, bought	Highly seasoned *3 months*
	Other *6 months*
Meat	**Beef**
	Joints *12 months*
	Minced (ground) *4 months*
	Steaks *6 months*
	Sausages *3 months*
	Lamb
	Joints *12 months*
	Chops and cutlets *6 months*
	Pork
	Joints *8 months*
	Chops *3 months*
	Sausages *4 months*
	Offal (variety meat) *4 months*
	Bacon
	Joints *1 month*
	Smoked *1 month*
	Unsmoked *3 months*
	Vacuum-packed *2 months*
Poultry	Chicken *12 months*
	Duck *8 months*
	Goose *8 months*
	Turkey *8 months*
	Game *12 months*
	Giblets *3 months*
	Stuffing *3 months*

The times given above are all recommended storage times. Food can be kept longer, although there may be some loss of flavour and a drying out of texture. There is no danger to health.

Commercial packs often have shorter storage times given on the outside of the bag. Manufacturers are anxious that their products should be enjoyed at their prime and consequently they tend to err on the side of safety.

Thawing

To thaw or not to thaw? It is a question that bothers many people. Some things should be cooked straight from the freezer; others must be given time to thaw out before cooking. If in doubt, the best rule to follow is to thaw food. And the best place for thawing is in the refrigerator, overnight or longer if need be.

It is perfectly permissible to thaw food at room temperature and, indeed, sometimes necessary if you haven't left yourself enough time to thaw it in the fridge. But the refrigerator is the safest place, hidden away from household pets and children's inquisitive little fingers.

Many things are better, however, if they are not allowed to thaw at all. Frozen vegetables, for example, retain their flavour and colour best if they are popped straight into boiling water and cooked no longer than is necessary to make them ready for the table. Count the cooking time from the moment the water returns to the boil and remember that they will already have undergone a few minutes blanching time so they should not take as long to cook as raw, unfrozen vegetables. The only exception to the rule is corn on the cob, which should be allowed to defrost completely before being cooked, otherwise the middle will still be frozen when the corn itself is ready.

Most meat, even joints, can be cooked from the frozen state (see next chapter for instructions and cooking times). There are exceptions here, too — poultry and boned and rolled joints. The reason is the risk of contamination which is higher with poultry and rolled joints than with other meat. All poultry, including fresh, must be cooked thoroughly so that the heat penetrates to the bone. In order to do this properly with, say, a frozen chicken, the bird would have to stay so long in the oven that the outside would be scorched to a frazzle. With rolled joints the risk comes from the handling which they had to undergo during the boning and rolling. Thawing before thorough cooking ensures that micro-organisms are destroyed before the meat is eaten.

Some foods require only half-thawing. Soft fruits, for example, are nicest if they are thawed just enough to soften and separate them. Four hours at room temperature is about right for a pound of berries in their container. Apricots, peaches, cherries, apples and rhubarb need about five to six hours. Free flow packs require only a third of these times.

Bread should be thawed at room temperature and takes about two hours. However, if you are in a hurry, wrap the bread in foil, and thaw it in a hot oven, 200°C, 400°F, Gas Mark 6, for 5 to 10 minutes. Sliced bread may be toasted from frozen.

Preparing food for freezing

When the new freezer first arrives, there is a temptation to fill it with all manner of things, whether they are likely to be useful or not. It is reassuring to see the cabinet bulging with food. But, unless the contents have been carefully selected, it is not necessarily good planning.

Buying in bulk may save money, but if you pack the freezer with something that the family do not particularly like, just because it was a bargain, it is a waste of valuable freezer space.

It is also pointless to freeze items which will keep equally well in a cupboard, or which are so simple to make that their preparation takes less time than thawing them out. Rich fruit cake and Christmas pudding are examples of the former, egg custard and cooked spaghetti (unless in a sauce or prepared dish) of the latter.

But there should always be room in the freezer for time-savers — or cook's aids. Whatever kind of cook you are — adventurous, painstaking, enthusiastic, slap-happy or reluctant — you are bound to find any or all of the following items a boon.

— Cook's aids —

Breadcrumbs: many recipes call for fresh breadcrumbs and if you are in a hurry or running short of bread, it is a great help to have them ready for use in the freezer. Fresh breadcrumbs can be prepared quickly and easily in an electric blender. They freeze well and remain separate, so that they can be stored in a bag and used as required. Crumbs for stuffings, puddings and sauces do not have to thaw before use, but for coating fried foods, they should be allowed to thaw at room temperature for about 30 minutes.

Buttered crumbs: add 100 g. (4 oz.) or 2 cups fresh breadcrumbs to 50 g. (2 oz.) or $\frac{1}{4}$ cup melted butter. Blend in a frying pan and fry slowly until golden-brown. Use as a topping for both savoury and sweet dishes. These crumbs keep for about one month.

Bread: fried as croûtons or in fancy shapes, these should be made from slices of bread $\frac{3}{4}$ to 1.25 cm. ($\frac{1}{4}$ to $\frac{1}{2}$ inch) thick. Both cubes and shapes may be fried in shallow or deep fat until golden brown, well drained and packed into polythene bags. To use, place them, still frozen, in a hot oven, 200°C, 400°F, Gas Mark 6, and bake for 5 minutes. Storage time is three months.

Garlic-flavoured butter: cream well $\frac{1}{2}$ kg. (1 lb.) unsalted butter, beat in 8 crushed garlic cloves and season well. Chill in the refrigerator, then form into a roll. Chill again until firm and cut in slices. Pack each slice in foil. Storage time is two months.

Brandy butter: cream 200 g. (8 oz.) or 1 cup unsalted butter with 200 g. (8 oz.) icing sugar or $1\frac{1}{3}$ cups confectioners' sugar. Beat in 6 tablespoons brandy, a little at a time. Freeze in rigid containers. Make it before the Christmas rush is on, but not too far ahead as the best storage time is about two months.

Maître d'hôtel or parsley butter: prepare as for garlic butter, substituting the finely grated rind and juice of 1 lemon and 6 level tablespoons chopped parsley for the garlic. Storage time is six months.

Butter balls or curls: keep a few made from unsalted butter in the freezer for use when needed. Storage time is six months.

Garlic bread: make several 2.5 cm. (1 in.) slits in the top of French loaves. The cuts should reach to within 1.25 cm. ($\frac{1}{2}$ in.) of the base. Open up the loaves and spread with garlic-flavoured butter. Wrap each loaf tightly in foil and freeze. To use, place the loaves, still in their foil wrappings, in a hot oven 200°C, 400°F, Gas Mark 6, and bake for 30 to 40 minutes. These loaves do not keep much longer than a week as the crust tends to flake after this time. They are, however, a useful time-saver if you are planning to hold a large buffet party.

Cheese bites: any left-over trimmings from cheese pastry for flans may be rolled out and cut into shapes. Cut them first, pack in a polythene bag and freeze. Storage time is three months.

Chocolate decorations: these add a luxury touch to cakes, soufflés and mousses, and, provided they are kept in a box rather than a bag, will keep their shape in the freezer without breaking. Melt cooking chocolate and spread it thinly on silicone non-stick paper. When the chocolate is firm but not brittle, cut it into shapes with a sharp knife and leave to set. To remove the shapes from the paper, slide the paper to the edge of the work surface, pull it down and gently lift off each portion. Curls of chocolate, or caraque, are made in similar fashion, but the melted chocolate should be spread on a marble slab. At setting point, the chocolate should be shaved off in curls, using a sharp knife held at an angle to the slab. Storage time is two months.

Chestnuts: peeling fresh chestnuts takes time and, with all the other things that need doing before Christmas, it saves a great deal of frustration to complete this particular job well in advance. Wash the chestnuts, pierce them with a knife and put in cold water. Bring to the boil and boil for 5 minutes. The chestnuts can then be peeled and skinned without difficulty. Do only a few at a time, peeling and skinning one lot while the next batch is on the stove. The chestnuts can be packed in polythene bags and frozen, in which case they will store for about six months, or cooked for a further 45 minutes, made into chestnut stuffing and frozen. Stuffing, however, has a storage life of only one month.

Coffee: strong coffee may be poured into ice cube trays and frozen. Use it for iced coffee, which will not become diluted as the ice cube melts. Storage life is three months.

Ice cubes: keep a bag of ice cubes in the freezer for adding to drinks when needed.

Juice of lemons and oranges: keep fresh fruit juices in small containers, clearly labelled, and add to fillings, dressings and sauces as required. Storage life is six months.

Lemon or orange rind: grated rind from leftover lemon or orange halves may be kept in small pots for use when required. Both lemons and oranges are easier to grate if the fruit halves are frozen first.

Lemon slices: barmen know the value of a ready supply of frozen lemon slices, for adding to drinks. Open freeze the slices and pack in bags so that there is no difficulty in separating the slices.

Seville oranges: buy these when cheap and store in polythene bags until you have time to make marmalade from them. A recipe using the whole fruit is best for frozen oranges.

Herbs: many recipes call for fresh herbs, and if you have a herb garden it is useful to freeze a number of them for use when the season is over. Chives, mint, parsley and tarragon are particularly good, although most herbs freeze well. There is no need to blanch them — simply pick sprigs of the chosen herb, wash and dry them before packing the whole sprigs into bags for freezing. Leftover mint stalks, from which the leaves have been removed for mint sauce, may also be frozen and used to flavour new potatoes. Parsley, thyme and bay leaves may be tied together and frozen to provide a ready bouquet garni.

Chopped herbs may be packed into ice cube trays, covered with water and frozen. Tip the cubes into a polythene bag for storage. Small individual jam pots are also suitable for containers if your ice cube tray is in use.

Chopped mint, with a little vinegar and castor sugar added, can also be frozen as a base for quickly made mint sauce. To use, add neat vinegar or vinegar diluted with water, according to taste, and allow to thaw. The mint sauce will have a brighter colour if boiling water is used instead of vinegar at the freezing stage.

Mint leaves and parsley sprigs may be stored in separate bags. If crushed while they are still frozen, they will break up and there will be no need to chop them when they thaw out. The storage life of all the herbs is about six months.

Meringue shells: pipe or spoon the meringue mixture on to a baking sheet lined with silicone non-stick paper or oiled greaseproof (waxed) paper. Bake in a cool oven, 130°C, 250°F, Gas Mark $\frac{1}{4}$, until the meringues are firm and crisp. Pack in rigid containers after they have cooled completely and use straight from the freezer. Storage time is three months.

Nuts: hazelnuts keep very well in the freezer and will store for a year without losing their moistness and freshness. They should not be salted, but whole, flaked, chopped or toasted nuts are ideal. Put them in small cartons before freezing. Storage life is up to six months.

Sauces: many sauces freeze well, especially curry or tomato sauce. If small quantities are required, freeze in ice cube trays and store the cubes in a polythene bag. If larger amounts are wanted, pour into rigid containers, leaving room for expansion, cool, seal and freeze. A sauce such as Hollandaise is not suitable for freezing as it separates when thawed and no amount of stirring or whisking will return it to the right consistency. Storage time is up to three months.

Stock: home-made stock is an invaluable standby. This, too, can be frozen in cube form and used as required. Do not overseason in the initial making; extra seasoning can always be added as the stock thaws out. Storage time is two months. Chicken carcasses and trimmings may be wrapped and frozen for use later in making stock.

Yeast: fresh yeast can be kept in the freezer for up to 1 year. Measure it into suitable quantities before freezing, wrap each portion individually and store in a rigid container. Remember to mark each packet with the appropriate amount. Before using, it is best to give it 30 minutes thawing time, but if you are in a hurry, the frozen yeast can be coarsely grated.

— A-Z of freezing fruit —

Freezing, without doubt, is the best and easiest way of preserving fruit. In each case I have given the way I consider best first. For example, I always do raspberries 'au naturel' with no sugar or syrup because that gives the best result when thawed: the raspberries remain firm and full of flavour.

Quality of fruit
Only top quality, ripe, fresh fruit should be frozen. If fruit is slightly over-ripe, freeze in purée form.

Freezing in syrup
The sweetness of the syrup depends on how sweet you like your fruit. Syrup is best used for fruits which discolour easily such as peaches and apricots. Dissolve the sugar in boiling water then cool before using to cover the fruit. To prevent the top layer of fruit becoming discoloured by exposure to the air, place a clean piece of non-absorbent paper below the lid to force the fruit down. This is only needed with fruits such as peaches, apricots and pears.

Syrup strengths for freezing fruit
30 per cent Medium syrup use 200 g. (8 oz.) or 1 cup sugar to $\frac{1}{2}$ l. (1 pint) or $2\frac{1}{2}$ cups water
45 per cent Heavy sweet syrup use $\frac{1}{2}$ kilo (1 lb.) or 2 cups sugar to $\frac{1}{2}$ l. (1 pint) or $2\frac{1}{2}$ cups water

Ascorbic Acid—Vitamin C
Some fruits such as peaches, apricots and pears discolour on thawing, therefore it is best to add ascorbic acid to the syrup before freezing. To each $\frac{1}{2}$ l. (1 pint) or $2\frac{1}{2}$ cups of syrup add $\frac{1}{4}$ teaspoon ascorbic acid. Buy the ascorbic acid at chemists (pharmacies). The powder form is cheaper than tablets.

Layering fruit with sugar

Use caster (superfine) sugar for layering fruit as it dissolves more quickly on thawing. I use 100 g. (4 oz.) or ½ cup sugar per ½ kg. (1 lb.) of fruit. If you like your fruit tart add less. On thawing, the sugar will make its own juice.

Fruit purée

Raw ripe fruit, such as raspberries and strawberries, can be puréed and used to flavour ice cream, mousses and fools, or the purée can be used as a sauce for ice cream. Other cooked fruits such as apples or gooseberries are excellent puréed for sauces, or as part of a dessert. Make sure to label the purées with sugar content before freezing. Purées also take up a lot less space in the freezer than the whole fruit, particularly so with fruits such as apples.

Serving frozen fruit

When the fruit is raw, as in the case of strawberries and raspberries, it is best to thaw slowly, preferably in the refrigerator. Serve them cold and, with strawberries, barely thawed, otherwise they are apt to go mushy. The thawing time is about 8 hours in the refrigerator for a pound pack and 4 hours at room temperature. Free flow packs require only a third of these times.

Other cooked or blanched fruits can thaw at room temperature until the individual fruits break up. It takes about 4 hours for a ½ kg. (1 lb.) pack. If you are in a hurry and you want to serve the fruit hot you can carefully thaw by reheating on the stove in a non-stick pan, stirring frequently.

Storage times of fruits

One year unless stated differently.

APPLES

Preparation Peel, core and slice. Put in cold water to which you have added 1 tablespoon salt to 1 l. (2 pints) water. Putting them in salt water prevents discolouration.

Then freeze in any of these ways:

Sliced without sugar Rinse in cold water, blanch for 1 minute, drain on absorbent paper and cool. Open freeze for free flow pack (see page 26): spread apple on trays, freeze until frozen solid, then tip into polythene bag.

Use for pies and puddings.

Cooked with sugar Stew in sugar and minimum water until tender, adding 200 g. (4 oz.) or ½ cup sugar to each ½ kg. (1 lb.) of fruit. Cool and pack in rigid containers. Use for strudels, pies and puddings.

Purée Cook with sugar as above, or if you prefer without; take care to label which you have done. Sieve or purée in liquidizer. Cool and pack in rigid containers.

Use for apple sauce, baby food or in desserts.

APRICOTS

Preparation Prepare in small quantities because the fruit discolours quickly. Plunge in boiling water for 30 seconds to loosen skins, then put in cold water.

Half apricots in syrup Remove skins, cut in half and remove stones. Cover with medium syrup with added ascorbic acid. Cool and pack in rigid containers. Use for fruit salad or in flans.

Whole apricots in syrup Leave whole and pack as halved fruit. After 6 months you may notice an almond flavour in the fruit imparted by the stones.

Use for fruit salad.

Cooked Cook stoned apricots in a little water and 100 g. (4 oz.) or ½ cup sugar to each ½ kg. (1 lb.) apricots. Cool and pack in rigid containers.

Use for pies and flans.

Purée Cook as above, only in minimum water, then sieve or purée. Cool and pack in rigid container.

Use as a sauce for ice cream, or as filling with cream in sponge cakes.

BANANAS

Do not freeze as whole fruit.

Preparation Can be puréed by mashing or puréed in a liquidizer. Add juice of 1 lemon and 25 g. (1 oz.) or 2 tablespoons caster sugar to each ½ kg. (1 lb.) of bananas.

Pack in rigid container.

Use for sandwich filling or in a banana cake or loaf.

BILBERRIES or BLUEBERRIES

Pick ripe firm fruits.

Dry pack If the fruit is really dry put into rigid containers.

Open freeze If fruit is slightly damp, open freeze for free flow pack (see page 26).

Use for pies and tarts.

BLACKBERRIES

Pick on a dry day for best results. Pack and freeze the moment you get home from the fields.

Dry pack. Put in rigid containers.

Open freeze If fruit is slightly damp, open freeze for free flow pack (see page 26).

BLACKCURRANTS *See currants.*

CHERRIES

Choose ripe sweet cherries. Red freeze better than black; white are best frozen in syrup.

Preparation Remove stalks and stones if you like. If the stone is left in after 6 months you may get a slightly almondy flavour from it.

Dry pack Pack whole fruit in rigid containers.

Layered with sugar Layer either whole or stoned fruit with sugar, using 100 g. (4 oz.) or ½ cup sugar to each ½ kg. (1 lb.), in a rigid container.

CURRANTS, Black, red and white

Preparation Stem currants and wash if necessary.

Dry pack Put in rigid containers.

Use for pies, puddings and jam (for jam, blanch currants for 1 minute).

Layered with sugar Layer dry with sugar using 100 g. (4 oz.) or ½ cup sugar to each ½ kg. (1 lb.) of fruit with red and white currants. Use 100 g. to 150 g. (4 to 6 oz.) or ½ to ¾ cup sugar with blackcurrants.

Use for pies and puddings.

Stewed with sugar Squashed or slightly over-ripe blackcurrants can be stewed using 200 g. (8 oz.) or 1 cup sugar to each ½ kg. (1 lb.) fruit, with ½ l. (1 pint) or 2½ cups water. Strain and freeze cold. This makes syrup for adding to water for children's drinks.

CRAB APPLES

If you haven't time to make crab apple jelly, cook the fruit and strain the juice in the usual way. Measure and freeze the juice. Continue making the jelly at a future date when you have time. Storage time 6 months.

DAMSONS

It is best not to dry pack as the skins become tough.

Halved in syrup Cut in half, pack in a rigid container and cover with heavy sweet syrup with added ascorbic acid (see page 34).

Use for pies and puddings.

FIGS

Choose ripe fruits and handle carefully.

Dry pack Put in shallow rigid container.

Whole in syrup Peel fruit and pack in rigid container. Cover with medium syrup (see page 34).

GRAPEFRUIT

Preparation Peel, remove pips and pith and then segment. Slimmers can freeze fruit without sugar, just in its own juice.

Layered in sugar Layer fruit with 100 g. (4 oz.) or ½ cup sugar to each ½ kg. (1 lb.) of fruit in a rigid container.

GRAPES

Preparation Wash fruit. Seedless varieties may be packed whole; others should be skinned, pipped and halved.

Whole or halved in syrup Pack in rigid containers in medium syrup (see page 34).

GREENGAGES

Preparation Wash if necessary. It is best not to dry pack as the skins become tough.

Halved in syrup Cut in half, pack in a rigid container and cover with heavy sweet syrup with added ascorbic acid (see page 34).

Use for pies and puddings.

LOGANBERRIES
Pick on a dry day.
Dry pack Put in rigid containers.
Use for puddings and pies.
NECTARINES
Preparation Choose ripe fruit. Skin carefully under running water. Cut in half and remove the stone if you like. Brush with lemon juice to prevent discolouring.
Whole or halved in syrup Pack in rigid containers, cover with heavy sweet syrup with added ascorbic acid (see page 34).
Use for desserts. Add a little brandy to thawed syrup if you like.
ORANGES
Preparation Peel, remove pips and pith and then segment. Slimmers can freeze fruit without sugar.
Layered in sugar Layer fruit with 100 g. (4 oz.) or ½ cup sugar to each ½ kg. (1 lb.) of fruit in a rigid container.
For marmalade Freeze Seville oranges whole packed in polythene bags.
Use for making marmalade by the whole fruit method (see page 157).
PEACHES
Preparation Skin carefully under running water. Cut in half and remove the stone if you like. Brush with lemon juice to prevent discolouring.
Whole or halved in syrup Pack in rigid containers, cover with heavy sweet syrup with added ascorbic acid (see page 34).
Use for desserts. Add a little brandy to thawed syrup if liked.
PEARS
Although you can freeze pears, the results lack flavour and I don't consider it worthwhile unless you have a large crop to get rid of.
Preparation Wash fruit, peel, core and quarter.
In syrup Poach quarters at once in a medium syrup (see page 34) for 2 minutes. Drain, cool and pack in the cool syrup with added ascorbic acid in rigid containers.
Use for a fruit salad or alone.
PINEAPPLE
Preparation Peel, core and slice in rings or chop.
Dry pack Put in rigid containers with all the juice.
Use for fruit salad or adding to ice cream.
Layered in sugar Add 100 g. (4 oz.) or ½ cup sugar to each ½ kg. (1 lb.) of fruit.
Use as a dessert.

PLUMS

It is best not to dry pack as the skins become tough.

Halved in syrup Cut in half, pack in rigid containers and cover with heavy sweet syrup with added ascorbic acid (see page 34).

Use for pies and puddings.

RASPBERRIES

Preparation Really freshly picked raspberries freeze very well. Handle as little as possible. Avoid washing unless absolutely necessary. Remove stalks.

Dry pack Leave in punnet or carefully put in rigid container if dry. Open freeze if slightly damp (see page 26).

Use as a dessert.

Purée Sieve or purée fruit in a liquidizer, and add 150 g. (6 oz.) or ¾ cup sugar to each ½ l. (1 pint) or 2½ cups of purée. Pack in small containers or freeze as ice cubes.

Use for flavouring ice creams, sorbets and mousses.

RHUBARB

Preparation Choose young tender stalks picked early in the season. Wash, trim and cut into 2.5 cm. (1 in.) lengths.

Dry pack Pack in rigid containers or polythene bags.

Use for pies, puddings, crumbles and summer pudding.

STRAWBERRIES

Preparation Remove stalks, wash if absolutely necessary and dry on absorbent paper. Grade fruit into sizes and from choice freeze small fruit.

Dry pack Open freeze: spread fruit out on trays, freeze until frozen solid, then pack in rigid containers or polythene bags.

Use for adding to fruit salad, serving alone or decoration.

Layered with sugar Arrange fruit and sugar in layers in rigid container using 100 g. (4 oz.) or ½ cup sugar to each ½ kg. (1 lb.) of fruit. If liked the fruit may be halved or sliced.

Use for adding to fruit salad.

Purée Sieve or purée fruit in a liquidizer and add 150 g. (6 oz.) or ¾ cup sugar to each ½ l. (1 pint) or 2½ cups of purée. Pack in small containers or freeze as ice cubes.

Use for flavouring ice cream, sorbets and mousses.

Making jam from frozen fruit

With a freezer you can make jam when you feel like it, perhaps on a cold winter day and not in the height of summer when you may be tired from picking the fruit or you may just feel lazy and want to enjoy the sunshine. It means too that if you haven't sugar or other ingredients, you can just freeze the fruit. There are a few points to note when using frozen fruit for jam making.

The pectin content of some fruits is weakened by freezing and this is particularly noticeable with fruits which give a soft set, as for example strawberries. To counteract this an extra tenth (1/10) in weight of fresh fruit can be allowed when freezing the fruit, that is 200 g. (8 oz.) extra per 2½ kg. (5 lb.) fruit. When making the jam follow the original recipe for sugar and yield. (This can be worked in reverse by using the recipe's weight of fruit and reducing the sugar and yield by one tenth.) The addition of a small amount of pectin from a pectin rich fruit to the standard recipe improves the set. In all cases the pectin test is helpful in assessing the pectin present in frozen fruit.

Frozen blackcurrants often have tough skins when made into jam; this can be overcome by blanching the fruit for 1 minute before cooling and freezing.

When the fruit is required for jam making it can be placed, frozen, in the preserving pan with the water if required and heated gently until the fruit is thawed. The method is then as for fresh fruit. The fruit can also be thawed prior to making the jam but this requires a certain amount of forethought and tends to give a poorer colour to the jam.

When freezing Seville oranges or tangerines for subsequent marmalade making it is advisable to add one eighth (1/8) extra weight. This need not be too precise, adding an extra small orange will be sufficient. To make the marmalade put the whole frozen fruit in a saucepan with the water and simmer gently for 2 hours with the lid on the pan. Cut up the fruit, separate the pips and return to the water in which the fruit was cooked and boil for 5 minutes. Put the sliced fruit and liquid strained free from pips in a preserving pan, boil off excess water if necessary, add the sugar and complete. The pressure pan can also be used. Slow-thawed oranges (overnight in the refrigerator) seem to give a weaker set.

Freezer jam If you have a surplus of strawberries or raspberries use them to make this delicious uncooked jam that you store in the freezer. The flavour is really fresh — it is less set than ordinary jam — more like a Swiss conserve.
To make crush 1 kg. 200 g. (2½ lb.) of strawberries with 2 kg. (4 lb.) caster (superfine) sugar. Leave to stand in a china bowl for 1 hour in a warm kitchen, stirring from time to time. During this period the sugar should have dissolved. Add a bottle of liquid pectin and stir in the juice of one large lemon. Stir until well blended. Pour into small jars filling to within 1.25 cm. (½ in.) of the top of the jar and cover each jar with foil. Label then leave in warm kitchen to mature for 2 days. At this stage I pack the jars in a small cardboard box so that they don't get knocked in the freezer. Freeze and use within 6 months.

Making wine from frozen fruit
I am not a wine maker but I am told it is an advantage to freeze the fruit before making wine as it softens the skins. It also has the advantage that you may not have enough fruit gathered in one picking so freeze it and after a number of pickings you will have the required amount to get going.

⁓ A-Z of freezing vegetables ⁓

It is best to freeze only first quality vegetables, ideally those picked when young and tender. All vegetables are best blanched (plunged into boiling water for a given time) before freezing. This destroys the enzymes present and preserves the colour and flavour.

To blanch
Prepare according to type. Bring not less than 3 l. (6 pints) or 7½ pints of water to the boil in a large pan. Blanch ½ kg. (1 lb.) of vegetables at a time, putting them in either a nylon or muslin wine straining bag or in a wire basket to fit the pan. Time the blanching from when the water returns to a full rolling boil after the vegetables are added. Take care to be accurate if you want the best results. The blanching water can be used for the full batch of vegetables, thus not losing the Vitamin C in the blanching water. If doing more than 4 kg. (8 lb.) of vegetables, change the water.

To cool
This should be done as quickly as possible in iced water or cold running water. The cooling time is about the same time as the blanching time. The vegetables should be cold right through.

To freeze vegetables without blanching

If you are faced with a glut crop, by all means freeze without blanching, but use the vegetables within two months if you want them at their best. They should be treated when unblanched as short term and used first from the freezer. An exception to this rule, in my opinion, are carrots. I have found they freeze well for up to 9 months without blanching.

To thaw and cook

Cook all vegetables, except corn on the cob, from frozen in boiling salted water until just tender. If frozen in the block, break up by turning over in the water and separating the vegetables. Corn on the cob should be thawed before cooking otherwise the centre of the cob will be still cold when the corn is cooked.

To pack

Pack in $\frac{1}{4}$ or $\frac{1}{2}$ kg. ($\frac{1}{2}$ or 1 lb.) packs if freezing in block form. If open freezing for a free flow (see page 26), pack in larger strong (heavy-duty) polythene bags.

Storing time

One year unless otherwise stated.

ARTICHOKES, Globe
Choose preferably large artichokes.
Preparation Cut off stalk, remove outer leaves and blanch three at a time. Pack each in a separate polythene bag.
Blanching time 6 minutes small/8 minutes large.
To use plunge frozen in boiling, salted water and cook for about 5 minutes until outer leaves can be removed easily.

ASPARAGUS
Buy in season and at their cheapest. Stalks may be frozen separately for soups.
Preparation Grade according to thickness, cut into even lengths and scrape lower part of stem. After blanching and cooling, tie in 100 g. (4 oz.) bundles. Put in polythene bags.
Blanching time 4 minutes thick spears/2 minutes thin spears.
To use Plunge frozen in boiling, salted water and cook for 3 to 5 minutes.

AUBERGINES (EGGPLANTS)
Only freeze these if in prime condition and a reasonable price. Consider using a small amount for Moussaka (see page 82).
Preparation Peel and cut in 2 cm. ($\frac{3}{4}$ in.) slices. Blanch, cool and open freeze (see page 26).
Blanching time 3 minutes.
To use Plunge frozen in boiling, salted water and cook for 5 minutes.

BEANS, BROAD (LIMA)
Preparation Pod and grade according to size. Blanch and cool. Either open freeze for free flow pack (see page 26), or pack in polythene bags or rigid containers.
Blanching time 2 minutes small/3 minutes large
To use Plunge frozen in boiling, salted water and cook for 5 to 8 minutes.

BEANS, FRENCH (GREEN)
If you don't have time to prepare all one batch of beans on one day, wrap the remainder in newspaper and put in a cool larder or refrigerator until the next day.
Preparation Top and tail. Leave small beans whole and cut others in 3.75 cm. (1$\frac{1}{2}$ in.) pieces, and blanch separately. Blanch and cool. Either open freeze for free flow pack (see page 26) or pack in polythene bags or rigid containers.
Blanching time 3 minutes whole/ 2 minutes cut.
To use Plunge frozen in boiling, salted water and cook for about 5 minutes for cut beans, 7 minutes for whole beans.

BEANS, RUNNER (STRING)
See note above about keeping beans firm. It is essential to cut beans more coarsely than usual if you like them crisp when cooked.
Preparation String, top and tail. Slice into diagonal 1.25 cm. ($\frac{1}{2}$ in.) slices. Blanch and cool. Either open freeze for free flow pack (see page 26) or pack in polythene bags or rigid containers.

Blanching time 2 minutes.

To use Plunge frozen in boiling, salted water and cook for 5 to 8 minutes.

BEETROOT (BEETS)

Choose small beetroots the size of a golf ball.

Preparation Cook, unpeeled, in boiling, salted water until tender, taking care not to puncture the skin. Peel, then pack whole in polythene bags. If slightly larger beetroots are used, slice before packing.

Storage time whole 8 months/sliced 6 months.

To use thaw in refrigerator for 2 to 6 hours according to size of pack.

BROCCOLI

Preparation Remove outer leaves and trim off woody stem. Blanch and cool. Either open freeze for free flow pack (see page 26) or pack in polythene bags or rigid containers.

Blanching time 2 minutes thick stems/1 minute thin stems.

To use Plunge frozen in boiling, salted water and cook for 5 to 8 minutes.

BRUSSELS SPROUTS

Preparation Trim and grade. (There is no need to cut crosses on the bottom.) Blanch and cool. Either open freeze for free flow pack (see page 26) or pack in polythene bags or rigid containers.

Blanching time 3 minutes medium/1½ minutes small.

To use Plunge frozen in boiling, salted water and cook for 5 to 8 minutes.

CARROTS

Very small, whole carrots freeze well.

Preparation Grade according to size. Scrub small carrots and scrape large ones. Slice or dice large carrots. Blanch and cool. (Carrots may be frozen without blanching — see page 40.) Either open freeze for free flow pack (see page 26) or pack in polythene bags or rigid containers.

Blanching time 3 minutes small/4 minutes thick slices.

Storage time 12 months if blanched/9 months if unblanched.

To use Plunge frozen in boiling, salted water and cook for about 5 minutes. The diced or sliced carrots can be added to stews and casseroles when still frozen.

CAULIFLOWER

Choose only compact white cauliflowers.

Preparation Break into flowerets about 3.75 to 5 cm. (1½ to 2 ins.) across. Blanch and cool. Either open freeze for free flow pack (see page 26) or pack in polythene bags or rigid containers.

Blanching time 3 minutes.

To use Plunge frozen in boiling, salted water and cook for 5 to 8 minutes.

CELERY

Only suitable for serving cooked. Use young heads.

Preparation Trim off any green. Cut in 1.25 cm. (½ in.) slices. Blanch and cool. Pack in small quantities in polythene bags.

Blanching time 3 minutes.

To use add to stews and casseroles.

CHICORY (FRENCH OR BELGIAN ENDIVE)

Only suitable for serving cooked. Select fresh white heads.

Preparation Remove any discoloured leaves. To keep white add the juice of ½ lemon to blanching water. Drain well after blanching and cool. Pack in polythene bags or polythene containers.

Blanching time 3 minutes.

To use Plunge frozen in boiling, salted water, with 1 teaspoon sugar added, and cook for 8 minutes. Serve hot with white or brown sauce.

CORN ON THE COB

It is essential that this is young and fresh.

Preparation Remove husk and silk. Cut off stem. Blanch and cool. Pack in polythene bags, singly. If corn kernels are taken off the cob it is not so satisfactory. If preparing this way, scrape off after blanching.

Blanching time 4 to 6 minutes.

To use Thaw before cooking, otherwise the inside of the cob will still be cold when the corn is cooked. When thawed boil in salted water for about 5 minutes.

COURGETTES (ZUCCHINI)

Pick even sized, young courgettes.

Preparation Cut in half if small, or in 2.5 cm. (1 in.) slices if larger. Blanch and cool. Either open freeze for free flow pack (see page 26) or pack in polythene bags or rigid containers.

Blanching time 1 minute.

To use Plunge frozen in boiling, salted water and cook for about 3 minutes, then toss in butter. Or allow to thaw and sauté in butter.

FENNEL

Only suitable for serving cooked.

Preparation Trim off any green. Cut in 1.25 cm. (½ in.) slices. Blanch and cool. Pack in small quantities in polythene bags.

Blanching time 3 minutes.

To use A very little goes a long way, so add sparingly to stews or casseroles. Or plunge frozen in boiling, salted water and cook for about 8 minutes and serve hot with cream sauce.

HERBS

Sprigs of herbs keep their colour but go limp on thawing; however, they are useful for flavour and for a bouquet garni. (For mint, see opposite.)

Preparation Chop herbs, separately or mixed. Either pack in clean 25 g. (1 oz.) butter containers (the kind you get on aeroplanes) or in ice cube trays and cover with water. Freeze, then turn out cubes and pack in polythene bags.

To use Add to stews, casseroles, soups or sauces. The chopped herbs can be used for dips, cheeses, etc.

KOHLRABI

Preparation Trim and peel. Leave very small ones whole and cube larger ones. Blanch and cool. Pack in polythene bags.

Blanching time 3 minutes whole/1 minute cubed.

To use Plunge frozen in boiling, salted water and cook for 8 to 12 minutes.

MARROW (SUMMER SQUASH)
Preparation Prepare as for courgettes (zucchini) only in bigger pieces, removing skin if tough.
Blanching time 2 minutes.
To use Plunge frozen in boiling, salted water and cook for about 5 minutes.
MINT SAUCE
Pick all the mint for freezing early in the season when full of flavour.
Preparation Chop mint finely, divide among ice cube tray section. Pour over sugar syrup made with 200 g. (8 oz.) or 1 cup sugar and 250 ml. ($\frac{1}{2}$ pint) or $1\frac{1}{4}$ cups water. Freeze, then put cubes in polythene bag.
To use Place one or two cubes in a sauceboat. Thaw a little, then thin down with vinegar.
MUSHROOMS
Freeze only fresh cultivated mushrooms. Small ones are best.
Preparation Wipe clean and slice if larger than button. Sauté in butter or freeze raw. Pack in small polythene containers.
Storage time 3 months cooked/1 month raw.
To use Add frozen cooked mushrooms to soup, sauces, casseroles or other dishes. Thaw raw mushrooms in container in refrigerator.

ONIONS
Label onions whether mild or strong. If freezing whole ones choose smallish ones, the size of golf balls. Not suitable for salads.
Preparation Peel onions. If freezing whole, blanch and cool. Either open freeze for free flow pack (see page 26) or pack in polythene bags or rigid containers. For sliced onion, cut in 1.25 cm. ($\frac{1}{2}$ in.) slices and pack in polythene bags. Put in second bag if storing for some time to prevent transfer of flavour.
Blanching time 2 minutes sliced/6 minutes whole.
To use Add to soups, stews and casseroles.
PARSNIPS
Choose young roots.
Preparation Trim and peel. Leave very small ones whole and cube larger ones. Pack in polythene bags.
Blanching time 4 minutes small/2 minutes cubed.
To use Plunge frozen in boiling, salted water and cook for about 15 minutes if whole, 10 minutes if cubed.
PEAS
Use only young peas.
Preparation Pod and either open freeze for free flow pack (see page 26) or pack in polythene bags or rigid containers.

Blanching time 1 minute.

To use Plunge frozen in boiling, salted water and cook for 4 to 7 minutes.

PEAS, Mange Tout, Sugar Peas or Podded Peas

Choose flat, tender young pods.

Preparation Top and tail. Remove any strings. Blanch in small quantities. Cool, then either open freeze for free flow pack (see page 26) or pack in polythene bags or rigid containers.

Blanching time 1 minute.

To use Plunge frozen in boiling, salted water and cook for about 4 minutes.

PEPPERS, RED OR GREEN

Freeze colours separately.

Preparation Freeze whole without blanching, or halve, cut out stem and seeds and blanch. Pack whole peppers (red and green separately) in polythene bags and cut peppers in polythene bags or polythene containers.

Blanching time 3 minutes.

Storage time 6 months raw/12 months blanched.

To use Raw peppers can be grilled (broiled), blanched halved peppers for stuffing or added to dishes. Plunge frozen in boiling, salted water and cook for 5 to 10 minutes according to use.

The best methods of freezing potatoes are those that use creamed potatoes or potatoes that are reheated or cooked in hot fat.

POTATOES, CHIPPED (FRENCH FRIED)

Preparation Deep fry in hot oil (180°C/360°F) until just tender but not browned. Drain on absorbent paper and cool quickly. Alternatively the uncooked chips (French fries) can be blanched in boiling water for 1 minute, then drained and cooled. Open freeze (see page 26).

To use Thaw, then turn straight into hot oil or fat and cook until golden brown. Drain

POTATOES, ROAST

Preparation Bring peeled potatoes to the boil in salted water, drain and dry. Roast in a hot oven, 200°C, 400°F, Gas Mark 6, in oil for about 1 hour, turning occasionally. Drain well and cool quickly. Pack in polythene bags, seal and label.

Storage time 6 months

To use Heat a little oil in a roasting tin and turn the frozen potatoes in this. Reheat in moderately hot oven, 190°C, 375°F, Gas Mark 5, for 30 minutes.

POTATOES, BAKED

Preparation Bake scrubbed potatoes in their jackets. Cut in half and scoop out the cooked potato. Mix with a little butter and seasoning and spoon the mixture back into the potato skins. Pack two stuffed potato halves face to face with a foil divider between them. Pack in freezer foil and label.

Storage time 6 months.

To use Place still wrapped in a hot oven, 200°C, 400°F, Gas Mark 6, and bake for 35 to 40 minutes, depending on the size. Unwrap, remove dividers, sprinkle with grated cheese and return to the oven for a further 10 minutes. If preferred, the potatoes may be served plain.

POTATOES, NEW

Preparation Wash and scrape or scrub the potatoes, choosing small even-sized ones. Cook in boiling, salted water until just tender. Drain well and toss in melted butter. Turn into a polythene bag and leave to cool. Seal, label and freeze.

Storage time 6 months.

To use Place the potatoes and butter in a casserole, cover and reheat in a moderate oven, 180°C, 350°F, Gas Mark 4, for 30 to 40 minutes, stirring from time to time. Sprinkle with chopped parsley, chives or mint.

POTATOES, DUCHESSE

Preparation Peel ½ kg. (1 lb.) potatoes and cook in boiling, salted water until tender, then drain and mash until smooth. Beat in 1 egg yolk, 25 g. (1 oz.) or 2 tablespoons butter and seasoning. Pipe in large rosettes on a greased baking sheet, then brush with a little beaten egg. Bake in a hot oven, 220°C, 425°F, Gas Mark 7, for about 10 minutes or until just golden. Cool. Open freeze (see page 26).

To use Place frozen on a baking sheet and reheat in a very hot oven, 220°C, 425°F, Gas Mark 7, for about 25 minutes.

SPINACH
Preparation Wash well in several waters. Blanch in small quantities. Drain thoroughly, press out excess moisture and cool. Pack in polythene bags or polythene containers.
Blanching time 2 minutes.
To use Plunge frozen in pan with 1.25 cm. ($\frac{1}{2}$ in.) water and a little salt. Cover and cook for 5 minutes, stirring frequently. Drain well. Add butter.
TOMATOES
Whole tomatoes freeze but are not suitable for salads.
Preparation Skin tomatoes. For tomato purée, simmer slowly in own juice until tender, then reduce to a purée and sieve if you like. Pack in small polythene containers or freeze in ice cube trays as herb cubes. Freeze whole tomatoes in polythene bags.
To use Add to soups, stews or casseroles.
TURNIPS
Choose young roots.
Preparation Prepare as for parsnips.
Blanching time 4 minutes small/2 minutes cubed.
To use Plunge frozen in boiling, salted water and cook for about 15 minutes whole, 10 minutes cubed.

—Freezing basic foodstuffs—

Baby foods
New mothers may be a little nervous about freezing food for the baby, fearing perhaps that it will be less nutritious or even harmful when it thaws out. But this, of course, need not be a worry.

Freezing baby food in meal-time quantities is a great economy, both in price and time. With three children of my own, I know how much I valued my freezer when the children were at the first-solids and early-toddler stages. In the past, busy mothers have relied on canned baby foods, feeling that the money they paid for the cans offset the time spent on preparing miniature meals. And the enthusiastic, no-cans-at-any-price cook resented the wastage of food that was almost inevitable.

A freezer puts an end to all that. The average family meal, unless it is highly spiced or very rich, nearly always yields enough food to be puréed and frozen for the baby. There is no need to doctor the flavour, because most babies enjoy savouries as much as sweet things. Home-made soup or stock, thickened with mashed potato or baby cereal, fish, liver and vegetables sieved or liquidized, stewed fruit sweetened with clear honey, can all be frozen and two or three weeks' supply stored in the freezer at one time. Containers can be old yogurt cartons or foil cases, sterilised in a Milton solution. Alternatively you can use ice cube trays for soups and other purées, each cube providing a sufficient meal-time quantity for a young baby.

Dairy produce

Most dairy products are fairly stable in price, and the only advantage of storing them in the freezer is as a standby should you forget — as we all do occasionally — to put them down on your weekly shopping list. Otherwise, storing them in great quantities means taking up freezer space which could be more sensibly used for meat and vegetables bought when the price was low. But if you suspect that any particular product is likely to shoot up in price in the next few months, it is as well to know what dairy produce can be frozen and how.

Butter: the blocks are a good shape for packing neatly in the freezer but should be wrapped in foil first. Salted butter will keep for 6 months, unsalted, 12 months.

Cheese: hard cheeses keep best when grated because they have a tendency to become dry and crumbly if stored in the block. Soft and cream cheeses with more than 40 per cent butter fat content freeze and keep well. Cottage cheese, however, tends to become acid after a few weeks and doesn't freeze well. Cheese dips for party use also freeze well if made from a rich cream cheese. Store hard cheese for 6 months, other cheese for 3 months. Thaw in the refrigerator before use and leave for 24 hours at room temperature to allow the full flavour to return.

Cream: the best results come from whipped cream, piped into rosettes before freezing, which can be used as a filling or mixed with a little sugar in a recipe. Single (light) cream *always* separates. Double (heavy) cream may separate, although Channel Island, Devonshire and Cornish clotted cream all freeze well if they are really fresh. Storage time is 3 months.

Eggs: if you keep hens, or want to buy eggs when the price is low, it is tempting to put whole eggs straight into the freezer. However, the lowering of the temperature causes the egg to expand and break the shell and the yolk becomes hard.

Successful freezing of whole eggs is only possible if the yolks and whites are mixed lightly together before freezing. A little salt or sugar (approx. $\frac{1}{2}$ teaspoon of either to 12 eggs) should be whisked in and the mixture poured into an ice-cube tray or other suitable container. Open freeze, then put the cubes in a polythene (plastic) bag, seal, label according to how many eggs were used and whether salt or sugar were added and return to the freezer.

To use, remove the amount required, place in a bowl and thaw for 2 to 3 hours. Whisk lightly with a fork and use as normal.

Yolks and whites may, however, be frozen separately (see photograph, page 15). Beat yolks with a stabilizer, such as sugar or salt, (using $\frac{1}{2}$ teaspoon to 6 yolks). Whites freeze well without any additive, just lightly mixed, and may be used for meringues when thawed. Pour yolks and whites — separately — into ice-cube trays or plastic egg cartons. Remember to indicate on the outside of the container of yolks which stabilizer was used and whether they are for sweet or savoury use. Open freeze and store the frozen eggs in polythene bags. Thaw and use as for whole eggs. Storage time, for separated or whole eggs, is 6 months.

Ice cream: bought in large packs, ice cream is an economical product to have in the freezer, particularly if you have small children in the family. Several different flavours are available, but the packs do take up a lot of room in the freezer. It is probably best to restrict your choice of ice cream to one or two flavours and, if these include vanilla, variety is possible by serving it with different toppings (see page124).Storage time 4 months.

Lard, cooking fat and margarine: useful standbys but not really necessary in a freezer. Storage time is 5 months.

Milk: buy homogenized milk and keep it in its cartons. Its freezer life is about 1 month, so make certain that the emergency carton is used and replaced at regular intervals.

Yogurt: home-made and bought yogurt separates when thawed from the freezer. Ready frozen yogurt can be bought in packs from a freezer centre and as this has a stabilizer added the product is very satisfactory.

Fish

The one, never-to-be-broken rule in freezing fish is that it must be fresh. Freshness means anything less than 24 hours after it has been caught, so that home-freezing must be confined to fish that you or your family have caught yourself, or for seaside dwellers fish that a local fisherman is selling direct.

Raw fish gives better results than cooked, but whether you freeze it whole, filleted, in cutlets or portions depends on your own preferences and on the size of the fish.

Quick freezing is best. Individual portions or fillets should be frozen in shallow packs, each portion separated from the next by a piece of thin plastic film. Mackerel, trout, mullet or herring can be frozen whole, and so can a salmon provided it is not more than 5 cm. (2 in.) thick.

To prevent the fish from drying out while it is in store, wrap it well, excluding as much air as possible. Foil is best for this purpose, doubled over for extra protection, before wrapping the fish. Heavy gauge polythene is also suitable, but the ends must be properly sealed with special freezer adhesive tape. Shallow foil dishes may be used provided the fish fits closely into them and they are also useful for cooked fish dishes. Small rigid containers are suitable for shellfish.

It is important not to overload the quick freezing compartment while freezing fish, or if your freezer has no special place for this purpose, put your fish where it will freeze the fastest, such as against the sides or base in chest models or over the evaporator coils in upright cabinets. Do not allow the fish to come into contact with other items in the freezer while the freezing process is going on.

Before preparing the fish for the freezer, set the fast freeze switch at least two hours in advance. Leave it on that setting for 24 hours and do not transfer the fish from the compartment for a further eight hours.

Large whole fish: scale, gut and remove fins and gills. The head and tail should be left on. Wash carefully and drain well. Wrap, seal and label, marking the date very clearly. Freeze only one fish at a time.

Small whole fish: prepare as above but the head and tail may be removed if wished. Open freeze (see photograph page 14) or package individually or separate with thin plastic and pack in quantities of from two to four.

Individual portions or fillets: whether the fish is cut into steaks or filleted is up to you. After preparing the fish, washing and draining, either open freeze (see page 26) or wrap the pieces, either individually or with separators, seal, label and freeze. Make the packages as flat as possible.

Shellfish: crab and lobster should be freshly cooked before freezing. Package whole, with a wrapping of heavy gauge polythene or foil, or remove the meat from the shell and put into small containers. Before serving, thaw for 6 to 8 hours in the refrigerator. Large prawns such as Dublin Bay, Gulf or Pacific, and scampi are best frozen raw, with the head, carapace, legs and claws removed and the washed tails packed into containers. The tails may be cooked from the frozen state by lowering them into boiling

water and simmering for 4 to 6 minutes. Shrimps and prawns should be similarly treated, but the tails are usually left in their shells. Alternatively, cook them lightly in salted water until they turn pink. Cool in the cooking liquid, drain and pack in suitable cartons. For scallops and similar shellfish, place in a hot oven, 200°C, 400°F, Gas Mark 6, until the shells open. Remove the black fringe from round the fish and cut the remainder from the shell. Rinse, drain and pack in containers. Leave to thaw in the refrigerator overnight before cooking as though they were fresh, or put into hot water or sauce in the frozen state.

Storage times for fish: this is fairly short because fish begin to lose their fresh flavour and texture if kept too long. Oily fish may develop a rancid flavour. For best results, these are the maximum storage times: white fish, 6 months; oily and smoked fish, 3 months; shellfish and cooked fish, 3 months.

Meat

Freezing is an excellent way of preserving fresh meat and the faster it is frozen the better the results.

The butchering and home-freezing of large quantities of meat, particularly beef, is not a task to be undertaken lightly, and few housewives have either the skill or the inclination to try it. I recommend buying meat from your own butcher who will in most cases give a discount for a bulk order. He will prepare the meat for you and pack it in the quantities you specify. He will remove the excess fat, which may become rancid in the freezer, but leave enough to prevent the meat from drying out. He will mince (grind) it, prepare chops and cut liver into convenient slices. He may be able to blast freeze the meat for you — this fast freezing method gives the best results. To have the meat prepared costs more than buying a carcass but is still a lot less than getting it retail every week. If you prefer, buy packs of selected cuts that your family enjoy from your freezer centre. Try a small amount first to test the quality.

Freezing meat at home: Freeze no more than 1/10th of the total capacity of the freezer at any one time. Freeze as quickly as possible using the fast freeze switch — see your manufacturer's book for special instructions for your freezer.

Packaging meat for the freezer

Joints boned and unboned: pack in polythene bags, preferably heavy duty. If there are any sharp bones pad them with foil so that they do not pierce the bag. Seal with a tie twist.

Minced (ground) meat, stewing meat: same as above. Pack in one meal or cooking session sized pack.

Steaks, chops, cutlets and escalopes: open freeze (see page 26). Pack closely together when each piece is absolutely frozen solid. Do not mix cuts together in one bag. Put in polythene bags, preferably heavy duty. If preferred you can separate each piece of meat with foil or with moisture-proof paper, then wrap tightly.

Cooking meat: Generally speaking, it is better to allow most cuts to thaw completely before roasting them. The thawing process should be carried out in the refrigerator, with the meat left in its original wrapping. This way, there is very little blood drip from the meat. If necessary, beef and lamb can be thawed at room temperature, which saves from three to five hours thawing time per $\frac{1}{2}$ kg. (1 lb.) in weight. But if you forget to remove the joint from the freezer the day before, it is possible to get satisfactory results from roasting frozen joints.

To cook meat from frozen: I have carried out a number of experiments in roasting frozen joints and the table below gives my conclusions. You may have to vary the time slightly because so much depends on the way you like your meat, the characteristics of your oven and the thickness of the joint. A meat thermometer, which is obtainable from freezer centres and kitchenware departments of large stores, is indispensable for good results every time.

The basic essential for success is longer slower cooking than usual.

The frozen middle takes longer to thaw and therefore to cook than the outside and in getting the inside cooked through the outside may become dryer, even scorched.

To roast the meat, cover loosely with foil for the first part of the cooking. If liked use roasting bags but I find that they stew rather than roast the meat and you don't get a crisp outside to the joint. You do, however, have a clean oven, so the choice is yours! If you use roasting bags, place the joint inside and close loosely with a tie twist.

Put the joint in a cold oven, set the thermostat to the appropriate temperature and let the cooking start. About 20 minutes before the joint should be ready, check the meat thermometer. Use scissors to snip the bag or lift a corner of the foil, and plunge the thermometer into the meat. For meat on the bone, try to get the thermometer near the bone without touching it. The temperature reading will show how well the inside is done (see the second chart below).

If cooking one of the cheaper roasting cuts of beef put an inch of water and a stock cube in the roasting pan (use the smallest one that will fit the joint), stand the joint in the water and cover it tightly with foil for three quarters of the cooking time. Roast at 170°C, 325°F, Gas Mark 3, for 60 minutes to the ½ kg. (1 lb.). Use the stock from the joint for the gravy.

COOKING TIME FROM FROZEN

Meat	Oven-setting	Time to allow per ½ kg. (1 lb.)
Beef	180°C, 350°F	55 minutes (well done)
	(Gas Mark 4)	50 minutes (rare)
Lamb	180°C, 350°F	45 minutes
	(Gas Mark 4)	
Pork	200°C, 400°F	60 minutes
	(Gas Mark 6)	

TEMPERATURE READINGS ON MEAT THERMOMETER

Meat	Temperature	State of meat
Beef	77°C/170°F	well done
	71°C/160°F	medium done
	65.5°C/150°F	rare
	60°C/140°F	very rare (best cold)
Lamb	82°C/180°F	well done
	77°C/170°F	pinkish
Pork	88°C/190°F	well done
	anything less	leave for longer as pork should never be underdone

Accompaniments to the meat must, of course, take into account the new times. Roast potatoes, for example, should be put in a separate dish with less fat than usual, and be given an hour's extra cooking time.

Smaller cuts, such as steaks or chops, can also be successfully cooked from the frozen state. If they are being grilled (broiled), place the pan 5 cm. (2 in.) further away from the heat than you would normally do. Bring them nearer to the heat to brown when they are almost cooked. If they are fried, start at a lower temperature and raise the heat at the end if the chops or steak are not brown.

49

Poultry

Freshly killed poultry should be plucked immediately, then hung for 24 hours before freezing at the lowest possible temperature. Freeze giblets separately, because their storage time is less than the rest of the birds. It is worth jointing some chickens and freezing the pieces individually by open freezing, partly because chicken joints are easier to pack in the freezer than the whole bird, partly because they are useful for all manner of dishes afterwards. If you are freezing a number of chickens, consider packing similar joints in the same wrapping, open freezing or using plastic film to separate the pieces. Some recipes call for several drumsticks or wings and it helps to have them all together. Pack as for meat. Chicken keeps for a year, giblets for two to three months.

Turkey is treated like chicken, but takes up a lot of room in the freezer and, although it will store for up to six months quite satisfactorily, it is a waste of space to keep it in the freezer except for a very short time. Cooked turkey slices should be frozen in gravy or stock to prevent them from becoming too dry. Use within 2 months.

Goose and duckling may also be frozen but choose young birds which are neither too fatty nor too lean. Storage time is five months.

Unlike meat, poultry must never be cooked from the frozen state. Thaw chicken in the refrigerator for about 24 hours and turkey for about 3 days. If you try to cook poultry from frozen, the result will be either harmful or inedible. Cooking the inside sufficiently to kill dangerous bacteria will mean scorching and drying the outside, however well wrapped the bird may be.

Game

Game birds, such as pheasant, grouse, partridge, snipe, woodcock, etc., should be well hung before the birds are plucked, drawn, washed and drained. Wrap in heavy gauge polythene or foil and freeze quickly. Like poultry, game birds must thaw completely before being cooked.

Hares should be hung by the feet for a week to 10 days. Save the blood. Leave whole or cut into joints after skinning and drawing. Freeze the blood separately to be added to the gravy when the hare is roasted or jugged. Rabbits may be treated in the same way, but it is not necessary to hang them. Storage time is 6 months. Thaw before cooking.

Venison is best if it is commercially frozen. It will store for 12 months and should be thawed before being cooked.

Bacon

Frankly, it is hardly worthwhile keeping bacon in the freezer since the storage time is fairly short. It has already been cured as a means of preserving it, and cured meats do not freeze well. If kept too long in the freezer it tends to go rancid.

However, if you want to keep *some* bacon in the freezer as a standby and you would prefer to freeze it yourself, then the bacon you buy for this purpose *must* be absolutely fresh. Tell your grocer what you intend to do with the bacon and ensure that you can collect it from him on the day he receives it from his supplier.

Vacuum-packed bacon is the best buy, both for joints and rashers, and it must be frozen as quickly as possible. If this is done, the storage time is 8 weeks, but after that period the flavour will be affected. If you wrap the bacon yourself, get as much air out of the package as you can and use heavy duty foil or polythene for the wrapping. Storage time for home-packed bacon joints is 7 to 8 weeks, and for home-packed rashers (slices), chops or steaks between 2 and 4 weeks. Unsmoked bacon keeps for about 2 weeks longer than smoked.

Before cooking, the bacon should be fully thawed, either in the refrigerator or at room temperature, and once thawed it should be cooked within 3 days.

Bulk preparation

Would you like to eat minced (ground) beef every day? Would your family rebel against a constant diet of chicken? Or do you prefer variety? The answers to these questions must be obvious and they point the way to what is one of the most interesting aspects of freezer cooking, one which gives the housewife the maximum opportunity for exercising her ingenuity and imagination.

Buying in bulk for the freezer is, as we have seen, a money-saver. Preparing in bulk is merely carrying things one logical step further. The truth is that with a supply of basic foodstuffs, ready prepared, you are in a position to ring the changes on an enormous number of meals from the freezer.

Meat To illustrate the advantages of bulk preparation, consider minced (ground) beef. The price of beef today makes all but the cheaper cuts a luxury. Good lean minced (ground) beef is still cheap to buy, especially in bulk, and it is the basic ingredient of a a great number of different dishes.

To use it to its best advantage, fry a good quantity of minced (ground) beef until it is pale golden and the fat has run out. Mix with chopped onions, add flour to thicken, and then stock or water and seasoning. Simmer until tender (see Lasagne, page 97). Store this mixture in the freezer to be used as required. From this you can produce enough variety to satisfy even the most demanding family: meat loaf, meatballs, shepherd's pie, fillings for pies and pasties, stuffed vegetables.

The same considerations apply to lamb or pork bought in quantity when in good supply.

Chicken Sometimes there is a glut of chicken on the market and it is worthwhile investing in several roasters to store in the freezer. Think what you can make from these, not forgetting to use the giblets and carcasses: eight 1½ kilo (just over 3 lb.) chickens will produce one roast chicken, eight fried chicken portions, four Coq au Vin portions, eight of orange tarragon chicken, four portions of chicken liver pâté, eight portions of chicken pie and 4 l. (8 pints) or 5 quarts of stock.

Soup Stock from a chicken carcass or beef or mutton bones is a most valuable part of your basic store. With a supply of stock in your freezer you have every kind of nourishing soup at your command. Simply put the bones, and giblets if any, with a few chopped onions, carrots, bay leaf, salt and pepper, into a large pan of water and bring to the boil. Skim, then simmer gently for about 3 hours, skimming occasionally and adding more water if necessary. Strain, cool and freeze in polythene containers.

Sauces A good sauce is vital for good cookery. Make life easier by doing most of the work in advance. You can make up, say, 2 l. (4 pints) or 5 pints of basic white sauce with milk, onion, butter, flour and seasoning. Freeze this and store it to make, later, cheese sauce, parsley sauce, shrimp or anchovy sauce, mushroom sauce, to name but a few. In the same way, make up and freeze a supply of basic brown sauce, using dripping, onion, carrot, celery, bacon, flour and stock. Develop it later according to the recipe you are following; serve it with meat dishes.

You can, of course, make up and store smaller quantities of individual sauces.

Plated Complete Meals It is a good idea if perhaps you have enough for a couple of extra platefuls at Sunday lunch to assemble two meals for the freezer to enjoy later. It is best to use divided foil plates if possible. Avoid freezing green vegetables. Yorkshire pudding, roast potatoes, root vegetables and sliced meat in gravy freeze well. Cover plate with foil before freezing. If possible freeze extra gravy in a small container so that it may be served with the meal. After freezing, reheat the plate, still covered, in the oven for 40–45 minutes at 200°C, 400°F, Gas Mark 6. Serve with extra gravy – if liked a portion of still frozen peas and a knob of butter can be slipped on the plate under the foil before going in the oven to reheat.

Bread If you enjoy baking your own bread, don't stick to one particular kind. With a basic mixture, prepared in bulk, you can make a whole repertoire of loaves, plain and fancy, rolls, plaits, fruit bread and buns. Basic mixtures can be for plain white bread and rolls or for wholemeal bread and scones or enriched for sweet loaves and buns of all kinds. Mixtures can be prepared and stored in the freezer as dough, risen or unrisen, or the baked end product can be frozen.

Cakes Basic home-made cake mixtures offer endless possibilities. One sponge mix can serve for cakes for tea or as the basis of any number of desserts with the addition of fruit and cream. It is a good idea to make a number of sponge cake layers and freeze them in packs, divided by foil between each layer. You can then – depending on inspiration or your family's demands — defrost two or more at a time and sandwich them together with whatever fits the mood of the moment. If your family is fond of chocolate — or ginger — cake, it is worth preparing a special supply of these basic mixes.

If sponges are filled with real cream it is best to slice them while still partially frozen. Fill sponges with more runny fillings after thawing otherwise the filling might soak into the sponge.

Pancakes or crêpes These are always popular, so make a supply when eggs are reasonably priced. The basic mixture is simple — flour, eggs, milk, salt and a little oil (see page 93). Pack the pancakes in layers for freezing. Unpacked, they defrost at room temperature in about 30 minutes. Serve them as a sweet with lemon juice and sugar, or use with savoury fillings. You can also pack them already rolled round the filling or folded over a fruit and sugar flavoured butter, in shallow foil containers ready for baking in the oven. (See Apple and Cinnamon Pancakes, page 119.)

Yorkshire Pudding Make the basic batter as usual. Well grease patty tins and pour in the amount of mixture that you generally make, then freeze. Foil patty tins may be used if liked. Wrap when frozen. Cook from frozen uncovered in the usual way. The only difference is that it will take a little longer.

No need to waste leftover cooked Yorkshire Puddings. Cool them, wrap and freeze. Put in a medium oven while still frozen to reheat — it will take between 10—20 minutes.

Pastry Make pastry in quantities and save time. Use shortcrust for flans, tartlets, fruit pies, pasties; flaky for savoury pies, mince pies, jam puffs; puff pastry for sausage rolls or vol-au-vents. All of these freeze well. To freeze, divide the pastry dough into 200 g. (8 oz.) or 2 cup and $\frac{1}{2}$ kilo (1 lb.) or 4 cup amounts, shape into neat rectangles and pack. When using, defrost only sufficiently to make rolling out possible. The resulting pies, tarts and flans can be frozen and stored either baked or unbaked.

Basic crumble mixes can be made and stored in polythene bags. They are quicker and easier to make than pastry, if you are short of time and energy.

Plate Pies If you like really crisp, not soggy pastry underneath fruit pies, freeze two circles of dough to fit a pie plate. Freeze them both on the plate separated with a piece of greaseproof (waxed) paper (ideally the plate should be enamel or tin so that when baking the heat gets through to the base of the pastry quickly). The filling is then added before baking.

If you do want to freeze the pie with the fruit filling in, thicken the juice of the fruit with cornflour (cornstarch), a scant level tablespoon of cornflour (cornstarch) to 125 ml. ($\frac{1}{4}$ pint) or $\frac{5}{8}$ cup sweetened fruit juice. Cool filling before putting in the pie. Freeze before baking. Bake from frozen, making air vents in the top of the pastry when ready to bake or when partly thawed. Bake for 10—15 minutes longer than usual, lowering the oven temperature if the pastry is browning too much towards the end of the cooking time.

Do not be daunted by the thought of preparing in large quantities. Start with small amounts, if you like, and see how much time bulk preparation will save you in the end.

Using bulk packs from the freezer centre

Just as supermarkets use their glittering rows of shelves to tempt you to buy more than you really need, so freezer centres use their bulk packs to encourage you to fill your freezer with items your family will probably not be able to eat for many months.

The answer is to keep your head. It can be very exciting to walk round a freezer centre, opening lid after lid of the chest freezers on display to see what goodies they contain. But do bear in mind your family's likes and dislikes and your own style of living. That bulk pack of several different kinds of pâtés is fine if you have a party coming up or if pâté is a regular feature of your menu. It is quite a different matter if pâté is something you serve only occasionally. The chances are that once you have sampled the first, you will forget that you have all the others sitting in your freezer until long past their recommended storage time.

On the other hand, some bulk packs are not likely to last long in your freezer. A pack of 1 kg. (2 lb.) of peas or beans will be gone long before its storage time is up. And four dozen fish fingers in a family of children will disappear in a time that will amaze you.

Avoid the temptation of buying large numbers of a particular item all in one go. If the dish is unfamiliar – for example, curried meat pies – buy one or two to start with and try them out on your family first. If they are popular, you can always buy a larger quantity when you next visit the freezer centre.

Some bulk packs are designed to make menu planning a little easier. Vegetable stew packs, for example, containing a number of the root vegetables most popular in stews, are usually a good buy. Ready sliced, they can produce a satisfying stew in a comparatively short time.

Packs of chops are almost always excellent to have in the freezer. They usually come in quantities of 15 or 20, and a family of five will demolish them long before their storage time is up.

Compare large pack prices with small packs before buying. With fruit and vegetables compare with the cost of the fresh item in the greengrocers or local market. For example, I have found that pineapple pieces are nearly always cheaper when bought frozen and they are ideal for something like pineapple ice cream (see page 123).

Convenience foods

The range of convenience foods is very wide, and before buying them you should decide for yourself how convenient they are in terms of time saved. They are unlikely to save you money, for it is almost always cheaper to prepare from scratch at home, but they can be very useful to have as a standby in the freezer. Some of the boil-in-the-bag fish and meat dishes are very good and provide a tasty meal in a matter of minutes.

In most cases, the best convenience foods are the most expensive. With pies, for example, it is probably true to say that the cheaper the pie the smaller the filling. So in this case it is better to concentrate on quality rather than on cheapness.

Pizzas, however, are an exception. Here, cheapness doesn't really matter because the filling can easily be added to – sliced tomatoes or mushrooms, grated cheese or extra anchovies, anything that the family particularly enjoys, or even leftovers.

There are many more exotic dishes available these days from freezer centres or high-class delicatessens, and some of these are excellent value – in terms of taste and presentation if not in money. And they can be a godsend for the housewife who finds giving a dinner party a nerve-wracking chore.

In short, the whole secret of using your freezer wisely and well is by trial-and-error. It does not take long to evolve a system of buying and cooking for the freezer that suits the needs of your family. And when you do, you will wonder how you ever managed without one.

Starters

— Asparagus Rolls —

METRIC/IMPERIAL
2 small brown loaves,
   preferably 2 days old
50 g./2 oz. butter, softened
2 × 250 g./10 oz. cans
   asparagus, drained

Remove the crusts from the loaves with a sharp knife. Cut 40 wafer-thin slices of bread. Spread each slice of bread with butter. Place a piece of asparagus diagonally across each slice, then roll up the bread very carefully.
To freeze: wrap the rolls in aluminium foil, seal, label and freeze. Store no longer than 3 weeks.
To thaw and serve: leave to thaw overnight in the foil.

Makes 40 rolls.

AMERICAN
2 small brown loaves,
   preferably 2 days old
¼ cup butter, softened
2 × 10 oz. cans asparagus,
   drained

— Cheese Straws —

METRIC/IMPERIAL
100 g./4 oz. flour
¼ teaspoon salt
pinch of pepper
25 g./1 oz. butter
50 g./2 oz. Cheddar cheese,
   grated
25 g./1 oz. Parmesan cheese,
   grated
1 egg yolk
cold water

Sift the flour, salt and pepper into a bowl. Add the butter and cut it into small pieces with a table knife. Rub the fat into the flour until the mixture resembles breadcrumbs. Add the cheese with the egg yolk and stir well. Add enough water to make a firm dough.
   Roll out the dough on a floured surface to ¾ cm. (¼ in.) thickness. Trim the edges of the dough to make a neat square or rectangle, then cut into straws, each about ¾ cm. (¼ in.) wide and 6.25 cm. (2½ in.) long. Re-roll the trimmings and cut out four or five circles about 7.5 cm. (3 in.) in diameter. Then cut out the centres with a 5 cm. (2 in.) cutter to form rings.
To freeze: lay the straws and rings on a baking sheet or flat dish and open freeze. Pack in rigid containers, seal and label.
To thaw and serve: replace on the baking sheet or flat dish and bake in a hot oven, 200°C, 400°F, Gas Mark 6, for 15 minutes or until pale golden brown. Cool on a wire cake rack for 10 minutes, then thread 9 or 10 straws through each ring. Serve warm.

Makes about 40.

AMERICAN
1 cup flour
¼ teaspoon salt
pinch of pepper
2 tablespoons butter
½ cup grated Cheddar cheese
¼ cup grated Parmesan
   cheese
1 egg yolk
cold water

— Sausage Rolls —

METRIC/IMPERIAL
½ kg./1 lb. pork sausage meat
1 tablespoon chopped fresh
   mixed herbs
salt and pepper
1 × 325 g./13 cz. packet
   commercial frozen
   puff pastry, thawed
milk

Mix together the sausage meat, herbs and seasoning. Divide into four portions and roll out each on a floured board to make a 'worm' about 40 cm. (16 in.) long.
   Roll out the pastry dough and cut into four strips, each 40 by 7.5 cm. (16 by 3 in.). Place a sausage meat 'worm' on each piece of dough and fold the dough over to seal. Brush the edges with milk and seal well. Cut each into eight portions. Make two or three slashes with a sharp knife on top of each portion.
To freeze: open freeze, then pack in polythene (plastic) bags, seal and label.
To thaw and serve: place on a baking sheet, brush with milk and bake in a hot oven, 220°C, 425°F, Gas Mark 7, for 20 to 25 minutes or until golden brown.

Makes 32.

AMERICAN
1 lb. pork sausage meat
1 tablespoon chopped fresh
   mixed herbs
salt and pepper
1 × 13 oz. packet commercial
   frozen puff pastry, thawed
milk

Small Swiss Flans

METRIC/IMPERIAL

Shortcrust pastry
200 g./8 oz. flour
½ teaspoon salt
50 g./2 oz. butter
50 g./2 oz. lard
2 tablespoons cold water
Filling
100 g./4 oz. streaky bacon
½ small onion, chopped
75 g./3 oz. Emmenthal or
    Gruyère cheese, grated
2 eggs
6 tablespoons single cream
    or creamy milk
2 teaspoons chopped chives
salt and pepper
12½ g./½ oz. butter

AMERICAN

Shortcrust pastry
2 cups flour
½ teaspoon salt
¼ cup butter
¼ cup lard
2 tablespoons cold water
Filling
4 oz. fatty bacon
½ small onion, chopped
¾ cup grated Emmenthal or
    Gruyère cheese
2 eggs
6 tablespoons light cream or
    half and half
2 teaspoons chopped chives
salt and pepper
1 tablespoon butter

Preheat the oven to fairly hot, 190°C, 375°F, Gas Mark 5. Grease 20 deep patty (muffin) tins.

Sift the flour and salt into a bowl and rub in the butter and lard until the mixture resembles fine breadcrumbs. Add the water and mix to a smooth dough. Roll out the dough on a floured surface and cut out 20 circles, large enough to line the patty (muffin) tins. Put the dough circles in the tins and line them with greaseproof (waxed) paper and dried beans. Bake in the centre of the oven for 15 minutes. Remove the tins from the oven and discard the paper and beans.

To prepare the filling, remove the rind from the bacon and cut it into small pieces. Fry the bacon and onion together for 5 minutes. Drain on kitchen paper and then divide between the pastry cases. Sprinkle over the cheese. Blend together the eggs, cream or milk (half and half), chives, salt and pepper. Spoon this mixture into the pastry cases. Dot with butter and bake in a warm oven, 170°C, 325°F, Gas Mark 3, for 20 minutes or until the filling is firm to the touch.

To freeze: cool, pack in a polythene (plastic) bag, seal, label and freeze.

To thaw and serve: place in a moderate oven, 180°C, 350°F, Gas Mark 4, and reheat for 15 to 20 minutes. Serve hot.

Makes 20 flans.

Smoked Salmon Flans

METRIC/IMPERIAL

125 g./5 oz. flour
salt and pepper
50 g./2 oz. butter or
    margarine
water
2 eggs
125 ml./¼ pint single cream
5 tablespoons milk
pinch of grated nutmeg
75 g./3 oz. smoked salmon
    pieces, cut into strips

AMERICAN

1¼ cups flour
salt and pepper
¼ cup butter or margarine
water
2 eggs
¾ cup light cream
¼ cup milk
pinch of grated nutmeg
3 oz. smoked salmon pieces,
    cut into strips

This can also be made in a 20 cm. (8 in.) flan case, when it will serve 6 portions.

To make the pastry, sift the flour and a pinch of salt into a bowl. Add the butter or margarine and cut it into small pieces with a table knife. Rub the fat into the flour until the mixture resembles breadcrumbs. Add enough water to make a firm dough. Divide the dough into four portions and roll out each one into a circle 12.5 cm. (5 in.) in diameter. Use these to line four 10 cm. (4 in.) diameter patty (muffin) tins. Press up the edges and flute.

Blend together the eggs, cream and milk. Season with salt, pepper and nutmeg. Strain the egg mixture into the flan cases and add the strips of salmon. Bake in a fairly hot oven, 190°C, 375°F, Gas Mark 5, for 35 to 40 minutes or until the filling is set and the pastry golden. Cool, then remove the flans from the tins.

To freeze: pack in a polythene (plastic) bag, seal, label and freeze.

To thaw and serve: replace in the tins and reheat in a moderate oven, 180°C, 350°F, Gas Mark 4, for 30 minutes. Serve warm with a green salad.

Serves 4.

~Bitterballen~

METRIC/IMPERIAL
6 g./¼ oz. or 2 teaspoons
  powdered gelatine
250 ml/½ pint beef stock or
  stock made with a beef
  stock cube
30 g./1¼ oz. butter
30 g./1¼ oz. flour
150 g./6 oz. cooked ham,
  finely chopped
2 teaspoons chopped parsley
¼ teaspoon grated nutmeg
salt and pepper
1 egg, beaten
about 75 g./3 oz. browned
  breadcrumbs
deep fat for frying

AMERICAN
2 teaspoons powdered
  gelatin
1¼ cups beef stock or stock
  made with a beef stock
  cube
2½ tablespoons butter
2½ tablespoons flour
1 cup finely chopped cooked
  ham
2 teaspoons chopped parsley
¼ teaspoon grated nutmeg
salt and pepper
1 egg, beaten
about 1 cup browned
  breadcrumbs
deep fat for frying

These are small meatballs, crisp on the outside and soft in the middle. In the Netherlands, they are served with drinks in most bars and restaurants.

Put the gelatine in a heatproof bowl with 3 tablespoons stock (or water) with the crumbled cube, if used. Place over a pan of simmering water and leave to stand until the gelatine has dissolved. Remove from the heat and stir in the remaining water.

Melt the butter in a saucepan and stir in the flour. Cook, stirring, for 2 minutes, then blend in the gelatine mixture. Bring to the boil, stirring, and simmer for 2 to 3 minutes, or until the sauce thickens.

Add the ham to the sauce with the parsley, nutmeg, salt and pepper. Turn on to a plate and leave in a cool place for several hours, or overnight, until set.

Roll the mixture into small balls. Coat the balls with egg and breadcrumbs twice.

To freeze: open freeze, then place in a polythene (plastic) bag, seal and label.

To thaw and serve: thaw in the refrigerator for 6 hours. Fry in hot fat until golden brown, drain on kitchen paper and serve hot with mild mustard.

Makes 30 to 40.

~Kidney, Bacon and Mushroom Kebabs~

METRIC/IMPERIAL
5 lamb's kidneys
10 streaky bacon rashers
100 g./4 oz. button
  mushrooms, halved
oil

AMERICAN
5 lamb's kidneys
10 fatty bacon slices
4 oz. button mushrooms,
  halved
oil

Remove the fat and membrane from the kidneys. Cut each in half and remove the core with scissors. Cut each half into three pieces.

Remove the rind from the bacon and stretch each rasher (slice) on a board with the back of a knife. Cut each into three pieces and roll them up.

Assemble the kebabs with a piece of kidney, bacon roll and mushroom half on a wooden cocktail stick. Place the kebabs on a baking sheet or grill (broiler) pan, brush with oil and grill (broil) for 5 minutes on each side.

To freeze: cool, wrap in aluminium foil, seal, label and freeze.

To thaw and serve: remove from the foil wrapping, place on a lightly greased ovenproof dish or baking sheet, lightly cover with foil and reheat in a warm oven, 170°C, 325°F, Gas Mark 3, for 20 to 25 minutes. Serve hot.

Makes 30 kebabs.

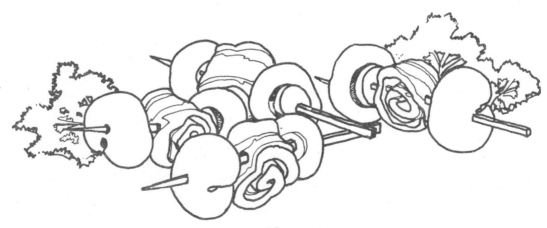

—Avocado Dip—

METRIC/IMPERIAL
2 avocado pears
juice of ½ lemon
1 tablespoon oil
1 teaspoon prepared mustard
1 teaspoon caster sugar
salt
freshly ground black pepper
125 ml./¼ pint double cream

Cut the avocado pears in half and remove the stones. Scoop out the flesh and place it in a bowl. Mash well with a fork. Mix the lemon juice, oil, mustard, sugar, salt and pepper together and stir into the mashed avocado. Whisk the cream until it is thick and forms soft peaks. Fold it into the avocado mixture.

To freeze: place in a small rigid container, cover, label and freeze.
To thaw and serve: leave to thaw at room temperature for 6 hours. Turn into a bowl and serve with potato crisps (chips), sticks of celery, chicory (endive) and carrot, sprigs of raw cauliflower or small sausages.

Serves 6.

AMERICAN
2 avocados
juice of ½ lemon
1 tablespoon oil
1 teaspoon prepared mustard
1 teaspoon superfine sugar
salt
freshly ground black pepper
⅝ cup heavy cream

—Red House Dip—

METRIC/IMPERIAL
4 tablespoons mango
   chutney, finely chopped
200 g./8 oz. rich cream cheese
¼ teaspoon dry mustard
1 teaspoon curry powder

Mix all the ingredients together well.
To freeze: place in a small rigid container, cover, label and freeze.
To thaw and serve: thaw in the refrigerator for 8 hours. Turn into a bowl or half a fresh pineapple shell and serve with potato crisps (chips), sticks of carrot and celery and sprigs of raw cauliflower.

Serves 6.

AMERICAN
4 tablespoons mango
   chutney, finely chopped
8 oz. rich cream cheese
¼ teaspoon dry mustard
1 teaspoon curry powder

—Blender Pâté—

METRIC/IMPERIAL
5 streaky bacon rashers
1 egg
100 g./4 oz. fresh
   breadcrumbs
200 g./8 oz. chicken livers
4 tablespoons dry sherry
100 g./4 oz. bacon trimmings
200 g./8 oz. pig's liver
½ garlic clove
1½ teaspoons salt
pinch of pepper
¼ teaspoon grated nutmeg
¼ teaspoon ground cloves
½ teaspoon dried mixed herbs
100 g./4 oz. lard, melted

This is a smooth pâté that is quick to make.

Remove the rind from the bacon. Place the rashers (slices) on a board and stretch with the back of a knife. Line the bottom and sides of a 1 kg. (2½ lb.) loaf tin or deep pie dish with the bacon rashers (slices).
   Using a liquidizer, reduce the egg, breadcrumbs, chicken livers and sherry to a purée. Pour into a bowl. Cut the bacon trimmings into small pieces and place in the liquidizer with the pig's liver, garlic, salt, pepper, nutmeg, cloves and herbs. Blend to a purée and add to the first mixture. Stir in the lard and mix well. Pour into the tin or dish and cover tightly with foil. Place in a roasting tin half full of warm water and bake in a warm oven, 170°C, 325°F, Gas Mark 3, for 2 hours.
To freeze: cool, turn out of the tin and wrap in a double thickness of aluminium foil. Label and freeze.
To thaw and serve: leave to thaw at room temperature for 6 hours. Serve with hot toast and butter.

Serves 4 to 6.

AMERICAN
5 fatty bacon slices
1 egg
2 cups fresh breadcrumbs
8 oz. chicken livers
4 tablespoons dry sherry
4 oz. bacon trimmings
8 oz. pig's liver
½ garlic clove
1½ teaspoons salt
pinch of pepper
¼ teaspoon grated nutmeg
¼ teaspoon ground cloves
½ teaspoon dried mixed herbs
½ cup lard, melted

~Terrine~

METRIC/IMPERIAL
300 g./12 oz. salt streaky pork
200 g./8 oz. pig's liver
200 g./8 oz. chicken livers
1 teaspoon chopped fresh
  thyme or ½ teaspoon dried
  thyme
2 tablespoons chopped
  parsley
2 garlic cloves, crushed
1½ teaspoons salt
¼ teaspoon pepper
50 g./2 oz. fresh brown
  breadcrumbs
5 tablespoons Madeira or
  sherry
¼ teaspoon ground mace
5 streaky bacon rashers

Mince (grind) the pork and livers together. Turn the meat into a bowl and mix in the thyme, parsley, garlic and seasoning. Soak the breadcrumbs in the Madeira or sherry until soft, then mash with a fork. Stir into the pork mixture with the mace.

Remove the rind from the bacon. Place the rashers (slices) on a board and stretch with the back of a knife. Line the bottom and sides of a 1 l. (2 pint) terrine with the bacon rashers (slices). Pour in the meat mixture and cover tightly with foil. Place in a roasting tin half full of warm water and bake in a cool oven, 150°C, 300°F, Gas Mark 2, for 2¼ hours.

To freeze: cool, cover the terrine with a lid of aluminium foil, label and freeze.

To thaw and serve: leave to thaw in the refrigerator overnight. Serve with hot toast and butter.

Serves 6.

AMERICAN
12 oz. salt streaky pork
8 oz. pig's liver
8 oz. chicken livers
1 teaspoon chopped fresh
  thyme or ½ teaspoon dried
  thyme
2 tablespoons chopped
  parsley
2 garlic cloves, crushed
1½ teaspoons salt
¼ teaspoon pepper
1 cup fresh brown
  breadcrumbs
5 tablespoons Madeira or
  sherry
¼ teaspoon ground mace
5 fatty bacon slices

~Spanish Pâté~

METRIC/IMPERIAL
200 g./8 oz. chicken livers
½ kg./1 lb. pig's liver
200 g./8 oz. chuck steak
600 g./1¼ lb. belly pork
300 g./12 oz. fat bacon
3 garlic cloves, crushed
1 tablespoon chopped fresh
  mixed herbs or 2 teaspoons
  dried mixed herbs
1 tablespoon salt
¾ teaspoon ground mace
1 egg
5 tablespoons sherry
4 tablespoons brandy
75 g./3 oz. Spanish stuffed
  green olives
black pepper

Mince (grind) the chicken livers, pig's liver, chuck steak, belly pork and bacon together. Add all the remaining ingredients and mix well. Put into two well-greased baking dishes or terrines and cover with aluminium foil. Stand in a roasting tin containing about 2.5 cm. (1 in.) of water and bake in a warm oven, 150°C, 300°F, Gas Mark 2, for 2 hours. Remove from the water bath and cool.

To freeze: cover with fresh foil, seal, label and freeze.

To thaw and serve: leave to thaw for 6 hours or overnight in the refrigerator. Turn out of the dishes or tins and decorate with extra sliced olives. Serve chilled with hot toast.

Serves 8.

AMERICAN
8 oz. chicken livers
1 lb. pig's liver
8 oz. chuck steak
1¼ lb. belly pork
12 oz. fat bacon
3 garlic cloves, crushed
1 tablespoon chopped fresh
  mixed herbs or 2 teaspoons
  dried mixed herbs
1 tablespoon salt
¾ teaspoon ground mace
1 egg
5 tablespoons sherry
4 tablespoons brandy
3 oz. stuffed green olives
black pepper

~Salmon Pâté~

METRIC/IMPERIAL
200 g./8 oz. smoked salmon
  pieces
juice of ½ lemon
freshly ground black pepper

There is no need to use prime smoked salmon for this pâté. You can usually buy salmon pieces — sometimes called trimmings — which are the slivers of salmon near the skin or any other chunky pieces that wouldn't sell as slices.

Put the salmon pieces in a liquidizer a few at a time and blend until coarsely chopped. Add the lemon juice and enough pepper to season well.

To freeze: place in a small rigid container, cover, label and freeze.

To thaw and serve: leave to thaw at room temperature for 6 hours. Serve on brown bread fingers or cheese sablés garnished with parsley sprigs, or serve as an hors d'oeuvre with buttered brown toast and lemon wedges.

Serves 4.

AMERICAN
8 oz. smoked salmon pieces
juice of ½ lemon
freshly ground black pepper

Kipper Pâté

METRIC/IMPERIAL
1 × 250 g./10 oz. packet
    buttered kipper fillets
125 ml./¼ pint double cream
pinch of cayenne pepper
parsley sprig

Cook the kipper fillets as directed on the packet. Remove them from the bag, drain off the butter and reserve. Remove all the dark skin and bones from the kipper fillets.

Put the fillets in a liquidizer with the cream, reserved butter and cayenne and blend until smooth. Alternatively, place all the ingredients in a bowl and mash well with a fork.

To freeze: place in a small rigid container, cover, label and freeze.
To thaw and serve: leave to thaw at room temperature for 3 hours or overnight in the refrigerator. Serve garnished with parsley, with hot toast and butter.

Serves 4.

AMERICAN
1 × 10 oz. packet buttered
    kipper fillets
⅝ cup heavy cream
pinch of cayenne pepper
parsley sprig

Smoked Trout Pâté

METRIC/IMPERIAL
2 large smoked trout
250 g./10 oz. butter, melted
75 g./3 oz. rich cream cheese
juice of ½ lemon
salt and pepper
parsley sprigs to garnish

This pâté may also be made with smoked mackerel.

Line a ½ kg. (1 lb.) loaf tin with foil.

Remove the skin and bones from the trout and purée in a liquidizer or mash well with a fork. Gradually add the butter, cream cheese, lemon juice and seasoning and blend or mash until smooth. Turn into the prepared tin and smooth the top.

To freeze: freeze for about 8 hours or until firm. Turn out of the tin, wrap in foil, label and return to the freezer.
To thaw and serve: leave to thaw for 8 hours in the refrigerator. Remove the foil and garnish with parsley. Serve with hot toast and butter.

Serves 6.

AMERICAN
2 large smoked trout
1¼ cups butter, melted
3 oz. rich cream cheese
juice of ½ lemon
salt and pepper
parsley sprigs to garnish

Buckling Mousse

METRIC/IMPERIAL
12½ g./½ oz. gelatine
3 tablespoons water
25 g./1 oz. butter
25 g./1 oz. flour
250 ml./½ pint milk
3 buckling, skinned and
    filleted
4 hard-boiled eggs, yolks
    sieved and whites finely
    chopped
salt and pepper
2 pinches of cayenne pepper
3 tablespoons mayonnaise
lemon wedges and parsley
    sprigs to garnish

This mousse can also be made using smoked trout.

Put the gelatine in a small heatproof bowl with the water. Leave to soak for 5 minutes. Stand the bowl in a pan of simmering water and stir until the gelatine has dissolved.

Melt the butter in a saucepan and stir in the flour. Cook, stirring, for 1 minute. Gradually add the milk, stirring constantly. Simmer for 3 minutes or until the sauce has thickened. Stir in the dissolved gelatine. Cool the sauce, stirring frequently so that a skin does not form.

Mash the buckling fillets with any soft roes. Add to the sauce with the eggs, seasoning, cayenne and mayonnaise. Turn the mixture into a mould.

To freeze: cover the mould with a lid of aluminium foil, label and freeze.
To thaw and serve: leave to thaw overnight in the refrigerator. Decorate with lemon wedges and parsley.

Serves 4.

AMERICAN
½ oz. gelatin
3 tablespoons water
2 tablespoons butter
¼ cup flour
1¼ cups milk
3 buckling, skinned and
    filleted
4 hard-boiled eggs, yolks
    sieved and whites finely
    chopped
salt and pepper
2 pinches of cayenne pepper
3 tablespoons mayonnaise
lemon wedges and parsley
    sprigs to garnish

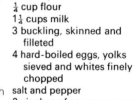

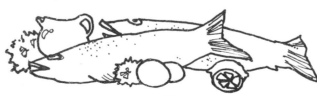

~Egg Mousse~

METRIC/IMPERIAL
18 g./¾ oz. gelatine
125 ml./¼ pint water
1 × 250 g./10 oz. can
    condensed consommé
12 hard-boiled eggs, chopped
250 ml./½ pint double cream,
    whipped until thick
250 ml./½ pint mayonnaise
salt and pepper
1 tablespoon chopped parsley

Incorporated into this mousse, chopped hard-boiled eggs freeze very well, as does the mayonnaise since it is mixed with whipped cream.

Put the gelatine in a small heatproof bowl with the water. Leave to soak for 5 minutes. Stand the bowl in a pan of simmering water and stir until the gelatine has dissolved. Add the gelatine to the undiluted consommé.

Mix together the eggs, cream, mayonnaise and three-quarters of the consommé. Check the seasoning, then pour the mixture into a serving dish. Chill the mousse until it is set.

Mix the chopped parsley with the remaining consommé and pour it carefully over the mousse. Chill until set.

To freeze: cover the dish with a lid of aluminium foil, label and freeze.

To thaw and serve: leave to thaw in the refrigerator overnight.

Serves 10 to 12.

AMERICAN
¾ oz. gelatin
⅝ cup water
1 × 10 oz. can condensed
    consommé
12 hard-boiled eggs, chopped
1¼ cups heavy cream,
    whipped until thick
1¼ cups mayonnaise
salt and pepper
1 tablespoon chopped parsley

~Smoked Haddock Creams~

METRIC/IMPERIAL
750 g./1½ lb. smoked
    haddock fillets
250 ml./½ pint milk
125 ml/¼ pint water
1 bay leaf
¼ teaspoon ground mace
6 peppercorns
25 g./1 oz. butter
25 g./1 oz. flour
salt and pepper
4 tablespoons single cream
25 g./1 oz. fresh breadcrumbs,
    toasted

Poach the haddock in the milk and water with the bay leaf, mace and peppercorns for 10 minutes. Remove the fish from the pan and strain the poaching liquid. Set aside.

Remove the skin and bones from the fish and flake it.

Melt the butter in a saucepan and stir in the flour. Cook, stirring, for 1 minute. Gradually add the reserved poaching liquid, stirring constantly. Bring to the boil and simmer for 3 minutes or until the sauce is thick. Add the fish and check the seasoning. Stir in the cream.

Divide the mixture between six scallop shells and sprinkle over the breadcrumbs.

To freeze: cool in the refrigerator, then cover each scallop with a lid of aluminium foil. Label and freeze.

To thaw and serve: remove the foil lids, place the scallop shells in a hot oven, 200°C, 400°F, Gas Mark 6 and reheat for 25 to 30 minutes.

Serves 6.

AMERICAN
1½ lb. smoked haddock fillets
1¼ cups milk
⅝ cup water
1 bay leaf
¼ teaspoon ground mace
6 peppercorns
2 tablespoons butter
¼ cup flour
salt and pepper
4 tablespoons light cream
½ cup fresh breadcrumbs,
    toasted

~Taramasalata~

METRIC/IMPERIAL
200 g./8 oz. smoked cod's roe
2 small slices white bread
2 tablespoons milk
6 tablespoons olive oil
2 tablespoons lemon juice
freshly ground black pepper

Remove the skin from the cod's roe. Place the roe in a mortar or bowl and pound with a pestle or mash with a fork until smooth.

Remove the crusts from the bread. Soak the slices in the milk, then squeeze out as much of the milk as possible. Add to the cod's roe and mash again. Add the oil a teaspoon at a time, mixing well. Stir in the lemon juice and pepper.

To freeze: place in a rigid polythene (plastic) container, cover, label and freeze.

To thaw and serve: leave to thaw at room temperature for 3 hours or overnight in the refrigerator. Serve with hot toast and butter.

Serves 4.

AMERICAN
8 oz. smoked cod's roe
2 small slices white bread
2 tablespoons milk
6 tablespoons olive oil
2 tablespoons lemon juice
freshly ground black pepper

─Ratatouille─

METRIC/IMPERIAL
50 g./2 oz. butter
2 large green peppers, pith
and seeds removed, cut
into strips
2 medium-sized onions, sliced
2 small aubergines, sliced
200 g./8 oz. tomatoes,
skinned, quartered and
seeds removed
5 tablespoons water
salt and pepper

Melt the butter in a saucepan and add the peppers and onions. Fry for about 5 minutes or until the onions are soft and golden brown. Add the aubergines (eggplants) and tomatoes with the water and seasoning to taste. Cook for 5 minutes.
To freeze: cool, place in a polythene (plastic) bag, seal, label and freeze.
To thaw and serve: to serve hot, thaw slowly in a non-stick pan over low heat or in a warm oven, 170°C, 325°F, Gas Mark 3, for about 30 minutes. To serve cold, leave to thaw at room temperature for 4 to 5 hours. Serve as an appetizer or as a vegetable with grilled (broiled) meat.

Serves 4.

AMERICAN
¼ cup butter
2 large green peppers, pith
and seeds removed, cut
into strips
2 medium-sized onions, sliced
2 small eggplants, sliced
8 oz. tomatoes, skinned,
quartered and seeds
removed
5 tablespoons water
salt and pepper

─Moules Marinières─

METRIC/IMPERIAL
3 l./6 pints mussels
4 shallots, chopped
25 g./1 oz. butter
4 parsley stalks
2 fresh thyme sprigs or ¼
teaspoon dried thyme
1 bay leaf
freshly ground black pepper
250 ml./½ pint dry white wine
12½ g./½ oz. butter mixed to a
paste with 12½ g./½ oz. flour
salt
chopped parsley to garnish

Scrape each mussel with a strong knife, removing every trace of seaweed, mud and beard. Wash in several changes of water, discarding any mussels which are badly chipped or cracked or ones which are not tightly closed. (Mussels that stay open are dead and should not be used.) Drain the mussels in a colander.

Fry the shallots in the butter until they are translucent but not browned. Add the herbs, pepper and wine and stir well. Then add the mussels. Cover the pan with a tight-fitting lid and cook for about 5 to 6 minutes, shaking the pan constantly, or until the mussels open. Discard any which remain closed. Lift the mussels out of the pan and discard the empty half of the shells.

Put the mussels in a rigid container and the remaining half shells in a polythene (plastic) bag. Bring the cooking liquid to the boil and boil until it has reduced to 250 ml. (½ pint) or 1¼ cups. Remove the parsley, fresh thyme (if used) and the bay leaf.

Form the butter and flour paste (beurre manié) into small balls and drop them, one at a time, into the simmering cooking liquid, stirring constantly. Cook until the liquid has thickened, then adjust the seasoning. Pour the liquid over the mussels.
To freeze: cool, cover, label and freeze. Use within two months.
To thaw and serve: leave to thaw overnight in the refrigerator. Turn into a saucepan and reheat gently, then bring to the boil. Arrange the shells in a dish, pour over the mussels and liquid and sprinkle with parsley. Serve with French bread and butter.

Serves 4 to 6.

AMERICAN
6 pints mussels
4 shallots, chopped
2 tablespoons butter
4 parsley stalks
2 fresh thyme sprigs or ¼
teaspoon dried thyme
1 bay leaf
freshly ground black pepper
1¼ cups dry white wine
1 tablespoon butter mixed to a
paste with 2 tablespoons
flour
salt
chopped parsley to garnish

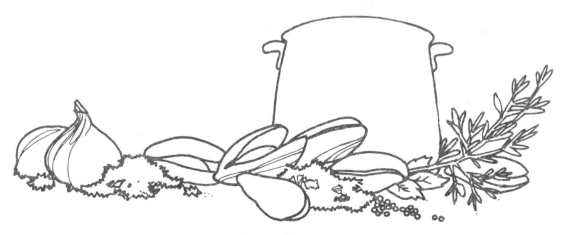

~ Prawns Provençale ~

METRIC/IMPERIAL
1 small onion, finely chopped
25 g./1 oz. butter
1 garlic clove, crushed
½ kg./1 lb. tomatoes, skinned,
    quartered and seeds
    removed
1 teaspoon chopped parsley
1 tablespoon dry sherry
    (optional)
1 teaspoon chopped chives
200 g./8 oz. shelled prawns
salt and pepper

Fry the onion gently in the butter until it is soft but not brown. Stir in the garlic and tomatoes and simmer until the tomatoes are soft but still retain their shape. Add the parsley, sherry (if used), chives and prawns (shrimp) and bring to the boil. Season to taste.
To freeze: turn into a boil-in-the-bag or small rigid container, cool, seal or cover, label and freeze.
To thaw and serve: either place the bag in a saucepan of boiling water and boil for 15 minutes, or turn the prawns (shrimp) and sauce into a saucepan and heat through slowly, stirring. Serve with plain boiled rice or brown bread and butter.

Serves 4.

AMERICAN
1 small onion, finely chopped
2 tablespoons butter
1 garlic clove, crushed
1 lb. tomatoes, skinned,
    quartered and seeds
    removed
1 teaspoon chopped parsley
1 tablespoon dry sherry
    (optional)
1 teaspoon chopped chives
8 oz. shelled baby shrimp
salt and pepper

~ Mint and Melon Cocktail ~

METRIC/IMPERIAL
1 small ripe melon
2 tablespoons lime juice
125 ml./¼ pint sweet white
    wine
4 mint sprigs

Halve the melon and remove the seeds. Peel the melon halves and discard the skin. Cut the flesh into cubes and place them in a rigid container with the lime juice and wine.
To freeze: cover, label and freeze.
To thaw and serve: leave to thaw in the refrigerator overnight. Divide between four individual glasses and top each with a mint sprig.

Serves 4.

AMERICAN
1 small ripe melon
2 tablespoons lime juice
⅝ cup sweet white wine
4 mint sprigs

~ Artichoke Soup ~

METRIC/IMPERIAL
½ kg./1 lb. Jerusalem
    artichokes
625 ml./1¼ pints chicken
    stock or stock made with a
    chicken stock cube
½ teaspoon dried basil
1 bay leaf
2 parsley sprigs
1 onion, quartered
25 g./1 oz. butter
25 g./1 oz. flour
250 ml./½ pint milk
salt and pepper
125 ml./¼ pint single cream
chopped parsley to garnish

Put the artichokes in a saucepan and cover with cold water. Bring to the boil, cover and simmer for 15 minutes. Drain well.

Peel the artichokes and return them to the pan with the chicken stock, basil, bay leaf, parsley and onion. Bring to the boil, cover and simmer for 15 minutes or until the artichokes are tender. Strain and reserve the cooking liquid. Remove and discard the parsley sprigs and bay leaf. Purée the artichokes and onion in a liquidizer or by pushing them through a sieve.

Melt the butter in a saucepan and stir in the flour. Cook, stirring, for 1 minute. Gradually add the strained cooking liquid, stirring constantly. Stir in the milk and vegetable purée. Bring to the boil, stirring, and simmer for 5 minutes. Season to taste.
To freeze: turn into a rigid container, cool, cover, label and freeze.
To thaw and serve: turn the frozen soup into a saucepan and thaw gently, stirring frequently. Bring to the boil, adjust the seasoning, and stir in the cream. Pour into bowls and sprinkle with parsley.

Serves 4.

AMERICAN
1 lb. Jerusalem artichokes
3 cups chicken stock or stock
    made with a chicken stock
    cube
½ teaspoon dried basil
1 bay leaf
2 parsley sprigs
1 onion, quartered
2 tablespoons butter
¼ cup flour
1¼ cups milk
salt and pepper
⅝ cup light cream
chopped parsley to garnish

(Right) Kipper Pâté

Scottish Vegetable Soup

METRIC/IMPERIAL
1 knuckle of bacon
1 large onion, chopped
3 carrots, scraped and diced
2 potatoes, peeled and diced
3 celery stalks, sliced
25 g./1 oz. dripping
1 bay leaf
salt and pepper
100 g./4 oz. frozen peas

Soak the bacon (ham) overnight and drain. Place it in a saucepan and cover with cold water. Bring to the boil, drain off the water and add 1 l. (2 pints) or 5 cups fresh cold water. Bring to the boil and simmer for 40 minutes.

Fry the onion, carrots, potatoes and celery in the dripping in a large saucepan for 5 minutes, stirring. Drain the cooking liquid from the bacon (ham) and add to the pan with the bay leaf and seasoning. Cover and simmer for 30 minutes.

Remove the skin and fat from the bacon (ham) and cut the meat into small pieces. Add to the soup with the peas and cook for a further 5 minutes. Adjust the seasoning.

To freeze: pour into a rigid container, cool, cover, label and freeze.
To thaw and serve: leave to thaw overnight in the refrigerator. Turn into a large saucepan and reheat slowly, stirring occasionally. Serve very hot with rolls.

Serves 6.

AMERICAN
1 knuckle of smoked ham
1 large onion, chopped
3 carrots, scraped and diced
2 potatoes, peeled and diced
3 celery stalks, sliced
2 tablespoons dripping
1 bay leaf
salt and pepper
4 oz. frozen peas

Onion Soup au Gratin

METRIC/IMPERIAL
2 tablespoons oil
25 g./1 oz. butter
500 g./1 lb. onions, finely chopped
25 g./1 oz. flour
750 ml./1½ pints home-made chicken or game stock, or stock made with 2 chicken stock cubes
2 teaspoons tomato purée
salt and pepper
6 slices French bread
40 g./1½ oz. Cheddar cheese, grated

Heat the oil in a saucepan, then add the butter. When it has melted add the onions and fry until they are beginning to brown. Blend in the flour and cook gently, stirring, until brown. Gradually stir in the stock, tomato purée and seasoning. Bring to the boil and simmer, covered, for 40 minutes.

To freeze: cool, turn into a rigid container, cover, label and freeze.
To thaw and serve: turn the frozen soup into a saucepan and thaw slowly over low heat, stirring occasionally, or thaw at room temperature before reheating. Bring to the boil. Lightly toast the bread and sprinkle with the cheese. Brown under the grill (broiler) and float the bread on top of the soup.

Serves 6.

AMERICAN
2 tablespoons oil
2 tablespoons butter
1 lb. onions, finely chopped
¼ cup flour
3¾ cups home-made chicken or game stock, or stock made with 2 chicken stock cubes
2 teaspoons tomato purée
salt and pepper
6 slices French bread
½ cup grated Cheddar cheese

Green Pepper Soup

METRIC/IMPERIAL
2 tablespoons oil
50 g./2 oz butter
200 g./8 oz. green peppers, seeds and cores removed, diced
2 onions, chopped
38 g./1½ oz. flour
375 ml./¾ pint home-made chicken stock or stock made with 2 chicken stock cubes
salt and pepper
375 ml./¾ pint milk
2 to 3 tablespoons single cream

This is an unusual soup which takes up little room in the freezer as the milk is added after thawing and reheating the soup.

Heat the oil in a saucepan, then add the butter. When it has melted, add the green peppers and onions and cook gently for 5 minutes. Blend in the flour and cook for 1 minute. Gradually stir in the stock and bring to the boil. Season and simmer, covered, for 30 minutes or until the vegetables are soft.

Push the soup through a sieve or purée in a liquidizer.
To freeze: pour into a rigid container, cool, cover, label and freeze.
To thaw and serve: turn the frozen soup into a saucepan, add 2 tablespoons water and reheat gently, covered, stirring occasionally. When thawed, stir in the milk. Heat through and add the cream just before serving. If serving cold, add extra cream.

Serves 4.

AMERICAN
2 tablespoons oil
¼ cup butter
8 oz. green peppers, seeds and cores removed, diced
2 onions, chopped
6 tablespoons flour
2 cups home-made chicken stock or stock made with 2 chicken stock cubes
salt and pepper
2 cups milk
2 to 3 tablespoons light cream

—Watercress Soup—

METRIC/IMPERIAL
2 bunches of watercress
50 g./2 oz. butter
1 onion, sliced
300 g./12 oz. potatoes, peeled
  and sliced
500 ml./1 pint home-made
  chicken stock or stock
  made with a chicken stock
  cube
salt and pepper
1 mace blade
375 ml./¾ pint boiling milk
125 ml./¼ pint single cream

Wash the watercress but do not remove the stalks. Trim off a small bunch of leaves to use for garnish.

Melt the butter in a saucepan and gently cook the onion and potatoes for about 4 minutes, not letting them brown. Add the stock, seasoning and mace blade. Bring to the boil and simmer, covered, for 15 minutes.

Add the watercress, with stalks, and simmer for a further 10 minutes. Remove the mace blade and push the soup through a sieve or purée it in a liquidizer.

To freeze: pour into a rigid container, cool, cover, label and freeze.
To thaw and serve: turn the frozen soup into a saucepan and reheat gently until thawed. Stir until well blended and add the boiling milk. Stir in the cream and sprinkle each serving with the finely chopped reserved watercress leaves.

Serves 4 to 6

AMERICAN
2 bunches of watercress
¼ cup butter
1 onion, sliced
12 oz. potatoes, peeled and
  sliced
2½ cups home-made chicken
  stock or stock made with a
  chicken stock cube
salt and pepper
1 mace blade
2 cups boiling milk
½ cup light cream

—Gazpacho—

METRIC/IMPERIAL
500 g./1 lb. tomatoes,
  skinned and sliced
1 small onion, sliced
1 garlic clove, crushed
2 slices white bread
4 tablespoons wine vinegar
5 tablespoons olive oil
250 ml/½ pint home-made
  chicken stock or stock
  made with a chicken stock
  cube
¼ small green pepper, seeds
  and core removed, diced
1 to 2 tablespoons lemon juice
salt and pepper
¼ cucumber, diced
fried croûtons

The fried croûtons may be frozen separately from the soup. Try diced green pepper and onion as alternatives to serve with the soup.

Put the tomatoes, onion, garlic, bread, vinegar, oil and stock in a liquidizer. Blend for a few seconds until the mixture is well combined. If necessary, blend in two or three batches. Turn the mixture into a bowl. Stir in the green pepper, lemon juice and seasoning.
To freeze: turn into a rigid container, cover, label and freeze.
To thaw and serve: leave to thaw overnight in the refrigerator. Serve with diced cucumber and fried croûtons.

Serves 4.

AMERICAN
1 lb. tomatoes, skinned and
  sliced
1 small onion, sliced
1 garlic clove, crushed
2 slices white bread
4 tablespoons wine vinegar
5 tablespoons olive oil
1¼ cups home-made chicken
  stock or stock made with a
  chicken stock cube
¼ small green pepper, seeds
  and core removed, diced
1 to 2 tablespoons lemon juice
salt and pepper
¼ cucumber, diced
fried croûtons

Green Pepper Soup

(right) Prawns Provençale

— Iced Cucumber Soup —

METRIC/IMPERIAL
1 large cucumber, peeled and
  roughly chopped
500 ml./1 pint home-made
  chicken stock or stock
  made with a chicken stock
  cube
¼ teaspoon dried mixed herbs
small bunch of chives
125 ml./¼ pint soured cream
salt and pepper

Put the cucumber, stock, herbs and most of the chives (reserve a few for garnish) in a saucepan. Bring to the boil and simmer, covered, for 10 minutes or until the cucumber is tender. Push the soup through a sieve or purée in a liquidizer.
To freeze: turn into a rigid container, cool, cover, label and freeze.
To thaw and serve: leave to thaw overnight in the refrigerator. Blend a little of the soup with the soured cream, then add this to the remaining soup with the seasoning. Sprinkle with the chopped reserved chives.

Serves 4.

AMERICAN
1 large cucumber, peeled and
  roughly chopped
2½ cups home-made chicken
  stock or stock made with a
  chicken stock cube
¼ teaspoon dried mixed herbs
small bunch of chives
⅝ cup sour cream
salt and pepper

— Hot Curry and Apple Soup —

METRIC/IMPERIAL
25 g./1 oz. butter
1 onion, finely chopped
38 g./1½ oz. flour
1 tablespoon curry powder
750 ml./1½ pints home-made
  chicken stock or stock
  made with 2 chicken stock
  cubes
700 g./1½ lb. cooking apples,
  peeled, cored and roughly
  sliced
juice of ½ lemon
salt and pepper
125 ml./¼ pint single cream

Melt the butter in a saucepan and add the onion. Fry gently until it is soft but not brown. Stir in the flour and curry powder and cook, stirring, for 1 minute. Add the stock, apples and lemon juice and stir well. Bring to the boil and simmer for 15 minutes. Leave the soup to cool slightly then push it through a sieve or purée it in a liquidizer. Adjust the seasoning.
To freeze: cool, pour into a rigid container, cover, label and freeze.
To thaw and serve: turn the frozen soup into a saucepan, add 2 tablespoons water and reheat gently, stirring occasionally. Bring to the boil. If necessary, add a little more stock to thin down the soup. Serve with a swirl of cream in each bowl of soup.

Serves 6.

AMERICAN
2 tablespoons butter
1 onion, finely chopped
6 tablespoons flour
1 tablespoon curry powder
3¾ cups home-made chicken
  stock or stock made with
  2 chicken stock cubes
1½ lb. cooking apples, peeled,
  cored and roughly sliced
juice of ½ lemon
salt and pepper
⅝ cup light cream

Main dishes

Beef Rouladen

(right) Preparing Jugged Chuck Steak

Jugged Chuck Steak

METRIC/IMPERIAL
¾ kg./1½ lb. chuck steak, cut
   into chunks
38 g./1½ oz. lard
2 small onions, each stuck
   with 2 cloves
1 celery stalk, sliced
6 peppercorns
thinly pared rind of ½ lemon
pinch of cayenne pepper
1 mace blade
1 thyme sprig
1 bay leaf
2 parsley sprigs
salt and pepper
½ l./1 pint water
25 g./1 oz. flour
125 ml./¼ pint port wine
1 tablespoon redcurrant jelly

Brown the meat chunks quickly in the lard, drain on absorbent paper towels and place in a casserole. Add the onions, celery, peppercorns, lemon rind, cayenne, mace, thyme, bay leaf, parsley, seasoning and water. Cover and braise in a warm oven, 170°C, 325°F, Gas Mark 3, for 1½ to 2 hours or until the meat is tender.

Remove the pieces of meat and place them in a rigid container. Strain the cooking liquid into a saucepan. Blend the flour with a little of the cool liquid and stir into the saucepan. Bring to the boil. stirring, and simmer until the sauce has thickened. Add the port and redcurrant jelly and blend well. Pour the sauce over the meat.
To freeze: cool, cover, label and freeze.
To thaw and serve: put into a casserole, preferably nonstick, cover and reheat in a warm oven, 170°C, 325°F, Gas Mark 3, for 45 minutes, stirring occasionally.

Serves 4.

AMERICAN
1½ lb. chuck steak, cut into
   chunks
3 tablespoons lard
2 small onions, each stuck
   with 2 cloves
1 celery stalk, sliced
6 peppercorns
thinly pared rind of ½ lemon
pinch of cayenne pepper
1 mace blade
1 thyme sprig
1 bay leaf
2 parsley sprigs
salt and pepper
2½ cups water
¼ cup flour
⅝ cup port wine
1 tablespoon redcurrant jelly

Steak and Kidney Pie

METRIC/IMPERIAL
600 g./1¼ lb. stewing steak
200 g./8 oz. ox kidney
25 g./1 oz. flour
100 g./4 oz. streaky bacon,
   cut into strips
1 large onion, chopped
25 g./1 oz. dripping
250 ml./½ pint beef stock or
   stock made with a stock
   cube
1 teaspoon Worcestershire
   sauce
1 tablespoon tomato ketchup
1 teaspoon salt
¼ teaspoon pepper
1 × 175 g./7 oz. packet
   commercial frozen puff
   pastry, thawed

Cut the steak and kidney into 2.5 cm. (1 in.) pieces and put in a polythene (plastic) bag with the flour. Toss until well coated, then fry with the bacon and onion in the dripping until browned. Stir in any flour left in the bag.

Add the stock and bring to the boil, stirring. Blend in the Worcestershire sauce, ketchup and seasoning. Cover and simmer for 1½ to 2 hours or until the meat is tender.

Turn into an aluminium foil pie dish and allow to cool completely. Roll out the pastry dough and place over the pie dish. Seal and crimp the edges.
To freeze: cover with foil, label and freeze.
To thaw and serve: remove the foil, brush the dough with milk and bake in a hot oven, 220°C, 425°F, Gas Mark 7, for 30 minutes. Reduce the oven temperature to moderate, 180°C, 350°F, Gas Mark 4, and bake for a further 20 minutes or until the pastry is well risen and golden brown.

Serves 6.

AMERICAN
1¼ lb. stewing steak
8 oz. ox kidney
¼ cup flour
4 oz. fatty bacon, cut into
   strips
1 large onion, chopped
2 tablespoons dripping
1¼ cups beef stock or stock
   made with a stock cube
1 teaspoon Worcestershire
   sauce
1 tablespoon tomato ketchup
1 teaspoon salt
¼ teaspoon pepper
1 × 7 oz. packet commercial
   frozen puff pastry, thawed

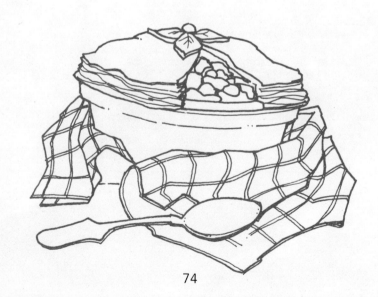

Beef Stroganoff

METRIC/IMPERIAL
1 large onion, chopped
63 g./2½ oz. butter
100 g./4 oz. button
  mushrooms, sliced
2 tomatoes, skinned, seeded
  and chopped
1 tablespoon oil
600 g./1¼ lb. fillet steak, cut
  into strips 5 cm./2 in. long
salt and pepper
125 ml./¼ pint soured cream

Fry the onion in 25 g. (1 oz.) or 2 tablespoons of the butter until soft but not brown. Remove the onion from the pan. Add the mushrooms to the pan with 13 g. (½ oz.) or 1 tablespoon of the remaining butter and fry for 2 minutes. Stir in the tomatoes and cook for a further 2 minutes. Add the mushroom and tomato mixture to the onion.

Melt the remaining butter in the pan with the oil. Add half the steak and fry for 4 minutes, turning frequently, or until just tender. Remove from the pan and cook the remaining steak.
To freeze: put the vegetables and steak in a rigid container, cool, cover, label and freeze.
To thaw and serve: put into a saucepan and reheat gently to simmering. Season to taste, remove from the heat and stir in the soured cream. Serve at once.

Serves 4.

AMERICAN
1 large onion, chopped
5 tablespoons butter
4 oz. button mushrooms,
  sliced
2 tomatoes, skinned, seeded
  and chopped
1 tablespoon oil
1¼ lb. tenderloin steak, cut
  into strips 2 in. long
salt and pepper
⅝ cup sour cream

Meatballs in Piquant Onion Sauce

METRIC/IMPERIAL
300 g./12 oz. minced beef
50 g./2 oz. fresh white
  breadcrumbs
1 egg
salt and pepper
¼ teaspoon dried marjoram
25 g./1 oz. dripping
200 g./8 oz. onions, sliced
25 g./1 oz. flour
250 ml./½ pint beef stock or
  stock made with a stock
  cube
1 tablespoon tomato ketchup
1 tablespoon Worcestershire
  sauce
¼ teaspoon gravy browning

Mix together the beef, breadcrumbs, egg, seasoning and marjoram. Turn out onto a floured board and shape into 16 balls. Fry the meatballs in the dripping until they are brown on all sides. Transfer them to a plate. Fry the onions for 3 minutes, stirring occasionally. Blend in the flour. Add the stock and bring to the boil, stirring. Stir in the ketchup, Worcestershire sauce, gravy browning and seasoning. Return the meatballs to the pan, cover and cook gently for 30 minutes.
To freeze: turn into a rigid container, cool, cover, label and freeze.
To thaw and serve: put into a casserole, preferably nonstick, cover and reheat in a warm oven, 170°C, 325°F, Gas Mark 3, for 40 minutes, stirring occasionally. Serve with creamed potatoes.

Serves 4.

AMERICAN
12 oz. ground beef
1 cup fresh white
  breadcrumbs
1 egg
salt and pepper
¼ teaspoon dried marjoram
2 tablespoons dripping
8 oz. onions, sliced
¼ cup flour
1¼ cups beef stock or stock
  made with a stock cube
1 tablespoon tomato ketchup
1 tablespoon Worcestershire
  sauce
¼ teaspoon gravy browning

Spiced Casserole

METRIC/IMPERIAL
1 kg./2 lb. neck of beef, cut
  into chunks
38 g./1½ oz. flour
salt and pepper
50 g./2 oz. dripping
200 g./8 oz. onions, sliced
2 garlic cloves, crushed
100 g./4 oz. mushrooms,
  sliced
½ green pepper, pith and seeds
  removed and diced
2 tablespoons sweet chutney
625 ml/1¼ pints beef stock or
  stock made with 2 beef
  stock cubes
½ teaspoon dried rosemary
4 tablespoons port or
  Madeira

Put the meat in a polythene (plastic) bag with the flour and seasoning and toss until well coated. Brown the meat quickly in the dripping in a flameproof casserole or saucepan. Add all the remaining ingredients, including any flour left in the bag, and bring to the boil. Cover and simmer for 2½ hours, stirring occasionally.
To freeze: turn into a rigid container, cool, cover, label and freeze.
To thaw and serve: leave to thaw overnight in the refrigerator, then reheat gently in a saucepan for 30 minutes. Otherwise, put the frozen mixture in a saucepan with 3 tablespoons water, cover and reheat gently, stirring occasionally, until simmering. Simmer for 20 minutes.

Serves 6.

AMERICAN
2 lb. chuck steak, cut into
  chunks
⅜ cup flour
salt and pepper
¼ cup dripping
8 oz. onions, sliced
2 garlic cloves, crushed
4 oz. mushrooms, sliced
½ green pepper, pith and seeds
  removed and diced
2 tablespoons sweet chutney
3 cups beef stock or stock
  made with 2 beef stock
  cubes
½ teaspoon dried rosemary
4 tablespoons port or
  Madeira

Hungarian Pork
(right) Moussaka

—Irish Beef with Dumplings—

METRIC/IMPERIAL

2 streaky bacon rashers, cut into small pieces
25 g./1 oz. lard or dripping
¾ to 1 kg./1½ to 2 lb. lean beef (flank, skirt, chuck or brisket), cut into large chunks
200 g./8 oz. onions, chopped
200 g./8 oz. carrots, scraped and diced
½ teaspoon salt
125 ml./¼ pint Guinness
¼ teaspoon pepper
375 ml./¾ pint beef stock or stock made with a stock cube

Dumplings
100 g./4 oz. self-raising flour
salt and pepper
50 g./2 oz. shredded suet
4 tablespoons water

Fry the bacon in the lard or dripping until it is just golden brown. Transfer it to a large saucepan. Brown the meat in the fat remaining in the frying-pan and transfer it to the saucepan. Put the vegetables on top of the meat and add the salt, Guinness, pepper and stock. Bring to the boil, cover and simmer for 1¾ hours or until the meat is nearly tender.

To make the dumplings, sift the flour and seasoning into a bowl. Add the suet and enough water to make a soft dough. Roll into eight small balls and add them to the saucepan. Simmer, covered, for 15 to 20 minutes longer or until the meat is tender and the dumplings are cooked. Do not lift the lid of the pan while the dumplings are cooking.

To freeze: turn the stew into a large foil dish with the dumplings on top, cool, cover, label and freeze.

To thaw and serve: remove the lid, cover lightly with a piece of foil and reheat in a moderate oven, 180°C, 350°F, Gas Mark 4, for 1 hour.

Serves 4 to 6.

AMERICAN

2 fatty bacon slices, cut into small pieces
2 tablespoons lard or dripping
1½ to 2 lb. lean beef (flank, skirt, chuck or brisket), cut into large chunks
8 oz. onions, chopped
8 oz. carrots, scraped and diced
½ teaspoon salt
⅝ cup Guinness
¼ teaspoon pepper
2 cups beef stock or stock made with a stock cube

Dumplings
1 cup self-rising flour
salt and pepper
¼ cup shredded suet
4 tablespoons water

—Beef Stuffed Peppers—

METRIC/IMPERIAL

½ kg./1 lb. minced beef
2 onions, chopped
2 tablespoons flour
250 ml./½ pint beef stock or stock made with a stock cube
salt and pepper
2 carrots, scraped and grated
4 large green peppers, halved and pith and seeds removed

Cheese sauce
25 g./1 oz. butter
25 g./1 oz. flour
250 ml./½ pint milk
½ teaspoon prepared mustard
50 g./2 oz. grated cheese
salt and pepper

Fry the beef and onions together for 5 minutes, stirring frequently, then stir in the flour. Add the stock and seasoning and bring to the boil. Stir in the carrots, cover and simmer for 30 minutes.

Meanwhile, blanch the peppers in boiling water for 5 minutes. Drain well and set aside.

To make the cheese sauce, melt the butter in a saucepan and stir in the flour. Cook, stirring, for 1 minute. Gradually add the milk, stirring constantly. Bring to the boil, stirring, and simmer until the sauce has thickened. Stir in the mustard, cheese and seasoning.

Fill each pepper half with the beef mixture and place in a foil dish. Pour the cheese sauce around.

To freeze: cool, cover with a lid of foil, label and freeze.

To thaw and serve: place in a fairly hot oven, 190°C, 375°F, Gas Mark 5, and bake for 40 minutes. Remove the foil lid and bake for a further 10 to 15 minutes. Serve with French bread or soft rolls.

Serves 4.

AMERICAN

1 lb. ground beef
2 onions, chopped
2 tablespoons flour
1¼ cups beef stock or stock made with a stock cube
salt and pepper
2 carrots, scraped and grated
4 large green peppers, halved and pith and seeds removed

Cheese sauce
2 tablespoons butter
¼ cup flour
1¼ cups milk
½ teaspoon prepared mustard
½ cup grated cheese
salt and pepper

~Swiss Steak~

METRIC/IMPERIAL

¾ kg./1½ lb. chuck steak,
   2.5 cm./1 in. thick, cut into
   8 pieces
38 g./1½ oz. flour
salt and pepper
38 g./1½ oz. lard
2 onions, sliced
2 celery stalks, chopped
1 × 200 g./8 oz. can tomatoes
2 teaspoons tomato purée
½ teaspoon Worcestershire
   sauce
125 ml./¼ pint water

Coat the meat with the flour which has been seasoned, pressing the flour on so that all is used. Brown the meat quickly in the lard, then transfer it to a casserole. Add the onions and celery to the fat remaining in the frying-pan and fry until they are pale golden brown. Add the vegetables to the casserole with all the remaining ingredients and mix well. Cover and braise in a warm oven, 170°C, 325°F, Gas Mark 3, for 2½ hours or until the meat is tender.
To freeze: turn into a rigid container, cool, cover, label and freeze.
To thaw and serve: put into a casserole, preferably nonstick, cover and reheat in a warm oven, 170°C, 325°F, Gas Mark 3, for 45 minutes, stirring occasionally.

Serves 4.

AMERICAN

1½ lb. chuck steak, 1 in. thick,
   cut into 8 pieces
⅜ cup flour
salt and pepper
3 tablespoons lard
2 onions, sliced
2 celery stalks, chopped
1 × 8 oz. can tomatoes
2 teaspoons tomato purée
½ teaspoon Worcestershire
   sauce
⅝ cup water

~Prestbury Meat Loaf~

METRIC/IMPERIAL

1 small onion, quartered
300 g./12 oz. pig's liver
½ kg./1 lb. pork sausage meat
½ kg./1 lb. lean minced beef
1 teaspoon dried mixed herbs
1 teaspoon salt
1 teaspoon pepper
5 tablespoons cider
parsley to garnish

Put the onion and pig's liver through a mincer (grinder) or food mill. Add to all the remaining ingredients and mix well. Press the mixture firmly into a 1 kg. (2 lb.) loaf tin. Stand the tin in a roasting tin containing 2.5 cm. (1 in.) depth of water and bake in a moderate oven, 180°C, 350°F, Gas Mark 4, for 1½ hours. Cool in the tin.
To freeze: wrap the loaf in foil, label and freeze.
To thaw and serve: leave to thaw overnight in the refrigerator or for 6 hours at room temperature. Place on a serving dish and garnish with parsley.

Serves 8 to 10.

AMERICAN

1 small onion, quartered
12 oz. pig's liver
1 lb. pork sausage meat
1 lb. lean ground beef
1 teaspoon dried mixed herbs
1 teaspoon salt
1 teaspoon pepper
5 tablespoons cider
parsley to garnish

~Beef Rouladen~

METRIC/IMPERIAL

4 slices beef topside, ¾ cm./
   ¼ in. thick
4 teaspoons horseradish
   cream
salt and pepper
2 small carrots, scraped and
   cut into strips
1 small onion, finely chopped
1 celery stalk, cut into strips
18 g./¾ oz. flour
2 tablespoons oil
375 ml./¾ pint tomato juice
5 tablespoons red wine

Remove the fat from the meat. Place the slices between two sheets of dampened greaseproof (waxed) paper and beat with a rolling pin until they are very thin. Remove the paper. Spread each meat slice with a spoonful of the horseradish cream and season. Lay the vegetables on top and roll up the meat slices. Fasten with string and coat the rolls in the flour.
   Brown the rolls in the oil. Add the tomato juice and wine and bring to the boil. Cover and simmer gently for 1¾ to 2 hours or until the meat is tender.
To freeze: turn into a rigid container, cool, cover, label and freeze.
To thaw and serve: put into a casserole and reheat in a moderate oven, 180°C, 350°F, Gas Mark 4, for 45 minutes. Serve with noodles.

Serves 4.

AMERICAN

4 slices round steak, ¼ in. thick
4 teaspoons horseradish
   cream
salt and pepper
2 small carrots, scraped and
   cut into strips
1 small onion, finely chopped
1 celery stalk, cut into strips
3 tablespoons flour
2 tablespoons oil
2 cups tomato juice
5 tablespoons red wine

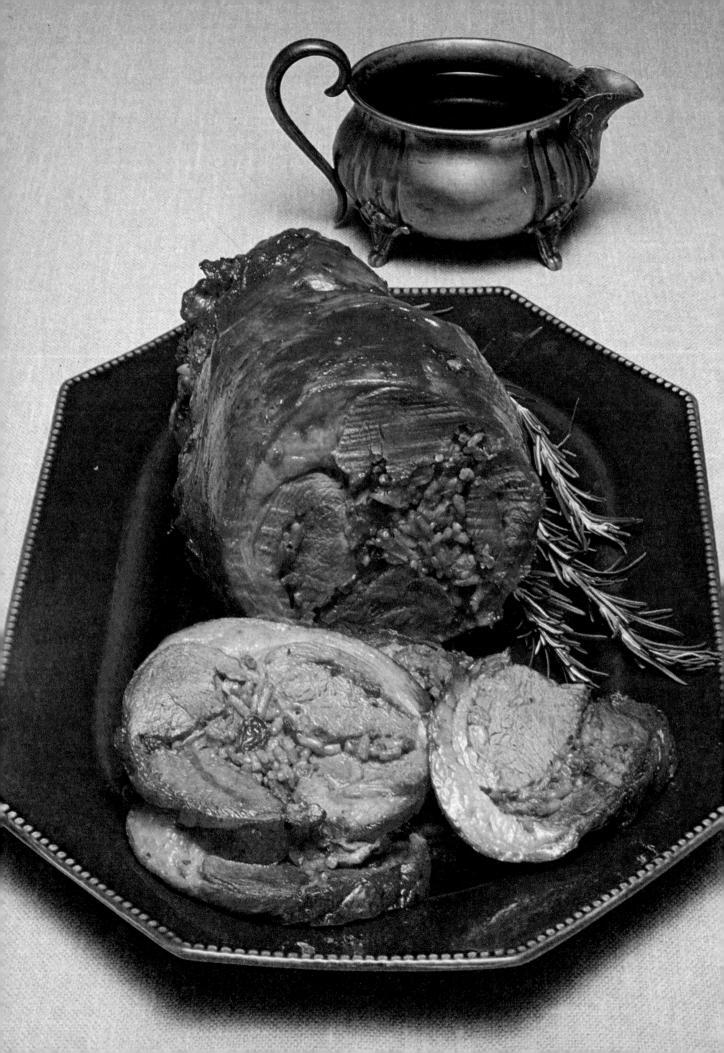

Veal Fricassé

METRIC/IMPERIAL
¾ kg./1½ lb. stewing veal, cut into chunks
2 onions, quartered
2 large carrots, scraped and quartered
3 bay leaves
1 parsley sprig
1 tablespoon lemon juice
salt and pepper
150 g./6 oz. mushrooms, sliced
38 g./1½ oz. butter
38 g./1½ oz. flour
125 ml./¼ pint single cream

Put the veal in a saucepan and cover with water. Bring to the boil, drain, rinse off the scum and return the veal to the pan. Add the onions, carrots, herbs, lemon juice, seasoning and 1 l. (2 pints) or 5 cups water. Bring to the boil, cover and simmer for 1 hour. Add the mushrooms and simmer for a further 30 minutes or until the meat is tender.

Put the veal and vegetables in a rigid container, removing the bay leaves and parsley. Reduce the cooking liquid to ½ l. (1 pint) or 2½ cups by boiling rapidly.

Melt the butter in a saucepan and stir in the flour. Cook, stirring, for 1 minute. Gradually add the cooking liquid, stirring constantly. Bring to the boil, stirring, and simmer for 5 minutes. Pour this sauce over the veal and vegetables.
To freeze: cool, cover, label and freeze.
To thaw and serve: put into a saucepan and reheat gently until simmering. Remove from the heat and stir in the cream. Serve at once.

Serves 4.

AMERICAN
1½ lb. stewing veal, cut into chunks
2 onions, quartered
2 large carrots, scraped and quartered
3 bay leaves
1 parsley sprig
1 tablespoon lemon juice
salt and pepper
6 oz. mushrooms, sliced
3 tablespoons butter
⅜ cup flour
⅝ cup light cream

Veal Wellington

METRIC/IMPERIAL
800 g./1¾ lb. pie veal, cut into chunks
3 tablespoons oil
38 g./1½ oz. butter
1 large onion, sliced
1½ tablespoons paprika
1½ tablespoons flour
375 ml./¾ pint chicken stock or stock made with a chicken stock cube
100 ml./4 fl. oz. white wine
1 teaspoon tomato purée
salt and pepper
200 g./8 oz. small button mushrooms
5 tablespoons double cream
chopped parsley to garnish

Fry the veal quickly in the oil and butter in a saucepan until it is just beginning to brown. Remove from the pan and drain on absorbent paper towels. Fry the onion in the fat remaining in the pan until it is soft and pale golden brown. Blend in the paprika and flour and cook for 1 minute, stirring. Add the stock, wine, tomato purée and seasoning and bring to the boil, stirring. Return the veal to the pan, cover and simmer for 50 minutes, or until the meat is tender. Add the mushrooms and cook for 5 minutes longer. Cool.
To freeze: turn into a rigid container, cover, label and freeze.
To thaw and serve: put into a casserole, preferably nonstick, cover and reheat in a warm oven, 170°C, 325°F, Gas Mark 3, for 40 minutes, stirring occasionally. Just before serving stir in the cream and sprinkle with parsley.

Serves 6.

AMERICAN
1¾ lb. pie veal, cut into chunks
3 tablespoons oil
3 tablespoons butter
1 large onion, sliced
1½ tablespoons paprika
1½ tablespoons flour
2 cups chicken stock or stock made with a chicken stock cube
½ cup white wine
1 teaspoon tomato purée
salt and pepper
8 oz. small button mushrooms
5 tablespoons heavy cream
chopped parsley to garnish

Lamb Chops in Barbecue Sauce

METRIC/IMPERIAL
1 large onion, chopped
1 garlic clove, crushed
50 g./2 oz. butter
100 g./4 oz. mushrooms, sliced
1 × 375 g./15 oz. can tomatoes
1 tablespoon tomato purée
1 to 2 dessertspoons sugar
2 tablespoons vinegar
4 lamb chump chops

Fry the onion and garlic in the butter for 5 minutes. Add the mushrooms and cook for a further 2 minutes, stirring occasionally. Stir in the tomatoes, tomato purée, sugar and vinegar and bring to the boil.

Put the chops in an ovenproof dish and pour over the sauce. Cover and bake in a moderate oven, 180°C, 350°F, Gas Mark 4, for 45 minutes.
To freeze: cool quickly, cover and freeze. When frozen, transfer to a polythene (plastic) bag, seal, label and return to the freezer.
To thaw and serve: return to the dish and reheat in a moderate oven, 180°C, 350°F, Gas Mark 4, for 45 minutes.

Serves 4.

AMERICAN
1 large onion, chopped
1 garlic clove, crushed
¼ cup butter
4 oz. mushrooms, sliced
1 × 15 oz. can tomatoes
1 tablespoon tomato purée
1 to 2 tablespoons sugar
2 tablespoons vinegar
4 English lamb chops

(Left) Armenian Roast Lamb

~Moussaka~

METRIC/IMPERIAL

1 kg./2 lb. aubergines, sliced
salt and pepper
7 tablespoons oil
½ kg./1 lb. boned lamb
   shoulder, minced
200 g./8 oz. onions, chopped
1 garlic clove, crushed
25 g./1 oz. flour
1 × 375 g./15 oz. can
   tomatoes
¼ teaspoon dried mixed herbs
2 tablespoons chopped
   parsley
Cheese sauce
25 g./1 oz. butter
25 g./1 oz. flour
250 ml./½ pint milk
100 g./4 oz. Cheddar cheese,
   grated
½ teaspoon prepared mustard
salt and pepper

Sprinkle the aubergine (eggplant) slices with salt and leave for 30 minutes. Drain and dry on absorbent paper towels. Fry the slices in 6 tablespoons of the oil until they are brown on both sides. Remove from the pan and drain on absorbent paper towels.

Put the remaining oil in the pan with the lamb and brown. Add the onions and garlic and cook for 10 minutes. Blend in the flour, about 1 teaspoon salt, pepper, tomatoes, herbs and parsley.

Arrange the aubergine (eggplant) slices and lamb mixture in layers in a buttered shallow ovenproof dish.

To make the cheese sauce, melt the butter in a saucepan and stir in the flour. Cook, stirring, for 1 minute. Gradually add the milk, stirring constantly. Bring to the boil, stirring, and simmer for 3 minutes or until the sauce has thickened. Stir in three-quarters of the cheese, the mustard and seasoning. Pour the sauce over the lamb and aubergines (eggplants) and sprinkle with the remaining cheese. Cool.

To freeze: open freeze, remove from the dish, put in a polythene (plastic) bag, seal, label and freeze.

To thaw and serve: return to the dish and reheat in a moderately hot oven, 200°C, 400°F, Gas Mark 6, for 1 hour.

Serves 4.

AMERICAN

2 lb. eggplants, sliced
salt and pepper
7 tablespoons oil
1 lb. boned lamb shoulder,
   ground
8 oz. onions, chopped
1 garlic clove, crushed
¼ cup flour
1 × 15 oz. can tomatoes
¼ teaspoon dried mixed herbs
2 tablespoons chopped
   parsley
Cheese sauce
2 tablespoons butter
¼ cup flour
1¼ cups milk
1 cup grated Cheddar cheese
½ teaspoon prepared mustard
salt and pepper

~Armenian Roast Lamb~

METRIC/IMPERIAL

1¾ kg./about 3 lb. boned
   lamb shoulder
25 g./1 oz. dripping
2 rosemary sprigs
1 dessertspoon flour
1½ teaspoons tomato purée
250 ml./½ pint chicken stock
   or stock made with a
   chicken stock cube
salt and pepper
Stuffing
63 g./2½ oz. long-grain rice
salt and pepper
100 g./4 oz. lamb's liver,
   diced
25 g./1 oz. butter
1 large onion, finely chopped
1 garlic clove, crushed
50 g./2 oz. raisins
1½ tablespoons chopped fresh
   herbs

To make the stuffing, cook the rice in boiling salted water until it is tender. Drain and rinse thoroughly. Fry the liver quickly in the butter for 2 to 3 minutes. Add the onion and garlic and cook for 4 minutes. Stir in the rice, raisins, herbs and seasoning. Cool.

To freeze: place the meat in a polythene (plastic) bag, seal, label and freeze. Place the stuffing in a rigid container, cover, label and freeze. Use within 2 months.

To thaw and serve: leave the meat and stuffing to thaw overnight in the refrigerator. Put the stuffing into the cavity in the meat and sew up or secure with skewers. Place the meat in a roasting tin with the dripping and put the rosemary sprigs on top. Roast in a moderate oven, 180°C, 350°F, Gas Mark 4, for 1½ to 2 hours or until the meat is cooked.

Place the meat on a serving dish and keep hot. Pour off all but 1 tablespoon of fat from the roasting tin and stir in the flour. Cook, stirring, for 1 minute over low heat. Stir in the tomato purée, stock and seasoning and bring to the boil. Simmer for 2 minutes. Serve the sauce with the meat.

Serves 6 to 8.

AMERICAN

3 lb. boned lamb shoulder
2 tablespoons dripping
2 rosemary sprigs
1 tablespoon flour
1½ teaspoons tomato purée
1¼ cups chicken stock or
   stock made with a chicken
   stock cube
salt and pepper
Stuffing
½ cup long-grain rice
salt and pepper
4 oz. lamb's liver, diced
2 tablespoons butter
1 large onion, finely chopped
1 garlic clove, crushed
⅓ cup raisins
1½ tablespoons chopped fresh
   herbs

⟶ Hungarian Pork ⟵

METRIC/IMPERIAL

800 g./1¾ lb. pork fillet
2 tablespoons oil
25 g./1 oz. butter
1 onion, chopped
1 tablespoon paprika
1 tablespoon flour
250 ml./½ pint beef stock or
  stock made with a stock
  cube
5 tablespoons sherry
1 teaspoon tomato purée
salt and pepper
150 g./6 oz. small button
  mushrooms
125 ml./¼ pint soured cream

Cut the pork into 3.75 cm. (1½ in.) pieces. Fry quickly in the oil and butter until just beginning to turn brown. Remove the pork from the pan and drain on absorbent paper towels.

Fry the onion and paprika in the fat remaining in the pan for 2 minutes, stirring. Blend in the flour and cook for another minute. Remove the pan from the heat and stir in the stock, sherry and tomato purée. Return to the heat, bring to the boil and simmer until the mixture has thickened.

Return the meat to the pan with seasoning to taste, cover and simmer for 30 to 40 minutes or until the pork is tender. Stir in the mushrooms and simmer for 2 minutes.

To freeze: turn into a rigid container, cool, cover, label and freeze.
To thaw and serve: put into a casserole, preferably nonstick, cover and reheat in a warm oven, 170°C, 325°F, Gas Mark 3, for 40 minutes, stirring occasionally. Just before serving stir in the soured cream.

Serves 4.

AMERICAN

1¾ lb. pork tenderloin
2 tablespoons oil
2 tablespoons butter
1 onion, chopped
1 tablespoon paprika
1 tablespoon flour
1¼ cups beef stock or stock
  made with a stock cube
5 tablespoons sherry
1 teaspoon tomato purée
salt and pepper
6 oz. small button mushrooms
⅝ cup sour cream

⟶ Boiled Mutton with Caper Sauce ⟵

METRIC/IMPERIAL

1¾ kg./about 3½ lb. leg of
  mutton
2 onions, each stuck with 3
  cloves
2 carrots, scraped and sliced
3 celery stalks, sliced
juice of ½ lemon
¼ teaspoon dried thyme
1 parsley sprig
6 peppercorns
1 mace blade
Caper sauce
38 g./1½ oz. butter
38 g./1½ oz. flour
2 tablespoons capers
1 to 2 teaspoons vinegar
  from the capers
1 teaspoon prepared mustard
salt and pepper
2 tablespoons single cream or
  creamy milk

Mutton is not always available so you can use lamb instead. If the leg of mutton or lamb is frozen, leave it to thaw in the refrigerator for 24 hours. Make one meal from the joint, then slice the remainder of the meat and freeze in the remaining sauce.

Put the mutton in a large saucepan and cover with water. Bring to the boil, removing the scum as it forms. When the liquid is free of scum, add the vegetables. Stir in the lemon juice, thyme, parsley, peppercorns and mace. Cover and simmer gently for 1¾ to 2 hours (or allowing 25 minutes to the ½ kg. or 1 lb.).

To make the caper sauce, melt the butter in a saucepan and stir in the flour. Cook, stirring, for 1 minute. Measure ½ l. (1 pint) or 2½ cups of the cooking liquid from the mutton and add this gradually to the butter and flour roux, stirring constantly. Bring to the boil, stirring, and simmer until the sauce has thickened. Stir in the capers, vinegar, mustard and seasoning. Place half the sauce on one side and add the cream to the remainder.

Remove the mutton from the pan and place it on a warm serving dish. Serve with the sauce to which the cream was added.
To freeze: carve the remaining meat and place in a rigid dish. Pour over the sauce without cream, cool, cover, label and freeze.
To thaw and serve: put into a casserole with 2 tablespoons water, cover and reheat in a warm oven, 170°C, 325°F, Gas Mark 3, for 50 minutes.

Serves 8.

AMERICAN

3½ lb. leg of mutton
2 onions, each stuck with 3
  cloves
2 carrots, scraped and sliced
3 celery stalks, sliced
juice of ½ lemon
¼ teaspoon dried thyme
1 parsley sprig
6 peppercorns
1 mace blade
Caper sauce
3 tablespoons butter
⅜ cup flour
2 tablespoons capers
1 to 2 teaspoons vinegar
  from the capers
1 teaspoon prepared mustard
salt and pepper
2 tablespoons light cream or
  half and half

—Pig's Head Brawn—

METRIC/IMPERIAL
½ pig's head, cut into 2 or 3
   pieces
2 pig's trotters
salt and pepper
2 onions, quartered
1 large carrot, scraped and
   sliced
2 bay leaves
6 peppercorns
6 cloves
3 parsley sprigs
sliced tomatoes and
   watercress to garnish

If you buy a pig for freezing, it sometimes comes with the head, hocks, shanks and trotters, and this is an excellent way of using the head and trotters.

Put the head and trotters in a large bowl with a handful of salt. Cover with cold water and leave to soak for 8 hours or overnight. Drain and place in a large saucepan. Cover with fresh cold water and bring to the boil, removing the scum. When the liquid is free of scum, add the onions, carrot, bay leaves, peppercorns and cloves. Cover and simmer for 2½ hours or until tender.

Remove the head and trotters from the pan and separate the meat from the skin and bones. Cut the meat into neat pieces and set aside. Discard the skin.

Return the bones to the pan with 1 teaspoon salt and boil rapidly until the cooking liquid has reduced to about ½ l. (1 pint) or 2½ cups. Strain and set aside to cool completely.

Chop the parsley and mix with the meat. Remove any fat from the cooled cooking liquid and mix with the meat. Check the seasoning. Turn into a pudding basin and leave to set in a cool place.
To freeze: freeze in the bowl until solid then dip the bowl into hand-hot water to unmould the brawn. Put into a polythene (plastic) bag, seal, label and return to the freezer.
To thaw and serve: put on a dish and leave to thaw at room temperature for 8 hours or in the refrigerator for 24 hours. Decorate with tomato slices and watercress.

Serves 4.

AMERICAN
½ pig's head, cut into 2 or 3
   pieces
2 pig's trotters
salt and pepper
2 onions, quartered
1 large carrot, scraped and
   sliced
2 bay leaves
6 peppercorns
6 cloves
3 parsley sprigs
sliced tomatoes and
   watercress to garnish

—Pork in Cider Sauce—

METRIC/IMPERIAL
¾ kg./1½ lb. pork fillet
salt and pepper
63 g./2½ oz. butter
200 g./8 oz. mushrooms,
   sliced
25 g./1 oz. flour
250 ml./½ pint cider
pinch of dried mixed herbs
125 ml./¼ pint soured cream

Cut the pork into 1.25 cm. (½ in.) slices and season them well. Fry the slices gently in 38 g. (1½ oz.) or 3 tablespoons of the butter for 10 minutes, turning once. Transfer the pork to a rigid container.

Add the mushrooms to the pan with the remaining butter and fry gently for 3 to 4 minutes or until soft. Stir in the flour and cook for 1 minute. Add the cider and herbs and cook for 2 minutes, stirring constantly. Pour the sauce over the meat. Cover and cool quickly.
To freeze: label and freeze.
To thaw and serve: leave to thaw overnight in the refrigerator. Put into a saucepan, reheat gently to simmering and simmer 5 minutes. Stir in the soured cream and check the seasoning. Serve with noodles, broccoli and grilled (broiled) tomatoes.

Serves 4.

AMERICAN
1½ lb. pork tenderloin
salt and pepper
5 tablespoons butter
8 oz. mushrooms, sliced
¼ cup flour
1¼ cups cider
pinch of dried mixed herbs
⅝ cup sour cream

—Spare Ribs in Piquant Sauce—

METRIC/IMPERIAL
4 spare rib chops (about ¾ kg./
1½ lb. in weight)
12½ g./½ oz. lard or dripping
1 large onion, finely chopped
¼ teaspoon garlic powder
1 × 50 g./2 oz. can tomato
purée
4 tablespoons water
2 tablespoons soft brown
sugar
3 tablespoons vinegar
1 teaspoon Worcestershire
sauce
½ teaspoon salt
pinch of cayenne pepper
2 tablespoons dry mustard
pinch of dried mixed herbs

Brown the chops quickly in the lard or dripping, turning once.
Remove them from the pan. Add the onion to the pan and fry for 5
minutes. Stir in all the remaining ingredients. Return the chops to the
pan, cover and simmer for 25 minutes or until they are tender.
To freeze: turn into a rigid container, cool, cover, label and freeze.
To thaw and serve: put into a casserole, preferably nonstick, cover
and reheat in a warm oven, 170°C, 325°F, Gas Mark 3, for 45
minutes, stirring occasionally.

Serves 4.

AMERICAN
4 spare rib chops (about 1½ lb.
in weight)
1 tablespoon lard or dripping
1 large onion, finely chopped
¼ teaspoon garlic powder
1 × 2 oz. can tomato purée
4 tablespoons water
2 tablespoons soft brown
sugar
3 tablespoons vinegar
1 teaspoon Worcestershire
sauce
½ teaspoon salt
pinch of cayenne pepper
2 tablespoons dry mustard
pinch of dried mixed herbs

—Chicken Stock—

METRIC/IMPERIAL
2 or 3 chicken carcasses
2 carrots, scraped and sliced
2 onions, sliced
1 teaspoon salt
¼ teaspoon pepper
1 bay leaf
1 teaspoon dried mixed herbs
¼ teaspoon ground mace
a few bacon trimmings (if
available)

Chicken carcasses can be stored in the freezer until you have
enough.

Break up the chicken carcasses roughly with a rolling pin, then
put them in a large saucepan with water to cover. Add the
remaining ingredients, cover and bring to the boil. Simmer for 1
hour. Strain the stock and leave to cool. Remove any meat from the
carcasses.
To freeze: pour the strained stock into a rigid container, cover and
freeze. When solid, transfer to a polythene (plastic) bag, seal, label
and freeze. Put the chicken meat in a polythene (plastic) bag, seal,
label and freeze.
To thaw and serve: add the frozen stock to soups, casseroles, etc.
as required. Add the chicken meat to soups, fricasses, etc.
Note: make beef stock in the same way, using bones from a roast or
fresh bones from the butcher.

AMERICAN
2 or 3 chicken carcasses
2 carrots, scraped and sliced
2 onions, sliced
1 teaspoon salt
¼ teaspoon pepper
1 bay leaf
1 teaspoon dried mixed herbs
¼ teaspoon ground mace
a few bacon trimmings (if
available)

—Chicken Marengo—

METRIC/IMPERIAL
4 chicken joints
2 tablespoons oil
25 g./1 oz. butter
25 g./1 oz. flour
250 ml./½ pint dry white wine
125 ml./¼ pint chicken stock
or stock made with a stock
cube
50 g./2 oz. mushrooms, sliced
1 × 375 g./15 oz. can
tomatoes
1 garlic clove, crushed
1 bouquet garni
1 teaspoon salt
pepper

Fry the chicken joints (pieces) quickly in the oil and butter until
golden brown on all sides. Remove the chicken from the pan and
set aside. Stir the flour into the fat remaining in the pan and cook,
stirring, until it has browned slightly.
Gradually add the wine and stock, stirring constantly, and bring
to the boil. Simmer until the mixture has thickened. Add all the
remaining ingredients and stir well. Return the chicken to the pan
and simmer gently for 20 minutes. Check the seasoning, remove the
bouquet garni and cool quickly.
To freeze: turn into a rigid container, cover, label and freeze.
To thaw and serve: leave to thaw overnight in the refrigerator. Put
into a saucepan and reheat gently to simmering, then simmer for
10 minutes.

Serves 4.

AMERICAN
4 chicken pieces
2 tablespoons oil
2 tablespoons butter
¼ cup flour
1¼ cups dry white wine
1¼ cups chicken stock or
stock made with a stock
cube
2 oz. mushrooms, sliced
1 × 15 oz. can tomatoes
1 garlic clove, crushed
1 bouquet garni
1 teaspoon salt
pepper

—Country Chicken Pie—

METRIC/IMPERIAL
25 g./1 oz. butter
25 g./1 oz. flour
250 ml./½ pint milk
salt and pepper
juice of ½ lemon
200 g./8 oz. cooked chicken
 meat, cut into small pieces
100 g./4 oz. cooked ham or
 bacon, cut into small pieces
2 to 3 cooked carrots, diced
1 × 175 g./7 oz. packet
 commercial frozen puff
 pastry, thawed

Melt the butter in a saucepan and stir in the flour. Cook, stirring, for 1 minute. Gradually add the milk, stirring constantly. Bring to the boil, stirring, and simmer for 2 minutes. Add all the remaining pie ingredients and mix well. Turn into an aluminium foil pie dish. Roll out the dough and cover the pie. Use the trimmings to decorate the top.
To freeze: open freeze for 8 hours to prevent the decoration from being crushed. Put into a polythene (plastic) bag, seal, label and return to the freezer.
To thaw and serve: remove from the bag, leave to thaw for 3 hours at room temperature, then brush with milk and bake in a hot oven, 220°C, 425°F, Gas Mark 7, for 15 minutes. Reduce the oven temperature to moderate, 180°C, 350°F, Gas Mark 4, and bake for a further 15 minutes. Otherwise, brush the frozen pie with milk and bake in a hot oven, 220°C, 425°F, Gas Mark 4, for 30 minutes. Reduce the oven temperature to moderate, 180°C, 350°F, Gas Mark 4, and bake for a further 20 minutes.

Serves 4.

AMERICAN
2 tablespoons butter
¼ cup flour
1¼ cups milk
salt and pepper
juice of ½ lemon
8 oz. cooked chicken meat,
 cut into small pieces
4 oz. cooked ham or bacon,
 cut into small pieces
2 to 3 cooked carrots, diced
1 × 7 oz. packet commercial
 frozen puff pastry, thawed

—Chicken with Mushroom Sauce—

METRIC/IMPERIAL
4 chicken joints
½ teaspoon chopped fresh
 thyme
½ teaspoon chopped fresh
 marjoram or rosemary
1 teaspoon salt
pinch of pepper
1 teaspoon chopped chives
5 tablespoons dry sherry
38 g./1½ oz. butter
25 g./1 oz. flour
250 ml./½ pint milk
juice of ½ lemon
150 g./6 oz. mushrooms,
 sliced

Put the chicken joints (pieces) into a deep casserole large enough to hold the pieces in a single layer. Sprinkle with the herbs, seasoning, chives and sherry. Dot with 12½ g. (½ oz.) or 1 tablespoon of the butter cut into small pieces. Cover with aluminium foil or a lid and bake in a moderate oven, 180°C, 350°F, Gas Mark 4, for 45 minutes.
 Melt the remaining butter in a saucepan and stir in the flour. Cook, stirring, for 1 minute. Gradually add the milk, stirring constantly. Bring to the boil, stirring. Stir in the juices from the chicken, the lemon juice and mushrooms. Simmer for 2 minutes.
To freeze: put the chicken pieces in a rigid container. Pour over the sauce, cover and cool quickly. Label and freeze.
To thaw and serve: leave to thaw overnight in the refrigerator. Put into a saucepan, reheat gently to simmering and simmer for 15 minutes.

Serves 4.

AMERICAN
4 chicken pieces
½ teaspoon chopped fresh
 thyme
½ teaspoon chopped fresh
 marjoram or rosemary
1 teaspoon salt
pinch of pepper
1 teaspoon chopped chives
5 tablespoons dry sherry
3 tablespoons butter
¼ cup flour
1¼ cups milk
juice of ½ lemon
6 oz. mushrooms, sliced

Chicken with Orange and Tarragon Sauce

METRIC/IMPERIAL
1¾ kg./about 3½ lb. roasting chicken
2 tablespoons cornflour
juice and grated rind of 2 large oranges
250 ml./½ pint water
1 onion, chopped
4 fresh tarragon sprigs, chopped, or 1 tablespoon dried tarragon
salt and pepper
125 ml./¼ pint soured cream

Roast the chicken in a moderate oven, 180°C, 350°F, Gas Mark 4, for 1 hour. Reserve the juices, but not the fat. Take all the meat from the bones and put it in a boil-in-the-bag or a rigid container.

Blend together the cornflour (cornstarch) and orange juice in a saucepan. Add the orange rind, water, chicken juices and onion. Bring to the boil and simmer until the mixture has thickened. Stir in the tarragon and seasoning and pour the sauce over the chicken. Cool quickly.

To freeze: cover, label and freeze.

To thaw and serve: leave to thaw overnight in the refrigerator. If in boil-in-the-bag, reheat in simmering water. Otherwise, put into a saucepan and reheat gently to simmering, then simmer for 5 minutes. Just before serving stir in the soured cream.

Serves 4.

AMERICAN
3½ lb. roasting chicken
2 tablespoons cornstarch
juice and grated rind of 2 large oranges
1¼ cups water
1 onion, chopped
4 fresh tarragon sprigs, chopped, or 1 tablespoon dried tarragon
salt and pepper
⅝ cup sour cream

Summer Chicken Casserole

METRIC/IMPERIAL
4 chicken quarters (leg portions)
4 tablespoons oil
25 g./1 oz. butter
50 g./2 oz. mushrooms, sliced
1 small onion, chopped
1 garlic clove, crushed
200 g./8 oz. marrow, peeled, seeded and diced
8 tomatoes, skinned and quartered
salt and pepper

Fry the chicken quarters gently in the oil and butter for 15 minutes, turning once. Add the vegetables and seasoning. Cover and simmer gently for 10 minutes.

To freeze: turn into a rigid container, cool quickly, cover, and freeze. Remove from the container, put in a polythene (plastic) bag, seal, label and return to the freezer.

To thaw and serve: leave to thaw overnight in the refrigerator. Put into a saucepan, cover and reheat gently to simmering, then simmer for 10 minutes.

Serves 4.

AMERICAN
4 chicken quarters (leg portions)
4 tablespoons oil
2 tablespoons butter
2 oz. mushrooms, sliced
1 small onion, chopped
1 garlic clove, crushed
8 oz. summer squash, peeled, seeded and diced
8 tomatoes, skinned and quartered
salt and pepper

Madras Chicken Curry

METRIC/IMPERIAL
4 chicken joints
4 tablespoons oil
2 onions, chopped
25 g./1 oz. flour
2 tablespoons curry powder (or more to taste)
250 ml./½ pint chicken stock or stock made with a stock cube
2 tablespoons mango chutney
salt and pepper
25 g./1 oz. sultanas
1 eating apple, cored and chopped

This is quite a mild curry, so add more curry powder if you like it hot.

Fry the chicken joints (pieces) quickly in the oil until golden brown on all sides. Remove the chicken from the pan. Remove the skin and bones and cut the meat into small pieces.

Fry the onions in the oil remaining in the pan until soft. Blend in the flour and curry powder and cook for 1 minute, stirring. Gradually add the stock, stirring, then bring to the boil and simmer until the mixture has thickened. Stir in the chutney and seasoning and return the chicken meat to the pan. Cover and simmer gently for 30 minutes or until the chicken is tender.

Stir in the sultanas (raisins) and apple and cook for 5 minutes longer.

To freeze: turn into a rigid container, cool, cover, label and freeze.

To thaw and serve: put into a casserole, preferably nonstick, cover and reheat in a warm oven, 170°C, 325°F, Gas Mark 3, for 40 minutes, stirring occasionally. Serve with boiled rice, lemon wedges and side dishes, for example sliced bananas sprinkled with lemon juice, diced cucumber mixed with plain yogurt, wedges or slices of hard-boiled egg, fried poppadum, chopped cucumber and tomato, mango chutney and peanuts.

Serves 4.

AMERICAN
4 chicken pieces
4 tablespoons oil
2 onions, chopped
¼ cup flour
2 tablespoons curry powder (or more to taste)
1¼ cups chicken stock or stock made with a stock cube
2 tablespoons mango chutney
salt and pepper
3 tablespoons golden raisins
1 eating apple, cored and chopped

—Chicken with Prunes—

METRIC/IMPERIAL
4 chicken joints
100 g./4 oz. prunes, soaked
5 onions, 1 sliced and
    4 quartered
1 bay leaf
6 peppercorns
250 ml./½ pint red wine
2 tablespoons olive oil
25 g./1 oz. butter
25 g./1 oz. flour
125 ml./¼ pint chicken stock
    or stock made with a stock
    cube
½ teaspoon salt
pepper
1 tablespoon redcurrant
    jelly

Put the prunes in a saucepan with the sliced onion, bay leaf, peppercorns and wine. Bring slowly to the boil and then cool. Add the chicken joints (pieces). Turn into a bowl, cover and leave to marinate overnight or for several hours in the refrigerator.

Strain the marinade and set aside. Stone the prunes. Fry the chicken quickly in the oil and butter until golden brown on all sides. Remove the chicken from the pan. Fry the quartered onions in the fat remaining in the pan until they are golden brown. Remove the onions from the pan.

Blend the flour with the fat remaining in the pan and gradually add the marinade, stirring constantly. Bring to the boil, stirring. Add the stock, salt, pepper and jelly and stir well. Return the chicken, quartered onions and prunes to the pan. Cover and simmer for 45 minutes or until the chicken is tender.

To freeze: turn into a foil dish or rigid container, cool, cover, label and freeze.

To thaw and serve: leave to thaw overnight in the refrigerator. Put into a casserole, cover and reheat in a warm oven, 170°C, 325°F, Gas Mark 3, for 1 hour.

Serves 4.

AMERICAN
4 chicken pieces
1 cup prunes, soaked
5 onions, 1 sliced and
    4 quartered
1 bay leaf
6 peppercorns
1¼ cups red wine
2 tablespoons olive oil
2 tablespoons butter
¼ cup flour
⅝ cup chicken stock or stock
    made with a stock cube
½ teaspoon salt
pepper
1 tablespoon redcurrant
    jelly

—Chicken Ratatouille—

METRIC/IMPERIAL
4 chicken joints
50 g./2 oz. butter
1 tablespoon oil
2 large green peppers, pith
    and seeds removed and cut
    into strips
2 medium-sized onions, sliced
2 medium-sized aubergines,
    sliced
200 g./8 oz. tomatoes,
    skinned, quartered and
    seeded
125 ml./¼ pint white wine
125 ml./¼ pint stock
salt and pepper

Fry the chicken joints (pieces) quickly in the butter and oil until they are golden brown on all sides. Reduce the heat, cover and continue cooking for 25 to 30 minutes or until the chicken is tender. Remove from the pan and place in an aluminium foil dish.

Fry the peppers and onions in the fat remaining in the pan for 5 minutes or until the onion is pale golden brown. Add the aubergines (eggplants) and tomatoes and cook for a further 5 minutes. Stir in the wine, stock and seasoning and bring to the boil. Simmer for 2 minutes. Pour over the chicken and cool.

To freeze: cover, label and freeze.

To thaw and serve: leave to thaw overnight in the refrigerator. Remove the lid, cover lightly with foil and reheat in a moderate oven, 180°C, 350°F, Gas Mark 4, for 50 to 60 minutes.

Serves 4.

AMERICAN
4 chicken pieces
¼ cup butter
1 tablespoon oil
2 large green peppers, pith
    and seeds removed and cut
    into strips
2 medium-sized onions, sliced
2 medium-sized eggplants,
    sliced
8 oz. tomatoes, skinned,
    quartered and seeded
⅝ cup white wine
⅝ cup stock
salt and pepper

Piquant Chicken Pilaff

METRIC/IMPERIAL
1¼ kg./2½ lb. boiling chicken
2 carrots, scraped and sliced
2 onions, sliced
1 bay leaf
1 parsley sprig
1 thyme sprig
¼ teaspoon salt
¼ teaspoon pepper
Pilaff
1 large onion, thinly sliced
50 g./2 oz. butter
175 g./7 oz. long-grain rice
1 teaspoon salt
¼ teaspoon dried mixed herbs
1 teaspoon ground turmeric
1 × 75 g./7 oz. can pimento,
   drained and cut into strips
½ teaspoon cayenne pepper
2 tablespoons chopped
   parsley
50 g./2 oz. fresh or salted
   cashew nuts

Put the chicken in a large saucepan and cover with water. Add the carrots, onions, bay leaf, parsley and thyme sprigs, salt and pepper. Bring to the boil, then simmer for 1 hour or until the chicken is tender. Remove the chicken from the pan and cool. Strain and reserve ½ l. (1 pint) or 2½ cups of the cooking liquid. When the chicken is cool enough to handle, remove the meat and cut it into large pieces.

To make the pilaff, fry the onion gently in the butter until it is soft. Add the rice and cook, stirring, for 2 minutes. Add the reserved cooking liquid, salt, herbs and turmeric and stir well. Bring to the boil, cover and simmer for 20 minutes or until the rice is tender and all the liquid has been absorbed. Stir in the pimento, cayenne, parsley and chicken.

To freeze: turn into a foil dish, cool, cover, label and freeze.
To thaw and serve: leave to thaw overnight in the refrigerator. Remove the lid, cover lightly with foil and reheat in a warm oven, 170°C, 325°F, Gas Mark 3, for 45 minutes. Stir in the nuts and serve with a green salad.

Serves 6.

AMERICAN
2½ lb. boiling chicken
2 carrots, scraped and sliced
2 onions, sliced
1 bay leaf
1 parsley sprig
1 thyme sprig
¼ teaspoon salt
¼ teaspoon pepper
Pilaff
1 large onion, thinly sliced
¼ cup butter
1¼ cups long-grain rice
1 teaspoon salt
¼ teaspoon dried mixed herbs
1 teaspoon ground turmeric
1 × 7 oz. can pimento,
   drained and cut into strips
½ teaspoon cayenne pepper
2 tablespoons chopped
   parsley
⅓ cup fresh or salted cashew
   nuts

Coq au Vin

METRIC/IMPERIAL
1½ kg./3 lb. roasting chicken
   with giblets
150 g./6 oz. salt pork, cut into
   cubes
3 tablespoons oil
12 button onions
200 g./8 oz. button
   mushrooms
2 garlic cloves, crushed
25 g./1 oz. flour
½ l./1 pint red wine
1 bay leaf
¼ teaspoon dried thyme
salt and pepper
2 tablespoons chopped
   parsley

Cut the chicken into six portions. Fry the pork in the oil until golden brown. Remove from the pan and place in a large casserole. Fry the chicken in the fat remaining in the pan until golden brown, turning once. Put the chicken in the casserole.

Fry the onions, mushrooms and garlic in the fat remaining in the pan for 5 minutes. Drain well and add to the casserole. Blend the flour with the fat remaining in the pan and cook, stirring, until golden brown. Gradually add the wine, stirring constantly. Bring to the boil, stirring, and simmer until the mixture thickens. Add the bay leaf, thyme, seasoning and the giblets and stir well. Pour into the casserole. Cover and cook in a moderate oven, 180°C, 350°F, Gas Mark 4, for 1 hour or until the chicken is tender. Cool, then skim off any fat on the surface. Remove and discard the giblets and bay leaf.

To freeze: turn into a rigid container, cover, label and freeze. Use within 2 months because of the inclusion of salt pork.
To thaw and serve: leave to thaw overnight in the refrigerator. Return to the casserole, cover and reheat in a moderate oven, 180°C, 350°F, Gas Mark 4, for 45 to 50 minutes. Sprinkle with parsley.

Serves 6.

AMERICAN
3 lb. roasting chicken with
   giblets
6 oz. salt pork, cut into cubes
3 tablespoons oil
12 baby onions
8 oz. button mushrooms
2 garlic cloves, crushed
¼ cup flour
2½ cups red wine
1 bay leaf
¼ teaspoon dried thyme
salt and pepper
2 tablespoons chopped
   parsley

~Chicken Risotto~

METRIC/IMPERIAL
1¾ kg./about 3½ lb. roasting chicken
1 tablespoon oil
50 g./2 oz. butter
1 large onion, chopped
2 or 3 celery stalks, chopped
1 garlic clove, crushed
1 large red pepper, pith and seeds removed and cut into strips
300 g./12 oz. long-grain rice
⅞ l./1¾ pints chicken stock or stock made with 2 stock cubes
1 teaspoon curry powder
½ teaspoon dried mixed herbs
¼ teaspoon chilli powder
1 bay leaf
100 g./4 oz. mushrooms, sliced
1 × 100 g./4 oz. packet commercial frozen peas
1 × 175 g./7 oz. can sweetcorn, drained
salt and pepper

Cut the chicken into six or eight portions and fry them quickly in the oil and all but 12½ g. (½ oz.) or 1 tablespoon of the butter until they are golden brown on both sides. Reduce the heat, cover and continue cooking for 20 minutes or until the chicken is tender. Remove from the pan and drain on absorbent paper towels. Remove the meat from the bones and cut it into small pieces.

Fry the onion, celery, garlic and red pepper in the fat remaining in the pan for 5 minutes or until soft. Add the rice and fry for 2 minutes, stirring. Stir in the stock, curry powder, herbs, chilli powder and bay leaf. Bring to the boil, cover and simmer for 25 minutes or until the rice is tender and all the liquid has been absorbed.

Fry the mushrooms in the remaining butter until they are just tender. Stir the mushrooms, chicken pieces, peas and corn into the rice mixture and season to taste.

To freeze: turn into two foil dishes, cool, cover, label and freeze.
To thaw and serve: leave to thaw overnight in the refrigerator or for 6 hours at room temperature. Remove the lids, cover lightly with foil and reheat in a warm oven, 170°C, 325°F, Gas Mark 3, for 45 minutes, stirring occasionally with a fork. Serve with a green salad.

Serves 8.

AMERICAN
3½ lb. roasting chicken
1 tablespoon oil
¼ cup butter
1 large onion, chopped
2 or 3 celery stalks, chopped
1 garlic clove, crushed
1 large red pepper, pith and seeds removed and cut into strips
2 cups long-grain rice
4½ cups chicken stock or stock made with 2 stock cubes
1 teaspoon curry powder
½ teaspoon dried mixed herbs
¼ teaspoon chilli powder
1 bay leaf
4 oz. mushrooms, sliced
1 × 4 oz. packet commercial frozen peas
1 × 7 oz. can corn, drained
salt and pepper

~Duck Sevilliana~

METRIC/IMPERIAL
2 kg./4 lb. oven-ready duck with giblets
salt and pepper
1 large onion, finely chopped
1 garlic clove, crushed
100 g./4 oz. mushrooms, sliced
1 × 175 g./7 oz. can pimento, drained and chopped
4 medium-sized tomatoes, skinned and chopped
50 g./2 oz. stuffed green olives, halved
2 tablespoons sherry

Put the duck in a roasting tin and sprinkle it with salt. Prick all over with a fork. Roast in a moderately hot oven, 200°C, 400°F, Gas Mark 6, for 1½ hours. Remove the duck from the tin and set aside. Pour off all but 3 tablespoons of the fat from the tin, leaving the juices behind as well.

Add the onion and garlic to the tin and cook until soft but not brown. Add the mushrooms, pimento and tomatoes and cook gently for 15 minutes. Stir in the olives and seasoning. Cool.

Trim the wing tips and any loose skin from the duck. Divide it into four portions, cutting straight through the breastbone and backbone, then across each half.

To freeze: put the sauce in a rigid container and lay the duck pieces on top. Cover, label and freeze.

To thaw and serve: put into a casserole and reheat in a moderate oven, 180°C, 350°F, Gas Mark 4, for 1 hour. Place the duck pieces on a hot serving dish. Stir the sherry into the sauce and pour over the duck.

Serves 4.

AMERICAN
4 lb. oven-ready duck with giblets
salt and pepper
1 large onion, finely chopped
1 garlic clove, crushed
4 oz. mushrooms, sliced
1 × 7 oz. can pimento, drained and chopped
4 medium-sized tomatoes, skinned and chopped
⅓ cup halved stuffed green olives
2 tablespoons sherry

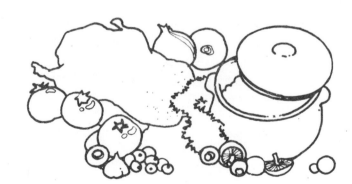

─Quick Hare Casserole─

METRIC/IMPERIAL
3 streaky bacon rashers, cut into pieces
2 tablespoons oil
1 small hare, jointed and trimmed
1 medium-sized onion stuck with 3 cloves
1 bouquet garni
1 × 175 g./15 oz. can oxtail soup
12½ g./½ oz. butter mixed to a paste with 12½ g./½ oz. flour
1 to 2 teaspoons redcurrant jelly
Forcemeat balls
75 g./3 oz. fresh white breadcrumbs
50 g./2 oz. shredded suet
salt and pepper
grated rind of ½ lemon
¼ teaspoon dried thyme
1 tablespoon chopped parsley
1 egg, beaten
oil for frying

Fry the bacon in the oil until it is golden. Transfer the bacon to a casserole. Fry the hare pieces in the fat remaining in the pan until they are lightly browned all over. Transfer the hare to the casserole. Add the onion, bouquet garni and soup and mix well. Cover and bake in a cool oven, 150°C, 300°F, Gas Mark 2, for 2 hours or until the hare is tender.

Remove the onion and bouquet garni. Gradually stir the butter and flour paste, in small pieces, into the liquid in the casserole. Mix in the jelly. Return the casserole to the oven and bake for a further 15 minutes.

Mix together all the ingredients for the forcemeat balls except the oil. Roll into eight balls.

To freeze: cool the hare mixture quickly, then turn into a rigid container, cover, label and freeze. Open freeze the forcemeat balls, then put them in a rigid container or polythene (plastic) bag. Seal, label and return to the freezer.

To thaw and serve: leave to thaw overnight in the refrigerator. Return the hare mixture to the casserole and reheat in a cool oven, 150°C, 300°F, Gas Mark 2, for 30 minutes. Fry the forcemeat balls in oil until they are golden. Drain on absorbent paper towels and serve with the hare casserole.

Serves 4.

AMERICAN
3 fatty bacon slices, cut into pieces
2 tablespoons oil
1 small hare, jointed and trimmed
1 medium-sized onion stuck with 3 cloves
1 bouquet garni
1 × 15 oz. can oxtail soup
1 tablespoon butter mixed to a paste with 2 tablespoons flour
1 to 2 teaspoons redcurrant jelly
Forcemeat balls
1½ cups fresh white breadcrumbs
¼ cup shredded suet
salt and pepper
grated rind of ½ lemon
¼ teaspoon dried thyme
1 tablespoon chopped parsley
1 egg, beaten
oil for frying

─Jugged Hare─

METRIC/IMPERIAL
1 hare, jointed and trimmed
50 g./2 oz. bacon fat
1 celery stalk, chopped
2 large onions, each stuck with 2 cloves
6 peppercorns
finely pared rind of ½ lemon
pinch of cayenne pepper
1 thyme sprig
1 bay leaf
2 parsley sprigs
1 mace blade
salt and pepper
1 l./2 pints water
50 g./2 oz. butter mixed to a past with 50 g./2 oz. flour
125 ml./¼ pint port or Madeira
2 tablespoons redcurrant jelly
fried bread croûtes
chopped parsley

Fry the pieces of hare in the bacon fat until they are lightly browned all over. Transfer the pieces to a casserole. Add the celery, onions, peppercorns, lemon rind, cayenne, thyme sprig, bay leaf, parsley sprigs, mace, seasoning and water. Cover tightly and cook in a warm oven, 170°C, 325°F, Gas Mark 3, for 2 hours or until the hare is tender.

Transfer the hare pieces to a rigid container. Strain the cooking liquid into a saucepan, discarding the flavourings. Gradually stir the butter and flour paste, in small pieces, into the liquid. When all has been added, bring to the boil and simmer gently until the sauce has thickened, stirring constantly. Stir in the port or Madeira and jelly and boil for 2 minutes. Pour the sauce over the hare pieces.

To freeze: cool, cover, label and freeze. Freezè the bread croûtes separately.

To thaw and serve: return to the casserole, cover and reheat in a warm oven, 170°C, 325°F, Gas Mark 3, for 40 minutes, stirring occasionally. Reheat the bread croûtes separately. Serve garnished with the croûtes and chopped parsley.

Serves 6 to 10.

AMERICAN
1 hare, jointed and trimmed
¼ cup bacon fat
1 celery stalk, chopped
2 large onions, each stuck with 2 cloves
6 peppercorns
finely pared rind of ½ lemon
pinch of cayenne pepper
1 thyme sprig
1 bay leaf
2 parsley sprigs
1 mace blade
salt and pepper
5 cups water
¼ cup butter mixed to a paste with ½ cup flour
⅝ cup port or Madeira
2 tablespoons redcurrant jelly
fried bread croûtes
chopped parsley

Pigeon Casserole with Chestnuts

METRIC/IMPERIAL
300 g./12 oz. chestnuts
3 plump pigeons
3 tablespoons oil
25 g./1 oz. butter
25 g./1 oz. flour
200 ml./8 fl. oz. red wine
250 ml./½ pint chicken stock
   or stock made with a stock
   cube
200 g./8 oz. onions, quartered
thinly pared rind and juice of
   1 orange
1 teaspoon redcurrant jelly
½ teaspoon salt
1 bouquet garni
pepper
parlsey sprigs

Simmer the chestnuts in boiling water for 2 minutes. Drain. Make a slit in each with a sharp knife and remove both the skins. Return to the boiling water and simmer for 20 minutes. Drain and set aside.

Split the pigeons in half and fry them in 2 tablespoons of the oil and the butter until they are browned on both sides. Transfer them to a casserole.

Add the chestnuts to the pan with the remaining oil and fry until they are evenly browned. Drain on absorbent paper towels.

Blend the flour with the fat remaining in the pan and cook gently, stirring, until brown. Gradually add the wine and stock, stirring constantly. Bring to the boil, stirring, and pour over the pigeons. Add the onions, orange rind and juice, redcurrant jelly, salt, bouquet garni and pepper. Cover and bake in a warm oven, 170°C, 325°F, Gas Mark 3, for 3 to 3½ hours or until the pigeons are tender. Add the chestnuts 45 minutes before the end of the cooking time.

Remove the bouquet garni and orange rind and check the seasoning.

To freeze: turn into a rigid container or aluminium foil dish, cool, cover, label and freeze.

To thaw and serve: leave to thaw overnight in the refrigerator. Put into a casserole, cover and reheat in a warm oven, 170°C, 325°F, Gas Mark 3, for 1 hour. Garnish with parsley sprigs and serve with braised root vegetables and creamed potatoes.

Serves 6.

AMERICAN
12 oz. chestnuts
3 plump pigeons
3 tablespoons oil
2 tablespoons butter
¼ cup flour
1 cup red wine
1¼ cups chicken stock or stock
   made with a stock cube
8 oz. onions, quartered
thinly pared rind and juice of
   1 orange
1 teaspoon redcurrant jelly
½ teaspoon salt
1 bouquet garni
pepper
parsley sprigs

Kidneys Turbigo

METRIC/IMPERIAL
1 medium-sized onion, finely
   chopped
63 g./2½ oz. butter
8 sheeps' kidneys, skinned,
   halved and cored
100 g./4 oz. button
   mushrooms, sliced
38 g./1½ oz. flour
375 ml./¾ pint chicken stock
   or stock made with a stock
   cube
1 tablespoon sherry
1 teaspoon tomato purée
salt and pepper
2 slices stale white bread
oil for frying
chopped parsley to garnish

Fry the onion in the butter until pale golden brown. Remove the onion from the pan and set aside. Fry the kidneys in the fat remaining in the pan for 1 minute on each side or until browned. Add the kidneys to the onion.

Fry the mushrooms in the fat remaining in the pan for 2 minutes. Stir in the flour and cook for 1 minute. Remove the pan from the heat and gradually add the stock, stirring constantly. Stir in the sherry and tomato purée. Return the pan to the heat and bring to the boil, stirring. Simmer until thickened.

Return the kidneys and onion to the pan and season to taste. Cover and simmer for 15 minutes.

Meanwhile, remove the crusts from the bread and cut each slice into four triangles. Fry the triangles in the oil until they are golden brown on both sides. Drain on absorbent paper towels, then place in a small rigid container.

To freeze: turn the kidney mixture into a rigid container, cool, cover, label and freeze. Cool the fried bread croûtes, cover, label and freeze.

To thaw and serve: put the kidney mixture into a casserole, cover and reheat in a warm oven, 170°C, 325°F, Gas Mark 3, for 45 minutes. Put the croûtes in the oven for the last 2 to 3 minutes. Turn the kidney mixture on to a serving dish and arrange the croûtes around the edge. Sprinkle with parsley.

Serves 4.

AMERICAN
1 medium-sized onion, finely
   chopped
5 tablespoons butter
8 sheeps' kidneys, skinned,
   halved and cored
4 oz. button mushrooms,
   sliced
⅜ cup flour
2 cups chicken stock or stock
   made with a stock cube
1 tablespoon sherry
1 teaspoon tomato purée
salt and pepper
2 slices stale white bread
oil for frying
chopped parsley to garnish

～Liver and Onions～

METRIC/IMPERIAL
½ kg./1 lb. calves' or lambs'
  liver
4 bacon rashers, roughly
  chopped
25 g./1 oz. dripping
2 large onions, sliced
25 g./1 oz. flour
250 ml./½ pint beef stock or
  stock made with a stock
  cube
2 teaspoons salt
¼ teaspoon pepper
chopped parsley to garnish

Thinly slice the liver and remove any large tubes. Wash in warm water and drain on absorbent paper towels.

Fry the bacon lightly in the dripping, then remove from the pan. Fry the onions gently in the fat remaining in the pan until they are just beginning to brown. Blend in the flour and cook for 1 minute, stirring. Gradually add the stock, stirring constantly, and season.

Bring to the boil, stirring. Add the liver and bacon, cover and simmer for 15 minutes. Cool.

To freeze: turn into a polythene (plastic) bag, seal, label and freeze.

To thaw and serve: put in a heatproof bowl over a pan of simmering water, cover with a lid and reheat for about 15 minutes. Turn into a serving dish, sprinkle with parsley and serve with mashed potatoes and buttered cabbage.

Serves 4.

AMERICAN
1 lb. calves' or lambs' liver
4 bacon slices, roughly
  chopped
2 tablespoons dripping
2 large onions, sliced
¼ cup flour
1¼ cups beef stock or stock
  made with a stock cube
2 teaspoons salt
¼ teaspoon pepper
chopped parsley to garnish

～Pancakes (Crêpes) Turbigo～

METRIC/IMPERIAL
Batter
100 g./4 oz. flour
¼ teaspoon salt
1 egg
1 tablespoon salad oil
250 ml./½ pint milk
oil for frying
Filling
1 onion, sliced
2 tablespoons oil
25 g./1 oz. butter
8 lambs' kidneys, skinned,
  cored and cut into
  1.25 cm./½ in. pieces
100 g./4 oz. button
  mushrooms, sliced
25 g./1 oz. flour
4 tablespoons Marsala or
  sherry
75 ml./3 fl. oz. water
salt and pepper

To make the batter, sift the flour and salt into a bowl. Blend in the egg, salad oil and enough milk to make a fairly thin batter. Heat a very little oil in a 20 cm. (8 in.) frying-pan or pancake (crêpe) pan. Drop 2 tablespoonsful of the batter into the centre of the pan and tilt and rotate to spread out the batter. Cook for 1 minute, then turn the pancake (crêpe) over and cook the other side for 1 minute. Turn the pancake (crêpe) out of the pan and make seven more pancakes (crêpes) in the same way.

For the filling, fry the onion gently in the oil and butter until soft but not brown. Add the kidneys and cook for 5 minutes, stirring occasionally. Add the mushrooms and cook for 2 minutes longer, then remove the onion, kidneys and mushrooms from the pan.

Stir the flour into the fat remaining in the pan. Gradually add the Marsala or sherry and water, stirring constantly. Bring to the boil, stirring, and season to taste. Return the onion, kidneys and mushrooms to the pan and stir well.

Divide the filling between the pancakes and roll them up.

To freeze: wrap in a double thickness of foil, seal, label and freeze.

To thaw and serve: unwrap and place in a shallow buttered dish. Lightly cover with foil and reheat in a moderate oven, 180°C, 350°F, Gas Mark 4, for 50 to 60 minutes.

Serves 4.

AMERICAN
Batter
1 cup flour
¼ teaspoon salt
1 egg
1 tablespoon salad oil
1¼ cups milk
oil for frying
Filling
1 onion, sliced
2 tablespoons oil
2 tablespoons butter
8 lambs' kidneys, skinned,
  cored and cut into ½ in.
  pieces
4 oz. button mushrooms,
  sliced
¼ cup flour
4 tablespoons Marsala or
  sherry
⅜ cup water
salt and pepper

~Kidneys in Red Wine~

METRIC/IMPERIAL

8 lambs' kidneys, skinned, halved and cored
50 g./2 oz. butter
1 large onion, sliced
1 large carrot, scraped and sliced
12½ g./½ oz. flour,
250 ml./½ pint red wine
250 ml./½ pint beef stock or stock made with a stock cube
1 teaspoon tomato purée
1 thyme sprig
1 bay leaf
200 g./8 oz. flat mushrooms
1 tablespoon chopped parsley to garnish

Brown the kidneys quickly in the butter, then remove them from the pan. Fry the onion and carrot in the fat remaining in the pan until golden. Blend in the floor and cook for 1 minute, stirring, then gradually stir in the wine, stock and tomato purée. Bring to the boil, stirring. Return the kidneys to the pan with the thyme and bay leaf, cover and simmer for 15 minutes. Add the mushrooms and simmer for 5 minutes longer. Discard the herbs and turn the mixture into a shallow ovenproof dish.
To freeze: cover and freeze until solid, then remove from the dish, put into a polythene (plastic) bag, seal, label and return to the freezer.
To thaw and serve: return to the dish and reheat in a fairly hot oven, 190°C, 375°F, Gas Mark 5, for 20 minutes. Sprinkle with the parsley.

Serves 4.

AMERICAN

8 lambs' kidneys, skinned, halved and cored
¼ cup butter
1 large onion, sliced
1 large carrot, scraped and sliced
2 tablespoons flour
1¼ cups red wine
1¼ cups beef stock or stock made with a stock cube
1 teaspoon tomato purée
1 thyme sprig
1 bay leaf
8 oz. flat mushrooms
1 tablespoon chopped parsley to garnish

~Casseroled Sweetbread~

METRIC/IMPERIAL

½ kg./1 lb. lambs' sweetbreads or 2 pairs calves' sweetbreads
250 ml./½ pint chicken stock or stock made with a stock cube
juice of ½ lemon
salt and pepper
100 g./4 oz. mushrooms, sliced
25 g./1 oz. butter
12½ g./½ oz. butter mashed to a paste with 12½ g./½ oz. flour
2 tablespoons creamy milk

Soak the sweetbreads in a bowl of cold water. When the water turns pink, replace it with fresh water. Continue replacing the water until it no longer turns pink. Place the sweetbreads in a saucepan and cover with fresh cold water. Bring to the boil and boil for 2 minutes. Drain thoroughly and remove as much skin and membrane as possible.

Put the sweetbreads in a casserole or ovenproof dish. Add the stock, lemon juice and seasoning.

Fry the mushrooms in the butter for 2 minutes, then add to the casserole. Cover and cook in a moderate oven, 180°C, 350°F, Gas Mark 4, for 25 to 30 minutes or until the sweetbreads are tender.

Drain the cooking liquid from the sweetbreads into a saucepan. Put the sweetbreads and mushrooms into a rigid container.

Add the butter and flour paste (beurre manié), in small pieces, to the cooking liquid, stirring constantly. Bring to the boil, stirring, and simmer until thickened. Adjust the seasoning and stir in the milk (half and half). Pour the sauce over the sweetbreads and cool.
To freeze: cover, label and freeze.
To thaw and serve: return to the casserole or ovenproof dish, cover and reheat in a warm oven, 170°C, 325°F, Gas Mark 3, for 45 minutes.

Serves 4.

AMERICAN

1 lb. lambs' sweetbreads or 2 pairs calves' sweetbreads
1¼ cups chicken stock or stock made with a stock cube
juice of ½ lemon
salt and pepper
4 oz. mushrooms, sliced
2 tablespoons butter
1 tablespoon butter mashed to a paste with 2 tablespoons flour
2 tablespoons half and half

─Easy Home-Made Fish Cakes─

METRIC/IMPERIAL
200 g./8 oz. cooked cod or haddock
1 large packet instant mashed potato
375 ml./¾ pint boiling water
25 g./1 oz. butter
1½ teaspoons chopped parsley
salt and pepper
1 egg, beaten
browned breadcrumbs
lard or oil for frying

Remove any skin and bones from the fish and flake.

Place the instant mashed potato in a bowl and stir in the boiling water. Add the butter, parsley, fish and seasoning and mix well. Set aside 2 tablespoons of the egg and stir the rest into the fish mixture. Divide the mixture into eight portions and shape into fish cakes. Brush the cakes with the reserved egg and coat with breadcrumbs.
To freeze: open freeze, pack in a polythene (plastic) bag, seal, label and return to the freezer.
To thaw and serve: fry the fish cakes in the lard or oil for 12 to 15 minutes, turning once, until golden brown and heated through.

Makes 8 fish cakes.

AMERICAN
8 oz. cooked cod or haddock
1 large packet instant mashed potato
2 cups boiling water
2 tablespoons butter
1½ teaspoons chopped parsley
salt and pepper
1 egg, beaten
browned breadcrumbs
lard or oil for cooking

─Seafood au Gratin─

METRIC/IMPERIAL
½ kg./1 lb. halibut or other white fish
125 ml./¼ pint dry white wine or dry cider
1 small onion, finely chopped
1 × 175 g./15 oz. can condensed lobster bisque
1 × 125 g./5 oz. packet commercial frozen dressed crab, thawed
100 g./4 oz. frozen peeled prawns, thawed
1 tablespoon chopped parsley
½ teaspoon salt
pinch of pepper
¾ kg./1½ lb. potatoes
25 g./1 oz. butter
milk
lemon wedges

Place the halibut in a saucepan with the wine or cider and onion. Cover and poach for 10 minutes. Lift the fish out of the pan and remove the skin and bones.

Blend the lobster bisque with the cooking liquid in the pan and simmer for 2 minutes. Add the fish, crab, prawns (shrimp), parsley and seasoning and bring to the boil, stirring. Cool.

Put the potatoes in cold water and bring to the boil. Simmer for 15 to 20 minutes or until the potatoes are tender. Drain and mash, then beat in the butter and enough milk to make a smooth consistency. Season to taste. Put the potato in a large piping bag fitted with a large fluted nozzle and pipe around the edge of a 20 cm. (8 in.) shallow oval ovenproof dish. Spoon the fish mixture into the centre and cool completely.
To freeze: open freeze until the pie is firm, then cover with a lid of aluminium foil, label and return to the freezer.
To thaw and serve: leave to thaw at room temperature for 4 hours or overnight in the refrigerator. Remove the foil lid and reheat in a hot oven, 220°C, 425°F, Gas Mark 7, for 30 to 40 minutes or until the potato is pale golden brown. Garnish with lemon wedges.

Serves 6.

AMERICAN
1 lb. halibut or other white fish
⅝ cup dry white wine or dry cider
1 small onion, finely chopped
1 × 15 oz. can condensed lobster bisque
1 × 5 oz. packet commercial frozen dressed crab, thawed
4 oz. frozen peeled baby shrimp, thawed
1 tablespoon chopped parsley
½ teaspoon salt
pinch of pepper
1½ lb. potatoes
2 tablespoons butter
milk
lemon wedges

Creamed Fish Pie

METRIC/IMPERIAL
½ kg./1 lb. cod or haddock
250 ml./½ pint milk
250 ml./½ pint water
few parsley stalks
50 g./2 oz. butter
25 g./1 oz. flour
100 g./4 oz. crabmeat or 2
  hard-boiled eggs, chopped
¼ teaspoon ground mace
salt and pepper
1½ lb. potatoes
1 egg, beaten
75 g./3 oz. Cheddar cheese,
  grated
milk

Put the fish in a saucepan with the milk, water and parsley stalks. Cover and poach for 10 minutes. Lift the fish out of the pan and remove the skin and bones. Flake the fish. Strain the cooking liquid and reserve 375 ml. (¾ pint) or 2 cups.

Melt half of the butter in a saucepan and stir in the flour. Cook, stirring, for 1 minute. Gradually add the reserved fish cooking liquid, stirring constantly. Bring to the boil, stirring, and simmer for 2 minutes. Remove the pan from the heat. Stir in the fish, crabmeat or eggs, mace and seasoning. Put the fish mixture into an ovenproof dish.

Put the potatoes in cold water and bring to the boil. Simmer for 15 to 20 minutes or until the potatoes are tender. Drain and mash, then beat in the remaining butter, the beaten egg, two-thirds of the cheese and enough milk to make a smooth consistency. Spoon the potato mixture on top of the fish mixture and mark it out with a fork. Sprinkle with the remaining cheese.

To freeze: open freeze until the pie is firm, then cover with a lid of foil, label and return to the freezer.

To thaw and serve: leave to thaw at room temperature for 4 hours or overnight in the refrigerator. Remove the foil lid and reheat in a hot oven, 220°C, 425°F, Gas Mark 7, for 30 minutes or until the potato is pale golden brown.

Serves 4.

AMERICAN
1 lb. cod or haddock
1¼ cups milk
1¼ cups water
few parsley stalks
¼ cup butter
¼ cup flour
4 oz. crabmeat or 2 hard-
  boiled eggs, chopped
¼ teaspoon ground mace
salt and pepper
1½ lb. potatoes
1 egg, beaten
¾ cup grated Cheddar cheese
milk

Kedgeree

METRIC/IMPERIAL
125 g./5 oz. long-grain rice
salt and pepper
1 onion, finely chopped
100 g./4 oz. butter
300 g./12 oz. cooked smoked
  haddock
4 hard-boiled eggs, finely
  chopped
1 tablespoon chopped
  parsley
3 tablespoons single cream

Cook the rice in boiling salted water until it is tender. Rinse well and drain.

Fry the onion in the butter until soft but not brown. Remove the skin and bone from the haddock and flake into large pieces. Add to the onion with the rice and eggs and mix well. Stir in the parsley and seasoning.

To freeze: turn into a well-greased aluminium foil dish, cool, cover, label and freeze.

To thaw and serve: remove the lid, lightly cover with foil and reheat in a moderately hot oven, 200°C, 400°F, Gas Mark 6, for 50 minutes, stirring occasionally with a fork. Just before serving stir in the cream.

Serves 4.

AMERICAN
¾ cup long-grain rice
salt and pepper
1 onion, finely chopped
½ cup butter
12 oz. cooked smoked
  haddock
4 hard-boiled eggs, finely
  chopped
1 tablespoon chopped parsley
3 tablespoons light cream

Haddock with Tomato Wine Sauce

METRIC/IMPERIAL
1 onion, chopped
2 tablespoons oil
1 × 200 g./8 oz. can tomatoes
50 g./2 oz. mushrooms, sliced
3 to 4 anchovies, chopped
125 ml./¼ pint white wine
1 tablespoon chopped parsley
salt and pepper
1 packet commercial frozen
  breaded haddock portions
fat or oil for frying

Fry the onion in the oil for 5 minutes or until soft but not brown. Add the tomatoes, mushrooms, anchovies, wine, parsley and seasoning. Cook gently, stirring frequently, for 20 minutes.

To freeze: turn the sauce into a rigid container, cool, cover, label and freeze.

To thaw and serve: put into a saucepan and reheat gently to simmering, then simmer for a few minutes. Fry the haddock according to the directions on the packet in fat or oil. Serve the haddock with the sauce.

Serves 4.

AMERICAN
1 onion, chopped
2 tablespoons oil
1 × 8 oz. can tomatoes
2 oz. mushrooms, sliced
3 to 4 anchovies, chopped
⅝ cup white wine
1 tablespoon chopped parsley
salt and pepper
1 packet commercial frozen
  breaded haddock portions
fat or oil for frying

—Lasagne—

Ragu Bolognese Sauce
2 streaky bacon rashers, cut into small pieces
1 large onion, chopped
½ kg./1 lb. minced beef
2 tablespoons oil
2 celery stalks, chopped
1 garlic clove, crushed
¼ teaspoon dried mixed herbs
2 teaspoons salt
½ teaspoon sugar
pinch of pepper
5 tablespoons tomato purée
250 ml./½ pint water
White sauce
25 g./1 oz. margarine
25 g./1 oz. flour
375 ml./¾ pint milk
salt and pepper
Pasta
2 teaspoons oil
2 teaspoons salt
100 g./4 oz. lasagne
100 g./4 oz. Gruyère cheese, grated
50 g./2 oz. Parmesan cheese, grated

Fry the bacon, onion and beef in the oil until brown, stirring frequently. Add all the remaining Bolognese sauce ingredients and stir well. Cover and simmer for 1 hour.

To make the white sauce, melt the margarine in a saucepan and stir in the flour. Cook, stirring, for 2 minutes. Gradually add the milk, stirring constantly. Bring to the boil, stirring, and simmer until the sauce has thickened. Season to taste, cover and keep hot.

To prepare the pasta, bring 2 l. (4 pints) or 5 pints of water to the boil with the oil and salt. Add the lasagne and boil for 8 minutes. Drain in a colander, rinse with cold water, then arrange on a damp towel so that the pieces don't stick together.

Assemble the lasagne in three layers in a shallow ovenproof dish lined with foil. Start with a layer of Bolognese sauce, then a layer of pasta, then a layer of white sauce and Gruyère cheese. Continue making layers, ending with one of white sauce. Sprinkle with the remaining Gruyère and the Parmesan.

To freeze: open freeze, remove from the dish and put in a polythene (plastic) bag, seal, label and return to the freezer.

To thaw and serve: return to the dish and reheat in a fairly hot oven, 190°C, 375°F, Gas Mark 5, for 1 hour or until golden brown. Serve with a green salad.

Serves 4 to 6.

Ragu Bolognese Sauce
2 fatty bacon slices, cut into small pieces
1 large onion, chopped
1 lb. ground beef
2 tablespoons oil
2 celery stalks, chopped
1 garlic clove, crushed
¼ teaspoon dried mixed herbs
2 teaspoons salt
½ teaspoon sugar
pinch of pepper
5 tablespoons tomato purée
1¼ cups water
White sauce
2 tablespoons margarine
¼ cup flour
2 cups milk
salt and pepper
Pasta
2 teaspoons oil
2 teaspoons salt
4 oz. lasagne
1 cup grated Gruyère cheese
½ cup grated Parmesan cheese

—Italian Tagliatelle—

½ kg./1 lb. pork sausage meat
25 g./1 oz. flour
salt and pepper
25 g./1 oz. dripping
½ head celery, sliced
1 small green pepper, pith and seeds removed and cut into strips
200 g./8 oz. onions, chopped
100 g./4 oz. mushrooms, sliced
1 × 250 g./10 oz. can condensed tomato soup
200 g./8 oz. tagliatelle
100 g./4 oz. strong Cheddar cheese, grated

Shape the sausage meat into 24 small balls and roll in the flour which has been seasoned. Fry the balls in the dripping for 5 minutes or until evenly browned. Add the celery, green pepper, onions, mushrooms and soup and stir well. Cover and simmer for 30 minutes.

Cook the tagliatelle in boiling salted water for 12 to 15 minutes or until tender. Rinse with cold water and drain well. Turn into a foil dish. Sprinkle over the cheese and pour over the meatballs and sauce.

To freeze: cool, cover, label and freeze.

To thaw and serve: leave to thaw overnight in the refrigerator. Remove the lid, lightly cover with foil and reheat in a warm oven, 170°C, 325°F, Gas Mark 3, for 1 hour. Serve with French bread and a green salad.

Serves 8.

1 lb. pork sausage meat
¼ cup flour
salt and pepper
2 tablespoons dripping
½ head celery, sliced
1 small green pepper, pith and seeds removed and cut into strips
8 oz. onions, chopped
4 oz. mushrooms, sliced
1 × 10 oz. can condensed tomato soup
8 oz. tagliatelle
1 cup grated strong Cheddar cheese

Country Chicken Pie

(right) Kedgeree

~Cannelloni~

METRIC/IMPERIAL
8 pieces of wide lasagne
½ quantity Ragu Bolognese sauce (see Lasagne recipe on page 00)
Cheese sauce
25 g./1 oz. butter
25 g./1 oz. flour
250 ml./½ pint milk
50 g./2 oz. Cheddar cheese, grated
½ teaspoon prepared mustard
salt and pepper

Cook the lasagne in boiling salted water for 8 to 10 minutes, or until it is tender. Drain, rinse and drain again. Arrange on a damp towel so that the pieces don't stick together.

Place a spoonful of the Bolognese sauce on each piece of lasagne and roll up. Put the lasagne rolls in a greased aluminium foil dish or rigid container.

To make the cheese sauce, melt the butter in a saucepan and stir in the flour. Cook, stirring, for 1 minute. Gradually add the milk, stirring constantly. Bring to the boil, stirring, and simmer until the sauce has thickened. Stir in the cheese, mustard and seasoning. Pour the sauce over the lasagne rolls.
To freeze: cool, then open freeze, remove from the dish and put in a polythene (plastic) bag, seal, label and return to the freezer.
To thaw and serve: return to the dish and bake in a hot oven, 200°C, 400°F, Gas Mark 6, for 1 hour or until golden brown. Serve with a green salad.

Serves 4.

AMERICAN
8 pieces of wide lasagne
½ quantity Ragu Bolognese sauce (see Lasagne recipe on page 00)
Cheese sauce
2 tablespoons butter
¼ cup flour
1¼ cups milk
½ cup grated Cheddar cheese
½ teaspoon prepared mustard
salt and pepper

~Pizzas~

METRIC/IMPERIAL
Yeast mixture
375 ml./¾ pint hand-hot water
1 teaspoon sugar
12½ g./½ oz. dried yeast
Dough
¾ kg./1½ lb. strong flour
2 teaspoons sugar
2 to 3 teaspoons salt
1 tablespoon oil
Topping 1
1 × 375 g./15 oz. can tomatoes, drained and roughly chopped
salt and pepper
8 black olives, halved and stoned
50 g./2 oz. grated cheese
Topping 2
1 small onion, finely chopped
1 green pepper, pith and seeds removed and cut into small pieces
1 tablespoon oil
100 g./4 oz. cooked ham, diced
100 g./4 oz. tomatoes, sliced
Topping 3
75 g./3 oz. liver sausage, sliced
1 × 200 g./8 oz. can tomatoes, drained and chopped
salt and pepper
3 streaky bacon rashers, halved
Topping 4
50 g./2 oz. sliced salami
100 g./4 oz. mushrooms, sliced
25 g./1 oz. butter, melted
75 g./3 oz. Emmenthal cheese, thinly sliced
paprika

To prepare the yeast mixture, combine the water and sugar and stir in the dried yeast. Leave in a warm place for 10 to 15 minutes or until frothy.

For the dough, sift the flour, sugar and salt into a bowl. Add the yeast mixture and oil and mix with a fork. Knead for about 10 minutes or until the dough is smooth and no longer sticky. Place in an oiled polythene (plastic) bag and leave until the dough has doubled in bulk. This will take about 1 hour at room temperature, or overnight in the refrigerator.

Turn the dough out on to a floured board and knead back to the original bulk. Divide the dough into four portions and roll out each portion into a 20 cm. (8 in.) circle. Brush each circle with a little oil.

To make Topping 1, mix together the tomatoes, seasoning and olives. Spread over one of the dough circles and sprinkle with the cheese.

To make Topping 2, fry the onion and green pepper in the oil until the onion is soft. Stir in the ham and spread over the second dough circle. Arrange the tomato slices on top.

To make Topping 3, cover the third dough circle with the liver sausage slices. Mix together the tomatoes and seasoning and spread over the liver sausage. Arrange the bacon on top like the spokes of a wheel.

To make Topping 4, cover the fourth dough circle with the salami slices. Fry the mushrooms in the melted butter and spread over the salami. Arrange the cheese slices on top and sprinkle with paprika.

Leave the pizzas in a warm place to prove for 20 minutes.
To freeze: wrap each pizza in foil, freeze flat until solid, then over-wrap in ones, twos or fours.
To thaw and serve: unwrap the pizzas and place on a lightly oiled baking sheet. Bake in a very hot oven, 220°C, 425°F, Gas Mark 7, for 25 to 30 minutes.

Makes 4 pizzas.

AMERICAN
Yeast mixture
2 cups hand-hot water
1 teaspoon sugar
½ oz. dried yeast
Dough
6 cups strong flour
2 teaspoons sugar
2 to 3 teaspoons salt
1 tablespoon oil
Topping 1
1 × 15 oz. can tomatoes, drained and roughly chopped
salt and pepper
8 black olives, halved and stoned
½ cup grated cheese
Topping 2
1 small onion, finely chopped
1 green pepper, pith and seeds removed and cut into small pieces
1 tablespoon oil
4 oz. cooked ham, diced
4 oz. tomatoes, sliced
Topping 3
3 oz. liver sausage, sliced
1 × 8 oz. can tomatoes, drained and chopped
salt and pepper
3 fatty bacon slices, halved
Topping 4
2 oz. sliced salami
4 oz. mushrooms, sliced
2 tablespoons melted butter
3 oz. Emmenthal cheese, thinly sliced
paprika

~Quiche Lorraine~

METRIC/IMPERIAL
Pastry
100 g./4 oz. flour
pinch of salt
63 g./2½ oz. butter
water
Filling
2 medium-sized onions,
    finely chopped
25 g./1 oz. butter
100 g./4 oz. bacon, cut into
    small pieces
1 egg
salt and pepper
125 ml/¼ pint single cream

To make the pastry, sift the flour and salt into a bowl. Add the butter and cut it into small pieces. Then rub it into the flour until the mixture resembles breadcrumbs. Mix in enough water to make a firm dough. Roll out the dough and use to line a 17.5 cm. (7 in.) flan ring placed on a baking sheet. Chill for 10 minutes, then line the pastry dough with a sheet of greaseproof (waxed) paper weighed down with dried beans. Bake 'blind' in a very hot oven, 220°C, 425°F, Gas Mark 7, for 15 minutes. Remove the beans and paper and set aside to cool.

To make the filling, fry the onions in the butter until soft but not brown. Add the bacon and fry until golden brown. Put the onion and bacon into the flan case. Mix together the egg, seasoning and cream and strain into the flan case. Bake in a moderate oven, 180°C, 350°F, Gas Mark 4, for 35 minutes or until the filling is set.
To freeze: cool, put in a polythene (plastic) bag, seal, label and freeze.
To thaw and serve: remove from the bag and reheat in a moderate oven, 180°C, 350°F, Gas Mark 4, for 30 to 40 minutes. Or leave to thaw at room temperature for 4 hours and then reheat in a moderate oven, 180°C, 350°F, Gas Mark 4, for 25 minutes. Serve with a green salad.

Serves 4.

AMERICAN
Pastry
1 cup flour
pinch of salt
5 tablespoons butter
water
Filling
2 medium-sized onions,
    finely chopped
2 tablespoons butter
4 oz. bacon, cut into small
    pieces
1 egg
salt and pepper
⅝ cup light cream

~Pissaladière~

METRIC/IMPERIAL
Dough base
200 g./8 oz. self-raising flour
½ teaspoon salt
25 g./1 oz. butter or margarine
125 ml./¼ pint milk
Topping
3 medium-sized onions, sliced
4 tablespoons oil
1 × 375 g./15 oz. can
    tomatoes, drained and
    roughly chopped
pepper
4 slices Mozzarella cheese
1 × 50 g./2 oz. can anchovy
    fillets, drained
about 20 stuffed green olives

To make the dough base, sift the flour and salt into a bowl. Add the butter or margarine and cut into small pieces. Rub into the flour until the mixture resembles breadcrumbs. Add the milk and mix to a soft dough. Knead the dough lightly, then roll it out into a 22.5 cm. (9 in.) circle. Place on a lightly greased baking sheet and using your thumb and forefinger, pinch up the edge of the dough to raise it slightly.

Fry the onions gently in the oil until they are soft but not brown. Spread the onions on the dough circle, cover with the tomatoes and sprinkle with pepper. Top with the cheese slices. Arrange the anchovy fillets in a lattice pattern on top and decorate with the olives.
To freeze: cover with polythene (plastic) wrap or put into a polythene (plastic) bag and freeze. When frozen, remove from the baking sheet, put into a polythene (plastic) bag, seal, label and return to the freezer.
To thaw and serve: replace on the baking sheet and bake in a very hot oven, 220°C, 425°F, Gas Mark 7, for 45 minutes or until the dough is browned and the cheese melted.

Serves 4 to 5.

AMERICAN
Dough base
2 cups self-rising flour
½ teaspoon salt
2 tablespoons butter or
    margarine
⅝ cup milk
Topping
3 medium-sized onions, sliced
4 tablespoons oil
1 × 15 oz. can tomatoes,
    drained and roughly
    chopped
pepper
4 slices Mozzarella cheese
1 × 2 oz. can anchovy fillets,
    drained
about 20 stuffed green olives

Cannelloni

(right) Quiche Lorraine and Pizzas

—Cauliflower Cheese—

METRIC/IMPERIAL
1 kg./2 lb. cauliflower,
  broken into flowerets
salt and pepper
38 g./1½ oz. butter
38 g./1½ oz. flour
375 ml./¾ pint milk
75 g./3 oz. Cheddar cheese,
  grated
½ teaspoon prepared mustard
1 tablespoon grated
  Parmesan cheese
2 tablespoons dry
  breadcrumbs

AMERICAN
2 lb. cauliflower, broken into
  flowerets
salt and pepper
3 tablespoons butter
⅜ cup flour
2 cups milk
¾ cup grated Cheddar cheese
½ teaspoon prepared mustard
1 tablespoon grated
  Parmesan cheese
2 tablespoons dry
  breadcrumbs

Cook the cauliflower in boiling salted water until barely tender. Drain, reserving 4 tablespoons of the cooking liquid.

Melt the butter in a saucepan and stir in the flour. Cook, stirring, for 1 minute. Gradually add the milk, stirring constantly. Bring to the boil, stirring, and simmer until the sauce has thickened. Stir in the Cheddar cheese, mustard, seasoning, cauliflower and reserved cooking liquid.

Turn into a foil container and sprinkle over the Parmesan cheese and breadcrumbs.

To freeze: cool, cover, label and freeze.

To thaw and serve: remove the foil lid and reheat in a hot oven, 200°C, 400°F, Gas Mark 6, for 30 minutes.

Note: leeks and chicory (French or Belgian endive) may be prepared in the same way. Add a little sugar to the cooking water of the chicory (endive) to reduce the bitter taste.

Serves 4.

—Basque Omelette—

METRIC/IMPERIAL
1 small green pepper, pith
  and seeds removed and
  thinly sliced
2 tablespoons olive oil
3 tomatoes, skinned, seeded
  and quartered
1 × 88 g./3½ oz. can tuna fish,
  drained and flaked
6 eggs
salt and pepper
1 × 50 g./2 oz. can anchovy
  fillets, drained

AMERICAN
1 small green pepper, pith and
  seeds removed and thinly
  sliced
2 tablespoons olive oil
3 tomatoes, skinned, seeded
  and quartered
1 × 3½ oz. can tuna fish,
  drained and flaked
6 eggs
salt and pepper
1 × 2 oz. can anchovy fillets,
  drained

Fry the green pepper gently in the oil in a 20 cm. (8 in.) nonstick frying-pan or omelette pan until soft. Add the tomatoes and tuna and cook for 2 minutes, stirring occasionally. Blend the eggs with the seasoning and add to the pan. Cook gently for 2 to 3 minutes. Arrange the anchovy fillets on top and cook under a hot grill (broiler) for 1 minute.

To freeze: slide the omelette on to a well-buttered piece of foil, cool, wrap, seal, label and freeze.

To thaw and serve: slide on to a well-buttered ovenproof dish, cover lightly with foil and reheat in a moderate oven, 180°C, 350°F, Gas Mark 4, for 25 to 30 minutes. Serve with French bread and a green salad.

Serves 4.

—Ham Omelette—

METRIC/IMPERIAL
6 eggs
salt and pepper
100 g./4 oz. cooked ham,
  diced
1 tablespoon chopped fresh
  herbs
1 tablespoon olive oil

AMERICAN
6 eggs
salt and pepper
4 oz. cooked ham, diced
1 tablespoon chopped fresh
  herbs
1 tablespoon olive oil

Blend the eggs with the seasoning and add the ham and herbs. Heat the oil in a 20 cm. (8 in.) nonstick frying-pan or omelette pan and pour in the egg mixture. Cook gently for 2 to 3 minutes, then cook under a hot grill (broiler) for 1 minute to set the egg lightly.

To freeze: slide the omelette on to a well-buttered piece of foil, cool, wrap, seal, label and freeze.

To thaw and serve: slide on to a well-buttered ovenproof dish, cover lightly with foil and reheat in a moderate oven, 180°C, 350°F, Gas Mark 4, for 25 to 30 minutes. Serve with French bread and a green salad.

Serves 4.

Vegetables

Broccoli Polonaise; Frozen Peas and Cucumber; Frozen Carrots and Fried Almonds
(right) Red Cabbage

Note: The majority of the recipes I have given here are for making frozen vegetables more interesting. Instructions for preparing and freezing the vegetables are given in the A–Z of vegetables on pages 39–45. The last three recipes are for vegetable dishes to be frozen.

Frozen Peas and Courgettes (Zucchini)

METRIC/IMPERIAL
200 g./8 oz. courgettes,
   sliced
50 g./2 oz. butter
200 g./8 oz. frozen peas
salt

Fry the courgettes (zucchini) gently in the butter, stirring frequently, until they are pale golden.

   Meanwhile, cook the peas in boiling salted water for 5 minutes. Drain and mix with the courgettes (zucchini).

Serves 4.

AMERICAN
8 oz. zucchini, sliced
$\frac{1}{4}$ cup butter
8 oz. frozen peas
salt

Frozen Peas and Cucumber

METRIC/IMPERIAL
1 medium-sized cucumber
25 g./1 oz. butter
200 g./8 oz. frozen peas
salt

Peel the cucumber and cut it into 1.25 cm. ($\frac{1}{2}$ in.) dice. Cook the cucumber dice gently in the butter, stirring frequently, until it is pale golden.

   Meanwhile, cook the peas in boiling salted water for 5 minutes. Drain and mix with the cucumber.

Serves 4.

AMERICAN
1 medium-sized cucumber
2 tablespoons butter
8 oz. frozen peas
salt

Mixed Vegetables au Gratin

METRIC/IMPERIAL
200 g./8 oz. mixed frozen
   vegetables
salt
Cheese sauce
25 g./1 oz. butter
25 g./1 oz. flour
250 ml./$\frac{1}{2}$ pint milk
75 g./3 oz. Cheddar cheese,
   grated
salt and pepper
2 tablespoons grated
   Parmesan cheese

Cook the vegetables in boiling salted water until tender and drain well.

   Meanwhile, to make the sauce, melt the butter in a saucepan and stir in the flour. Cook, stirring, for 1 minute. Gradually add the milk, stirring constantly. Bring to the boil, stirring, and simmer until the sauce has thickened. Add most of the Cheddar cheese with seasoning to taste. Stir in the mixed vegetables and turn into a flameproof dish.

   Mix the remaining Cheddar cheese with the Parmesan cheese and sprinkle over the top. Brown under a hot grill (broiler).

Serves 4.

AMERICAN
8 oz. mixed frozen vegetables
salt
Cheese sauce
2 tablespoons butter
$\frac{1}{4}$ cup flour
$1\frac{1}{4}$ cups milk
$\frac{3}{4}$ cup grated Cheddar cheese
salt and pepper
2 tablespoons grated
   Parmesan cheese

—Frozen Carrots and Fried Almonds—

METRIC/IMPERIAL
300 g./12 oz. frozen carrot
    slices
salt
50 g./2 oz. blanched almonds
25 g./1 oz. butter

Cook the carrot slices in boiling salted water for 5 minutes. Drain well.

Meanwhile fry the almonds in the butter, stirring, until they are golden brown. Mix the carrots with the almonds.

Serves 4.

AMERICAN
12 oz. frozen carrot slices
salt
$\frac{1}{3}$ cup blanched almonds
2 tablespoons butter

—Broccoli Polonaise—

METRIC/IMPERIAL
$\frac{1}{2}$ kg./1 lb. frozen broccoli
    spears
salt
75 g./3 oz. butter
100 g./4 oz. fresh white
    breadcrumbs
2 hard-boiled eggs, whites
    finely chopped and yolks
    sieved
2 tablespoons chopped
    parsley

Cook the broccoli in boiling salted water for 5 minutes. Drain well, put in a heated serving dish and add one-third of the butter. Set aside and keep hot.

Fry the breadcrumbs in the remaining butter until they are crisp and golden. Sprinkle them over the broccoli. Arrange a circle of egg white around the edge of the dish, then a circle of egg yolk and then a circle of parsley.

Serves 4.

AMERICAN
1 lb. frozen broccoli spears
salt
$\frac{3}{8}$ cup butter
2 cups fresh white
    breadcrumbs
2 hard-boiled eggs, whites
    finely chopped
    and yolks sieved
2 tablespoons chopped
    parsley

—Roasted Whole Frozen Onions—

METRIC/IMPERIAL
6 whole frozen onions
dripping or hot fat, melted

Put the onions in a roasting tin with the dripping or fat. If roasting a joint of meat, put the onions around it. Roast in a moderate oven, 180°C, 350°F, Gas Mark 4, for 45 minutes to 1 hour, basting occasionally, or until the onions are tender and golden brown.

Serves 6.

AMERICAN
6 whole frozen onions
dripping or hot fat, melted

Rosti

(right) Sweet and Sour Pork; Spring Rolls; Chinese Chicken
with Cashew Nuts; Hot Sauce Noodles

Mixed Root Vegetables in Onion Sauce

METRIC/IMPERIAL
200 g./8 oz. large carrots
1 parsnip
1 turnip
Onion sauce
1 large onion, chopped
25 g./1 oz. butter
25 g./1 oz. flour
250 ml./½ pint milk
salt and pepper

Peel the carrots, parsnip and turnip and cut them into 1.25 cm. (½ in.) dice. Blanch in boiling water for 3 minutes, then drain.

To make the sauce, fry the onion gently in the butter until it is soft but not coloured. Stir in the flour and cook for 1 minute. Gradually add the milk, stirring constantly. Bring to the boil, stirring, and simmer until the sauce has thickened. Season to taste and mix in the root vegetables.

To freeze: turn into a rigid container, cool, cover, label and freeze.
To thaw and serve: put into a saucepan with 1 tablespoon water and reheat gently to simmering, stirring frequently.

Serves 4.

AMERICAN
8 oz. large carrots
1 parsnip
1 turnip
Onion sauce
1 large onion, chopped
2 tablespoons butter
¼ cup flour
1¼ cups milk
salt and pepper

Red Cabbage

METRIC/IMPERIAL
1 medium-sized red cabbage, finely shredded
½ kg./1 lb. cooking apples, peeled, cored and sliced
125 ml./¼ pint water
3 tablespoons sugar
1 teaspoon salt
4 cloves
5 tablespoons vinegar
50 g./2 oz. butter
1 tablespoon redcurrant jelly

Put the cabbage and apples in a saucepan with the water, sugar, salt and cloves. Cover and simmer for about 45 minutes or until the cabbage is tender. Remove the cloves and stir in the vinegar, butter and redcurrant jelly.

To freeze: turn into a rigid container, cool, cover, label and freeze. Use within 2 months.
To thaw and serve: leave to thaw at room temperature for 5 to 6 hours. Put in a saucepan and reheat gently, stirring frequently, to simmering.

Serves 4.

AMERICAN
1 medium-sized red cabbage, finely shredded
1 lb. cooking apples, peeled, cored and sliced
⅝ cup water
3 tablespoons sugar
1 teaspoon salt
4 cloves
5 tablespoons vinegar
¼ cup butter
1 tablespoon redcurrant jelly

Rosti

METRIC/IMPERIAL
1 kg./2 lb. potatoes
salt and pepper
75 g./3 oz. Emmenthal or Gruyère cheese, grated
100 g./4 oz. streaky bacon, cut into thin strips
75 g./3 oz. butter

Put the unpeeled potatoes into a pan of salted water and bring to the boil. Simmer for 20 minutes or until the potatoes are just cooked. Drain and when cool peel off the skins. Grate into a bowl and add the cheese.

Fry the bacon strips in one-third of the butter for 3 to 4 minutes or until cooked. Drain and add to the potatoes. Season well. Turn the mixture on to a piece of aluminium foil and shape into a circle the size of the frying-pan.

To freeze: cover with foil, label and freeze.
To thaw and serve: melt the remaining butter in the frying-pan. Add the potato cake and cook gently for 15 minutes on each side. Turn out by placing a serving plate, upside-down, on the frying-pan and reversing the two.

Serves 4.

AMERICAN
2 lb. potatoes
salt and pepper
¾ cup grated Emmenthal or Gruyère cheese
4 oz. fatty bacon, cut into thin strips
⅜ cup butter

Chinese dishes

Note: These recipes may all be taken straight from the freezer and then cooked. However, you will need to stir-fry less if you thaw the dishes for 24 hours in the refrigerator, or 8 hours at room temperature. You will also find the foods heat considerably quicker when thawed first. All these dishes combined are plenty for a Chinese party for 12 guests and are authentic in flavour.

~Spring Rolls~

METRIC/IMPERIAL
100 g./4 oz. flour
1 egg
250 ml./½ pint water
oil for frying
Marinade
¼ teaspoon sugar
1 teaspoon cornflour
¼ teaspoon salt
pepper
2 teaspoons soya sauce
1 teaspoon water
Filling
100 g./4 oz. lean pork
oil for frying
100 g./4 oz. mushrooms, sliced
1 × ½ kg./1 lb. can bean sprouts, drained
¾ teaspoon salt
2 tablespoons water
1 garlic clove, crushed
1 teaspoon cornflour dissolved in 1 tablespoon water
pinch of salt
1 egg, beaten

AMERICAN
1 cup flour
1 egg
1¼ cups water
oil for frying
Marinade
¼ teaspoon sugar
1 teaspoon cornstarch
¼ teaspoon salt
pepper
2 teaspoons soy sauce
1 teaspoon water
Filling
4 oz. lean pork
oil for frying
4 oz. mushrooms, sliced
1 × 1 lb. can bean sprouts, drained
¾ teaspoon salt
2 tablespoons water
1 garlic clove, crushed
1 teaspoon cornstarch, dissolved in 1 tablespoon water
pinch of sugar
1 egg, beaten

Beat together the flour, egg and water to make a thin, smooth batter. Lightly oil a heavy 17.5 cm. (7 in.) diameter frying-pan and heat. Drop a generous tablespoonful of the batter into the centre of the pan and tilt and rotate it to spread out the batter. Cook for 1 minute, then turn the pancake (crêpe) over and cook the other side for 1 minute. Remove the pancake from the pan and use the remaining batter to make more pancakes in the same way. You should be able to make about 12.

Mix together the marinade ingredients. Cut the pork into slices, ¾ cm. (¼ in.) thick and 5 cm. (2 in.) long, and put them in the marinade. Leave for 10 minutes.

Heat 1 tablespoon oil in the frying-pan and add the mushrooms. Fry for 1 minute, stirring. Add the bean sprouts and cook for another minute, stirring. Add the salt and water, cover and cook for 2 minutes. Remove the mushrooms and bean sprouts from the pan and set aside.

Add the garlic and pork to the pan with 2 teaspoons oil. Fry for 2 minutes, stirring. Return the mushrooms and bean sprouts to the pan and mix well. Stir in the cornflour (cornstarch) and sugar and simmer until thickened.

Put about 1 tablespoon of the filling on each pancake and roll them up, folding in the ends like small parcels. Use the beaten egg to seal the edges.

To freeze: wrap the spring rolls in a single layer in aluminium foil, seal, label and freeze.

To thaw and serve: remove the foil and drop the frozen rolls carefully into hot deep fat, about three at a time. Fry for about 3 minutes or until golden brown, drain and serve hot.

Makes about 12.

~Rice and Sweetcorn~

METRIC/IMPERIAL
150 g./6 oz. long-grain rice
½ l./1 pint water
salt and pepper
200 g./8 oz. lean pork, finely chopped
oil for frying
2 garlic cloves, crushed
1 × 275 g./7 oz. can sweetcorn, drained
2 teaspoons cornflour dissolved in 2 tablespoons water
2 spring onions, chopped
1 egg, beaten
Marinade
1 teaspoon cornflour
1 teaspoon oil
1 tablespoon soya sauce

AMERICAN
1 cup long-grain rice
2½ cups water
salt and pepper
8 oz. lean pork, finely chopped
oil for frying
2 garlic cloves, crushed
1 × 7 oz. can corn, drained
2 teaspoons cornstarch dissolved in 2 tablespoons water
2 scallions, chopped
1 egg, beaten
Marinade
1 teaspoon cornstarch
1 teaspoon oil
1 tablespoon soy sauce

Put the rice and three-quarters of the water in a saucepan with 1 teaspoon salt. Cover and simmer for 15 minutes or until the rice is just tender and almost all the water has been absorbed. Drain, then turn the rice on to a plate and set aside.

Mix together the ingredients for the marinade, adding a pinch of pepper. Add the pork to the marinade and leave for 15 minutes.

Heat 1 tablespoon oil in a heavy frying-pan. Add the pork, garlic and 1 teaspoon salt and cook for 2 minutes, stirring. Add the corn and remaining water and simmer for 1 minute. Stir in the cornflour (cornstarch) and spring onions (scallions) and simmer for 1 minute. Turn into a shallow polythene (plastic) container. Cool, then stir in the rice.

To freeze: cover, label and freeze.

To thaw and serve: put in a saucepan with 1 tablespoon water. Cover and heat gently, stirring occasionally with a fork. When the mixture is just simmering, stir in the beaten egg. Cook for 1 minute longer.

Serves 3 to 4.

─Chicken Parcels─

METRIC/IMPERIAL
few drops chilli sauce
2 teaspoons medium dry
    sherry
½ teaspoon caster sugar
pepper
¼ teaspoon salt
1 teaspoon soya sauce
½ teaspoon sesame seeds
200 g./8 oz. chicken meat, cut
    into 2.5 cm./1 in. pieces
oil for frying

Blend together the chilli sauce, sherry, sugar, pepper, salt, soya sauce and sesame seeds. Add the chicken to this marinade and leave for 30 minutes.

Lightly oil six 15 cm. (6 in.) squares of aluminium foil. Divide the chicken between the pieces of foil, then wrap up firmly into small parcels.

To freeze: label and freeze.

To thaw and serve: drop the foil parcels into hot deep oil a few at a time and fry for 5 minutes. Drain and serve in the foil.

Serves 2 to 3.

AMERICAN
few drops chilli sauce
2 teaspoons medium dry
    sherry
½ teaspoon superfine sugar
pepper
¼ teaspoon salt
1 teaspoon soy sauce
½ teaspoon sesame seeds
8 oz. chicken meat, cut into
    1 in. pieces
oil for frying

─Chinese Chicken with Cashew Nuts─

METRIC/IMPERIAL
150 g./6 oz. chicken meat,
    cut in 1.25 cm./½ in. pieces
oil for frying
100 g./4 oz. cashew nuts
100 g./4 oz. mushrooms,
    thinly sliced
50 g./2 oz. canned bamboo
    shoots, drained and sliced
100 g./4 oz. frozen peas
125 ml./¼ pint water
½ teaspoon sugar
2 teaspoons cornflour
    dissolved in 2 tablespoons
    water
salt and pepper
Marinade
1 teaspoon medium dry
    sherry
2 teaspoons soya sauce
1 teaspoon oil
½ teaspoon sugar
2 teaspoons cornflour

Blend together the ingredients for the marinade. Add the chicken to the marinade and leave for 10 minutes.

Heat 1 tablespoon oil in a heavy frying-pan. Add the cashew nuts and fry until golden brown. Drain and set aside.

Add the mushrooms to the pan and fry for 1 minute, stirring. Remove them from the pan and set aside.

Add the bamboo shoots to the pan with 2 teaspoons oil and fry for 1 minute, stirring. Remove them from the pan and add to the mushrooms.

Add the chicken to the pan with 1 tablespoon oil and fry for 2 minutes, stirring, or until the chicken is firm. Return the mushrooms and bamboo shoots to the pan with the peas and water. Simmer for 2 minutes. Add the sugar and cornflour (cornstarch) and simmer until thickened. Adjust the seasoning if necessary.

To freeze: turn into a rigid container, cool, cover, label and freeze.

To thaw and serve: put in a saucepan with 2 tablespoons water. Cover and heat gently, stirring occasionally. As soon as the mixture is hot, turn it on to a serving dish and top with the cashew nuts.

Serves 2 to 3.

AMERICAN
6 oz. chicken meat, cut in ½ in.
    pieces
oil for frying
⅔ cup cashew nuts
4 oz. mushrooms, thinly sliced
2 oz. canned bamboo shoots,
    drained and sliced
4 oz. frozen peas
⅝ cup water
½ teaspoon sugar
2 teaspoons cornstarch
    dissolved in 2 tablespoons
    water
salt and pepper
Marinade
1 teaspoon medium dry sherry
2 teaspoons soy sauce
1 teaspoon oil
½ teaspoon sugar
2 teaspoons cornstarch

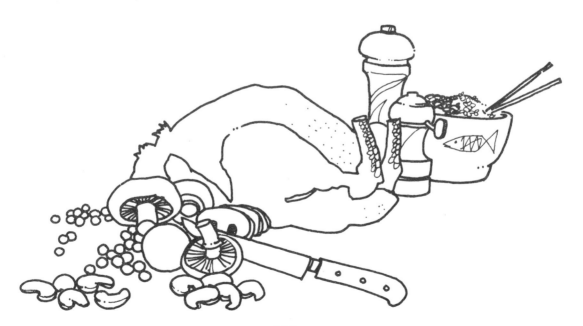

Sweet and Sour Pork

METRIC/IMPERIAL

Batter
100 g./4 oz. self-raising flour
½ teaspoon salt
125 ml./¼ pint water
Sweet and sour sauce
1 × 300 g./12 oz. can
    pineapple chunks
3 tablespoons malt vinegar
1 tablespoon tomato purée
2 teaspoons soft brown sugar
2 teaspoons cornflour
1 tablespoon water
1 spring onion, cut in 2.5 cm./
    1 in. pieces
1 green pepper, pith and seeds
    removed and sliced
oil for frying
Pork mixture
200 g./8 oz. lean pork, cut in
    1.25 cm./½ in. pieces
25 g./1 oz. flour
salt and pepper
oil for deep frying

Beat together the batter ingredients to make a smooth mixture. Set aside for 15 minutes.

Drain the pineapple chunks, reserving 4 tablespoons juice. Put the juice in a saucepan with the vinegar, tomato purée, sugar, cornflour (cornstarch) and water. Simmer for 2 minutes, stirring.

Meanwhile, fry the spring onion (scallion) and green pepper in 1 tablespoon oil for 30 seconds. Add to the saucepan with the pineapple and mix well. Turn the sauce into a rigid container and cool.

Toss the pork in the flour which has been seasoned with salt and pepper. Dip the pork pieces in the batter, then fry in hot deep oil for 5 minutes or until pale golden. Drain on absorbent paper, place in a second rigid container and cool.
To freeze: Cover, label and freeze.
To thaw and serve: drop the pork pieces into hot deep oil and fry for about 3 minutes or until golden brown. Drain on absorbent paper and keep hot. Put the frozen sauce in a saucepan with 1 tablespoon water. Cover and heat gently until just simmering, stirring occasionally. Put the pork on a hot serving dish and pour over the sauce.

Serves 3.

AMERICAN

Batter
1 cup self-rising flour
½ teaspoon salt
⅝ cup water
Sweet and sour sauce
1 × 12 oz. can pineapple
    chunks
3 tablespoons malt vinegar
1 tablespoon tomato purée
2 teaspoons soft brown
    sugar
2 teaspoons cornstarch
1 tablespoon water
1 scallion, cut in 1 in. pieces
1 green pepper, pith and
    seeds removed and sliced
oil for frying
Pork mixture
8 oz. lean pork, cut in ½ in.
    pieces
¼ cup flour
salt and pepper
oil for deep frying

Char Siu Barbecued Pork

METRIC/IMPERIAL
½ kg./1 lb. lean pork, e.g.
    fillet, shoulder or leg
1 tablespoon medium dry
    sherry
1 tablespoon soya sauce
1 tablespoon caster sugar
2 teaspoons salt
pepper

Cut the pork into strips, 10 cm. (4 in.) long and 2.5 cm. (1 in.) wide. Blend together all the remaining ingredients and put the pork strips into this marinade. Leave for 1 hour, turning occasionally.
To freeze: turn into a plastic container, cover, label and freeze.
To thaw and serve: leave to thaw overnight in the refrigerator or for 4 hours at room temperature. Place the pork strips on a grill (broiler) rack and pour over the marinade. Grill (broil) for 6 minutes. Turn the strips over and grill (broil) for a further 6 minutes.

Serves 4.

AMERICAN
1 lb. lean pork, e.g. tenderloin,
    shoulder or leg
1 tablespoon medium dry
    sherry
1 tablespoon soy sauce
1 tablespoon superfine sugar
2 teaspoons salt
pepper

Steak Chop Suey

METRIC/IMPERIAL
200 g./8 oz. steak
oil for frying
1 onion, sliced
1 large carrot, scraped and
    sliced
1 small piece preserved
    ginger, thinly sliced
200 g./8 oz. white cabbage,
    sliced
1 teaspoon sugar
1 teaspoon salt
125 ml./¼ pint water
2 teaspoons cornflour
1 teaspoon soya sauce
Marinade
1 tablespoon oil
2 teaspoons soya sauce
½ teaspoon sugar
salt and pepper
2 teaspoons cornflour

Mix together the ingredients for the marinade. Cut the steak into very thin slices and add to the marinade. Leave for 5 minutes.

Heat 1 tablespoon oil in a heavy frying-pan. Add the onion and carrot and fry for 1 minute, stirring. Remove the vegetables from the pan and set aside.

Add the ginger and cabbage to the pan and fry for 2 minutes, stirring. Return the onion and carrot to the pan with the sugar and salt. Mix well, then remove all from the pan and set aside.

Add the steak slices to the pan with 2 teaspoons oil and fry for 2 minutes, stirring. Mix together the water, cornflour (cornstarch) and soya sauce and add to the pan. Simmer until thickened, stirring. Stir the vegetable mixture into the steak and sauce.
To freeze: turn into a rigid container, cool, cover, label and freeze.
To thaw and serve: put in a saucepan with 2 tablespoons water. Cover and heat gently, stirring occasionally, until just simmering.

Serves 4.

AMERICAN
8 oz. steak
oil for frying
1 onion, sliced
1 large carrot, scraped and
    sliced
1 small piece preserved
    ginger, thinly sliced
8 oz. white cabbage, sliced
1 teaspoon sugar
1 teaspoon salt
⅝ cup water
2 teaspoons cornstarch
1 teaspoon soy sauce
Marinade
1 tablespoon oil
2 teaspoons soy sauce
½ teaspoon sugar
salt and pepper
2 teaspoons cornstarch

Shredded Pork Sauté

METRIC/IMPERIAL
200 g./8 oz. lean pork
oil for frying
1 × 100 g./4 oz. can bamboo
 shoots, drained and thinly
 sliced
100 g./4 oz. button
 mushrooms, thinly sliced
pinch of caster sugar
125 ml./¼ pint water
1 garlic clove, crushed
1 teaspoon salt
2 teaspoons cornflour
1 teaspoon medium dry
 sherry
1 teaspoon soya sauce
Marinade
2 teaspoons oil
1 teaspoon soya sauce
pepper
2 teaspoons cornflour

Mix the marinade ingredients together. Cut the pork into very thin slices and add to the marinade. Leave for 10 minutes.

Heat 1 tablespoon oil in a heavy frying-pan. Add the bamboo shoots and fry for 2 minutes, stirring. Remove from the pan and set aside.

Add the mushrooms to the pan and fry for 1 minute, stirring. Stir in the sugar and 1 tablespoon of the water. Cover and simmer for 1 minute. Remove the mushroom mixture from the pan and set aside.

Add the pork and garlic to the pan with 2 teaspoons oil and fry for 3 minutes, stirring. Drain off any excess fat, then return the bamboo shoots and mushroom mixture to the pan with the salt. Cook for 1 minute.

Mix together the remaining ingredients, including the rest of the water, and add to the pork mixture. Stir well and simmer until thickened.

To freeze: turn into a rigid container, cool, cover, label and freeze.
To thaw and serve: put in a saucepan with 2 tablespoons water and heat gently, stirring occasionally.

Serves 2.

AMERICAN
8 oz. lean pork
oil for frying
1 × 4 oz. can bamboo shoots,
 drained and thinly sliced
4 oz. button mushrooms,
 thinly sliced
pinch of superfine sugar
⅝ cup water
1 garlic clove, crushed
1 teaspoon salt
2 teaspoons cornstarch
1 teaspoon medium dry
 sherry
1 teaspoon soy sauce
Marinade
2 teaspoons oil
1 teaspoon soy sauce
pepper
2 teaspoons cornstarch

Hot Sauce Noodles

METRIC/IMPERIAL
200 g./8 oz. egg noodles
100 g./4 oz. lean pork
oil for frying
50 g./2 oz. shelled prawns,
 halved
50 g./2 oz. mushrooms,
 thinly sliced
1 canned pimento, thinly
 sliced
1 teaspoon salt
chilli sauce to taste (add drop
 by drop)
2 teaspoons vinegar
1 teaspoon cornflour
 dissolved in 2 tablespoons
 water
Marinade
1 garlic clove, crushed
pepper
1 teaspoon oil
2 teaspoons soya sauce
1 teaspoon cornflour

Cook the noodles in plenty of boiling salted water for 12 to 15 minutes or until they are just tender. Drain and set aside.

Mix together the ingredients for the marinade. Finely shred the pork and add to the marinade. Leave for 5 minutes, then drain the pork.

Heat 1 tablespoon oil in a heavy frying-pan. Add the pork and fry for 3 minutes, stirring. Add the prawns (shrimp) and fry for 1 minute, stirring. Add the mushrooms and fry for 1 minute, stirring. Add the pimento and fry for 1 minute, stirring. Stir in the remaining ingredients and simmer until thickened. Mix in the noodles.

To freeze: turn into a rigid container, cool, cover, label and freeze.
To thaw and serve: put in a saucepan with 4 tablespoons water. Cover and heat gently until just simmering, stirring occasionally with a fork.

Serves 4 to 6.

AMERICAN
8 oz. egg noodles
4 oz. lean pork
oil for frying
2 oz. shelled baby shrimp,
 halved
2 oz. mushrooms, thinly
 sliced
1 canned pimento, thinly
 sliced
1 teaspoon salt
chilli sauce to taste (add drop
 by drop)
2 teaspoons vinegar
1 teaspoon cornstarch
 dissolved in 2 tablespoons
 water
Marinade
1 garlic clove, crushed
pepper
1 teaspoon oil
2 teaspoons soy sauce
1 teaspoon cornstarch

Desserts

—Apple Jalousie—

If you have an abundance of apples or have apple purée in the freezer this is a good way of using it up.

Place the apples in a pan with the water, butter and sugar. Cover the pan and cook slowly until the apples are tender. Remove the lid and continue to cook the apples, mashing them with a wooden spoon as they simmer. Cook until the apple is a thick purée. Put on one side to cool.

Roll out the pastry on a floured board to a rectangle 20 by 30 cm. (8 by 12 in.) then cut it into two strips each 10 by 30 cm. (4 by 12 in.) long. Lay one strip on a baking dish. Brush the edges with water and spoon the cold apple purée down the centre.

Fold the second strip of pastry in half lengthways and cut with a sharp knife across the fold at 5 cm. (2 in.) intervals, leaving 2.5 cm. (1 in.) of pastry uncut at the sides. Unfold and place on top of the filling, press on firmly and knock up the edges with the back of a knife.

To freeze: open freeze the jalousie until it is firm, then wrap in foil and label.

To thaw and serve: Lightly beat the egg white and brush over the top. Bake in the centre of the oven 200°C, 400°F, Gas Mark 6 for 35 to 40 minutes or until the pastry is well risen and golden brown. Remove from the oven and brush again with egg white. Serve hot as a pudding or cold for tea.

Serves 6 to 8 portions.

METRIC/IMPERIAL
½ kg./1 lb. cooking apples, peeled, cored and sliced
2 tablespoons water
25 g./1 oz. butter
50 g./2 oz. granulated sugar
1 × 325 g./13 oz. packet commercial frozen puff pastry, thawed
1 egg white

AMERICAN
1 lb. cooking apples, peeled, cored and sliced
2 tablespoons water
2 tablespoons butter
¼ cup sugar
13 oz. packet commercial frozen puff pastry, thawed
1 egg white

—Cinnamon Apple Pancakes (Crêpes)—

To make the batter, sift the flour and salt into a bowl. Blend in the egg, salad oil and enough milk to make a fairly thin batter. Heat a very little oil in a 17.5 cm. (7 in.) frying-pan or crêpe pan. Drop 2 tablespoonsful of the batter into the centre of the pan and tilt and rotate to spread out the batter. Cook for 1 minute, then turn the pancake (crêpe) over and cook the other side for 1 minute. Turn the pancake (crêpe) out of the pan and make nine or ten more pancakes (crêpes) in the same way.

For the filling, put the apples, cinnamon, sugar and butter in a saucepan and simmer gently for about 20 minutes or until the apple is tender, stirring occasionally. Cool.

Divide the filling between the pancakes (crêpes) and roll them up.

To freeze: wrap in a double thickness of foil, seal, label and freeze.

To thaw and serve: unwrap and leave to thaw at room temperature for 4 hours. Fry the pancake (crêpe) rolls in the butter over moderate heat until they are golden brown all over. Pile on a warm serving dish and sprinkle with the sugar and cinnamon mixture. Serve with cream or ice cream. If it is more convenient, place the frozen pancake (crêpe) rolls on a baking sheet, brush with the butter which has been melted, and reheat in a moderately hot oven, 200°C, 400°F, Gas Mark 6, for 30 minutes.

Serves 5 to 6.

METRIC/IMPERIAL
Batter
100 g./4 oz. flour
¼ teaspoon salt
1 egg
1 tablespoon salad oil
250 ml./½ pint milk
oil for frying
Filling
4 very large Bramley apples, peeled, cored and sliced
¼ teaspoon ground cinnamon
150 g./6 oz. Demerara sugar
100 g./4 oz. butter
about 63 g./2½ oz. butter for frying
a little Demerara sugar mixed with cinnamon for sprinkling

AMERICAN
Batter
1 cup flour
¼ teaspoon salt
1 egg
1 tablespoon salad oil
1¼ cups milk
oil for frying
Filling
4 very large cooking apples, peeled, cored and sliced
¼ teaspoon ground cinnamon
1 cup light brown sugar
½ cup butter
about 5 tablespoons butter for frying
a little light brown sugar mixed with cinnamon for sprinkling

— Apple Charlotte —

METRIC/IMPERIAL
½ kg./1 lb. cooking apples,
    peeled, cored and sliced
75 g./3 oz. Demerara sugar
grated rind and juice of ½
    orange
small sliced loaf of brown
    bread
100 g./4 oz. unsalted butter,
    melted

AMERICAN
1 lb. cooking apples, peeled,
    cored and sliced
½ cup light brown sugar
grated rind and juice of ½
    orange
small sliced loaf of brown
    bread
½ cup unsalted butter, melted

Put the apples, 50 g. (2 oz.) or ⅓ cup of the sugar and the orange rind and juice in a saucepan and simmer gently for about 20 minutes or until the apples are tender, pounding occasionally with a wooden spoon. Cool.

Trim the crusts from most of the bread and cut into long strips. Cover the base and sides of a greased 17.5 cm. (7 in.) diameter sandwich (layer) cake tin with some of the strips. Sprinkle the bread with half of the remaining sugar and pour over half the melted butter.

Spread over the cold apple mixture and cover with the remaining bread strips, overlapping them. Pour over the remaining melted butter and sprinkle with the rest of the sugar.

To freeze: open freeze, then remove from the tin and put in a polythene (plastic) bag, seal, label and return to the freezer.

To thaw and serve: remove from the bag and replace in the tin. Bake in a moderately hot oven, 200°C, 400°F, Gas Mark 6, for about 40 minutes or until golden brown.

Serves 4 to 6.

— Mincemeat and Apple Pie —

METRIC/IMPERIAL
75 g./3 oz. cheap margarine,
    very cold
75 g./3 oz. lard, very cold
200 g./8 oz. flour
½ teaspoon salt
about 125 ml./¼ pint water
Filling
200 g./8 oz. mincemeat
200 g./8 oz. apples, peeled,
    cored, sliced and stewed
little milk
caster sugar

AMERICAN
½ cup cheap margarine, very
    cold
½ cup lard, very cold
2 cups flour
½ teaspoon salt
about ⅝ cup water
Filling
8 oz. mincemeat
8 oz. apples, peeled, cored,
    sliced and stewed
little milk
sugar

Grate the fats coarsely into a bowl. Sift in the flour and salt and stir in just enough water to make a firm dough. Roll out the dough to a strip about 1.25 cm. (½ in.) thick and 15 cm. (6 in.) wide. Fold the dough in three and roll it out again to a strip the same size. Fold in three once again, then wrap in greaseproof (waxed) paper and chill in the refrigerator for 30 minutes.

Roll out just under half the dough to a circle about ¾ cm. (¼ in.) thick and line a 20 cm. (8 in.) diameter foil pie plate. Spoon in the mincemeat, then the apple. Brush the edges of the dough with milk.

Roll out the remaining dough to ¾ cm. (¼ in.) thickness and use to cover the pie. Trim off any surplus dough and seal and flute the edges.

To freeze: open freeze, then cover with a lid of foil, label and return to the freezer.

To thaw and serve: remove the foil lid and bake in a very hot oven, 220°C, 425°F, Gas Mark 7, for 45 minutes or until golden brown. Serve sprinkled with sugar.

Serves 6.

─Christmas Pudding─

METRIC/IMPERIAL

150 g./6 oz. self-raising flour
1 teaspoon ground mixed
  spice
½ teaspoon grated nutmeg
1 teaspoon salt
½ kg./1 lb. fresh white
  breadcrumbs
½ kg./1 lb. shredded suet
100 g./4 oz. candied peel,
  finely chopped
100 g./4 oz. blanched
  almonds, shredded
grated rind of 2 oranges
1 kg./2 lb. seedless raisins,
  finely chopped, washed
  and dried
200 g./8 oz. currants, washed
  and dried
½ kg./1 lb. sultanas, washed
  and dried
300 g./12 oz. soft brown
  sugar
4 tablespoons black treacle
6 eggs, beaten
½ l./1 pint stout

Sift together the flour, mixed spice, nutmeg and salt. Mix with the
breadcrumbs, suet, candied peel, almonds, orange rind, raisins,
currants, sultanas (golden raisins), sugar and treacle (corn syrup or
molasses). Add the eggs and stout and mix well so that all the
ingredients are thoroughly blended.

Turn the mixture into well-greased pudding basins — either four
1 l. (2 pint) basins or several of different sizes — filling each basin
three-quarters full. Press the mixture down well to prevent air
bubbles forming. Cover each basin with a double thickness of
greased greaseproof (waxed) paper and then a lid of foil.

Steam or simmer the puddings for 6 to 8 hours, depending on
size. then lift them out of the pans and leave to cool.

To freeze: remove from the basins and wrap in a double thickness of
foil, label and freeze.

To thaw and serve: leave to thaw overnight in the refrigerator.
Return to the basins, which have been well greased, cover with a lid
of paper and foil as before and steam or simmer for 3 hours.

Makes 4 puddings.

The recipe for Brandy Butter is in the Cook's Aids section on
page 32.

AMERICAN

1½ cups self-rising flour
1 teaspoon ground mixed
  spice
½ teaspoon grated nutmeg
1 teaspoon salt
1 lb. (8 cups) fresh white
  breadcrumbs
1 lb. (2 cups) shredded suet
⅔ cup finely chopped candied
  peel
⅔ cup shredded blanched
  almonds
grated rind of 2 oranges
2 lb. seedless raisins, finely
  chopped, washed and
  dried
1⅓ cups currants, washed and
  dried
1 lb. golden raisins, washed
  and dried
2 cups dark brown sugar
4 tablespoons dark corn syrup
  or molasses
6 eggs, beaten
2½ cups stout

— Small Mince Pies —

METRIC/IMPERIAL
½ kg./1 lb. self-raising flour
100 g./4 oz. butter
100 g./4 oz. hard margarine
50 g./2 oz. lard
1 egg, separated
milk
¾ kg./1½ lb. mincemeat
caster sugar

Sift the flour into a bowl. Add the butter, margarine and lard and cut into small pieces, then rub the fats into the flour until the mixture resembles breadcrumbs. Add the egg yolk with enough milk to make a firm dough. Knead until well blended, then chill the dough in the refrigerator for 20 minutes.

Roll out half the dough thinly. Cut out about 35 circles, 7 cm. (2¾ in.) in diameter. Use these to line 35 tart tins. Fill with the mincemeat.

Roll out the remaining dough and cut out 35 circles, 5.75 cm. (2¼ in.) in diameter for the lids. Wet the edges of the dough circles in the tin and press the lids on gently to seal.

Lightly beat the egg white and brush over the tops of the pies. Dust lightly with sugar. Bake in a moderately hot oven, 200°C, 400°F, Gas Mark 6, for 20 minutes or until the pastry is crisp and golden brown. Leave to cool in the tins.
To freeze: freeze in the tins, then pack in a polythene (plastic) bag, seal, label and return to the freezer. Use within 3 months.
To thaw and serve: replace in the tins and reheat in a moderately hot oven, 200°C, 400°F, Gas Mark 6, for 25 minutes.

Makes 35 pies.

AMERICAN
1 lb. (4 cups) self-rising flour
½ cup butter
½ cup hard margarine
¼ cup lard
1 egg, separated
milk
1½ lb. mincemeat
sugar

— Baked Alaska —

METRIC/IMPERIAL
1 jam-filled Swiss roll
2 to 3 tablespoons sherry
2 egg whites
100 g./4 oz. caster sugar
1 × ½ kg./1 lb. block commercial raspberry ripple ice cream

Cut the Swiss (jelly) roll into nine slices and arrange them in an oblong on a 20 cm. (8 in.) foil pie plate. Sprinkle with the sherry.

Whisk the egg whites until they are stiff, then add half the sugar and continue whisking until the egg whites are very stiff. Carefully fold in the remaining sugar, cutting it in gently so as to lose as little air as possible.

Place the brick of ice cream in the centre of the pie plate and cover quickly with the egg white mixture. Bake in a hot oven, 220°C, 425°F, Gas Mark 7, for 5 minutes to set the meringue topping.
To freeze: freeze unwrapped until solid, then cover with a piece of nonstick silicone paper, pack in a polythene (plastic) bag, seal, label and return to the freezer.
To thaw and serve: unwrap and reheat in a hot oven, 220°C, 425°F, Gas Mark 7, for 5 minutes.

Serves 4 to 6.

AMERICAN
1 jam-filled jelly roll
2 to 3 tablespoons sherry
2 egg whites
½ cup superfine sugar
1 × 1 lb. block commercial raspberry ripple ice cream

~ Vanilla Ice Cream ~

METRIC/IMPERIAL
4 eggs, separated
100 g./4 oz. caster sugar
250 ml./½ pint double cream
½ teaspoon vanilla essence

AMERICAN
4 eggs, separated
½ cup superfine sugar
1¼ cups heavy cream
½ teaspoon vanilla essence

Whisk the egg yolks until well blended. Whisk the egg whites until they are stiff, then whisk in the sugar a teaspoonful at a time. Whisk the cream until it holds a soft peak, then fold it into the egg white mixture with the egg yolks and vanilla.
To freeze: turn into a rigid container, cover, label and freeze.
To thaw and serve: leave to thaw at room temperature for 5 minutes. Serve with sponge fingers or thin biscuits (cookies).

Serves 6 to 8.

Variations
Blackcurrant: add undiluted blackcurrant drink concentrate to taste, about 6 tablespoons, before freezing.
Strawberry or Raspberry: sieve 200 g./8 oz. fresh or thawed frozen fruit and fold into the mixture with a few drops of red food colouring before freezing.
Coffee: add 2 tablespoons strong coffee and 1 tablespoon rum or brandy before freezing.
Chocolate: add 6 tablespoons drinking chocolate to the egg yolks and mix well.
Gooseberry: stew 200 g./8 oz. gooseberries with 50 g./2 oz. or ¼ cup sugar and a little water, then purée in a sieve or liquidizer. Cool and add with a little green food colouring before freezing.
Pineapple: cut the flesh from a small pineapple, add the juice of ½ lemon and 50 g./2 oz. icing sugar or ⅓ cup confectioners' sugar. Purée in a liquidizer, freeze until just set, then fold into the ice cream before it is frozen. Alternatively, use frozen pineapple chunks or pieces.

~ Rice Krispie Flan with Caramel Sauce ~

METRIC/IMPERIAL
50 g./2 oz. butter
100 ml./4 fl. oz. golden syrup
50 g./2 oz. soft brown sugar
100 g./4 oz. marshmallows
75 g./3 oz. Rice Krispies
100 g./4 oz. caramel toffees
4 tablespoons milk
1 × ½ kg./1 lb. block vanilla
   ice cream

AMERICAN
¼ cup butter
½ cup light corn syrup
⅓ cup dark brown sugar
4 oz. marshmallows
2 cups Rice Krispies
4 oz. caramel toffees
4 tablespoons milk
1 × 1 lb. block vanilla ice
   cream

Put the butter, syrup and sugar in a large saucepan and heat gently until the butter has melted. Bring to the boil and boil for 1 minute. Remove from the heat. Add the marshmallows and stir until they have melted. Cool slightly.

Stir in the Rice Krispies, making sure they are mixed in thoroughly. Press the mixture into a greased 20 cm. (8 in.) diameter flan ring placed on a greased baking sheet. Leave in a cool place to set.

Place the toffees and milk in a heatproof bowl over a pan of hot water. Melt the toffees, stirring occasionally.

To serve, place the Rice Krispie base on a serving dish, arrange spoonsful of ice cream on top and pour over the toffee sauce.

Serves 6.

─Fruity Ice Cream─

METRIC/IMPERIAL
50 g./2 oz. seedless raisins
50 g./2 oz. walnuts, chopped
50 g./2 oz. glacé cherries, chopped
3 tablespoons orange juice or orange-flavoured liqueur to taste
1 × ½ kg./1 lb. block vanilla ice cream

Any glacé fruits can be used in this ice cream; chopped stem ginger is also good in it.

Put the raisins in a small bowl, cover with hot water and leave to stand for 10 minutes. Drain thoroughly and chop. Add the walnuts, cherries and orange juice or liqueur.
Put the ice cream in another bowl and mix until it has softened slightly. Do not let it melt completely. Mix in the fruit mixture.
To freeze: turn into an ice cube tray and freeze overnight.
To thaw and serve: leave to stand at room temperature for 5 minutes, then serve with wafers.

Serves 4.

AMERICAN
⅓ cup seedless raisins
⅓ cup chopped walnuts
⅓ cup chopped glacé cherries
3 tablespoons orange juice or orange-flavoured liqueur to taste
1 × 1 lb. block vanilla ice cream

─Caramel Raisin Sauce─

METRIC/IMPERIAL
200 g./8 oz. soft brown sugar
125 ml./¼ pint water
38 g./1½ oz. butter
1 strip of lemon rind
25 g./1 oz. cornflour mixed with 2 tablespoons water
1 teaspoon lemon juice
50 g./2 oz. seedless raisins

This and the following two sauces are good served with ice cream — either homemade or commercial. Try this one with coffee or vanilla ice cream.

Put the sugar and water in a heavy saucepan and stir over low heat until the sugar has dissolved. Add the butter and lemon rind and bring to the boil. Boil for 5 minutes. Add a little of the sugar syrup to the cornflour (cornstarch) mixture, mix well, and stir into the syrup in the saucepan. Bring to the boil again and simmer for 2 minutes, stirring constantly.
Remove the lemon rind. Add the lemon juice and raisins and stir well. Turn into a rigid container and cool.
To freeze: cover, label and freeze.
To thaw and serve: turn into a small heatproof bowl and place over a saucepan of hot water. Reheat slowly, stirring occasionally, until hot. Pour over ice cream.

Serves 6.

AMERICAN
1⅓ cups dark brown sugar
⅝ cup water
3 tablespoons butter
1 strip of lemon rind
¼ cup cornstarch mixed with 2 tablespoons water
1 teaspoon lemon juice
⅓ cup seedless raisins

─Butterscotch Sauce─

METRIC/IMPERIAL
1 tablespoon golden syrup
1 tablespoon lemon juice
1 tablespoon brown sugar
12½ g./½ oz. butter
1½ teaspoons custard powder
125 ml./¼ pint water
1 pineapple ring, chopped

Put the syrup, lemon juice, sugar and butter in a saucepan and heat gently until the butter has melted, stirring occasionally. Blend the custard powder with the water and add to the syrup mixture. Bring to the boil, stirring, and simmer until thickened. Add the pineapple. Pour over ice cream.

Serves 4.

AMERICAN
1 tablespoon light corn syrup
1 tablespoon lemon juice
1 tablespoon brown sugar
1 tablespoon butter
1½ teaspoons custard powder
⅝ cup water
1 pineapple ring, chopped

─Foamy Marshmallow Sauce─

METRIC/IMPERIAL
100 g./4 oz. marshmallows
juice of ½ lemon

Put the marshmallows and lemon juice in a small heatproof bowl and place over a pan of hot water. Stir until melted and frothy. Pour over chocolate ice cream.

Serves 4.

AMERICAN
4 oz. marshmallows
juice of ½ lemon

Fresh Pineapple Sorbet

METRIC/IMPERIAL
1 medium-sized pineapple
juice of 1½ lemons
about 375 ml./¾ pint water
150 g./6 oz. caster sugar

AMERICAN
1 medium-sized pineapple
juice of 1½ lemons
about 1⅞ cups water
¾ cup superfine sugar

Cut the pineapple in half lengthways and cut the hard core from the centre of each half. Scoop out all the flesh, keeping the shells intact. Set the shells aside. Chop the flesh finely, saving the juice.

Mix the chopped pineapple, pineapple juice and lemon juice together.

Put the water and sugar in a pan over low heat. Allow the sugar to dissolve slowly, then cool the syrup. Stir the syrup into the pineapple mixture.

Alternatively, put the pineapple flesh, juice and lemon juice in a liquidizer and blend to a purée. Then stir in the cooled sugar syrup.
To freeze: pour into a shallow rigid container, freeze until set but not hard, then turn into a bowl and whisk until the sorbet is broken up and light. Replace in the container, cover, label and return to the freezer.
To thaw and serve: scoop out the sorbet with a metal spoon that has been dipped in boiling water. Serve in the pineapple shells.

Serves 4.

Fresh Lemon Sorbet

METRIC/IMPERIAL
6 lemons
250 ml./½ pint water
150 g./6 oz. sugar
1 egg white

AMERICAN
6 lemons
1¼ cups water
¾ cup sugar
1 egg white

Peel the rind thinly from the bottom of each lemon using a potato peeler. Put these pieces of rind in a saucepan with the water and sugar. Heat gently until the sugar has dissolved, then simmer for 10 minutes. Leave to cool.

Cut the tops off the lemons and scoop out all the flesh, using a grapefruit knife or pointed spoon. Put the flesh into a bowl with any juice. Reserve the shells and tops.

Remove any pips from the flesh, then purée it in a liquidizer and strain. Strain the sugar syrup on to the lemon purée and mix well. Turn into a rigid container, cover and freeze until half frozen.

Trim a little from the bottom of each lemon shell so that they will stand upright. Put the lemon shells and lids into the freezer to chill.

Whisk the egg white until stiff. Turn the half-frozen lemon mixture into a bowl and whisk until smooth. Fold in the egg white. Pile the sorbet in the lemon shells and put on the lids.
To freeze: wrap individually in foil, label and freeze.
To thaw and serve: unwrap and leave to thaw in the refrigerator for 30 minutes.
Note: if you don't have the time to scoop out the lemon flesh, just cut the lemons in half and squeeze out the juice with a lemon squeezer. You can then fill each half lemon with sorbet and serve two halves for each person.

Serves 6.

~ Grapefruit Water Ice ~

METRIC/IMPERIAL
100 g./4 oz. caster sugar
250 ml./½ pint water
1 × 150 g./6 oz. can frozen
  concentrated grapefruit
  juice
3 egg whites

Dissolve the sugar in the water over low heat, then allow to cool. Blend the undiluted grapefruit juice with the sugar syrup and pour it into a shallow rigid container. Cover and freeze for 30 minutes or until the mixture is just beginning to set, then turn it into a bowl and mash until smooth.

Whisk the egg whites until they are stiff, then fold into the grapefruit mixture.
To freeze: replace in the container, cover, label and return to the freezer.
To thaw and serve: leave to thaw in the refrigerator for 30 minutes, then spoon into individual glasses.
Note: concentrated orange juice may be used instead.

Serves 6.

AMERICAN
½ cup superfine sugar
1¼ cups water
1 × 6 oz. can frozen
  concentrated grapefruit
  juice
3 egg whites

~ Danish Layer Dessert Cake ~

METRIC/IMPERIAL
163 g./6½ oz. butter
163 g./6½ oz. caster sugar
212½ g./8½ oz. flour
2 teaspoons ground
  cinnamon
250 ml./½ pint double cream
3 tablespoons top of the milk
raspberry jam
icing sugar
8 walnut halves

Cream the butter until it is soft, then add the sugar and continue to beat until the mixture is pale and fluffy. Sift the flour and cinnamon together and add to the butter mixture a tablespoonful at a time. The last few spoonsful may have to be worked in by hand. Divide the mixture into eight equal pieces.

Cut out eight squares of foil, about 22.5 cm. (9 in.) square. Put one piece of dough on a foil square and press out very thinly with your fingers to form a 17.5 cm. (7 in.) circle. Repeat the process with the remaining dough pieces.
To freeze: stack the foil squares on top of each other, wrap securely in foil, label and freeze.
To thaw and serve: peel the foil from the dough layers and place them on well-greased baking sheets. Bake in a moderately hot oven, 200°C, 400°F, Gas Mark 6, for about 8 minutes. Leave to cool and harden for a few minutes before transferring to a wire rack.

Whip the cream and milk (half and half) together until they will form a soft peak. Sandwich the layers together with the whipped cream and jam, leaving a little cream over for decoration. Sprinkle the top with icing (confectioners') sugar, mark into eight portions and decorate each portion with a whirl of cream and a walnut half.

Serves 8.

AMERICAN
¾ cup plus 1 tablespoon
  butter
¾ cup plus 1 tablespoon
  superfine sugar
2 cups plus 2 tablespoons
  flour
2 teaspoons ground
  cinnamon
1¼ cups heavy cream
3 tablespoons half and half
raspberry jam
confectioners' sugar
8 walnut halves

—Apple and Lemon Dessert—

METRIC/IMPERIAL
250 ml./½ pint apple purée
2 tablespoons caster sugar
1 teaspoon grated lemon rind
2 eggs, separated
125 ml./¼ pint double cream

Put the apple purée, sugar and lemon rind in the top of a double boiler and heat until the sugar dissolves. Add the egg yolks and cook, stirring constantly, until the apple mixture has thickened. Remove from the heat and cool.

Whisk the egg whites until stiff and whisk the cream until thick. Fold both into the apple mixture.

To freeze: turn into a serving dish, cover with a lid of foil, then freeze until solid. Dip the dish into hand-hot water to unmould the dessert, put it into a polythene (plastic) bag, seal, label and return to the freezer.

To thaw and serve: return to the dish and leave to thaw for 6 hours in the refrigerator.

Serves 4.

AMERICAN
1¼ cups apple purée
2 tablespoons superfine sugar
1 teaspoon grated lemon rind
2 eggs, separated
⅝ cup heavy cream

—Chocolate Cream Roll—

METRIC/IMPERIAL
Sponge cake roll
50 g./2 oz. self-raising flour
25 g./1 oz. cocoa powder
¼ teaspoon salt
3 eggs
75 g./3 oz. caster sugar
1 tablespoon hot water
Chocolate buttercream filling
50 g./2 oz. caster sugar
125 ml./¼ pint milk
50 g./2 oz. plain chocolate
2 egg yolks
150 g./6 oz. unsalted butter
chocolate curls to decorate

To make the cake, sift the flour, cocoa and salt into a bowl. Put the eggs and sugar in a heatproof bowl and place over a pan of gently simmering water. Whisk until the mixture is thick and mousse-like (with a rotary beater this will take about 5 minutes). Remove from the heat and whisk for 2 minutes longer. Fold in the sifted ingredients and the water, stirring just enough to blend the ingredients together evenly.

Pour into a Swiss (jelly) roll tin, 32.5 by 22.5 cm. (13 by 9 in.). which has been lined with greased greaseproof (waxed) paper. Bake in a moderately hot oven, 200°C, 400°F, Gas Mark 6, for 10 minutes or until the cake will spring back when lightly pressed with a fingertip.

Turn the cake out on to a sheet of greaseproof (waxed) paper which has been sprinkled with caster (superfine) sugar. Roll up the cake immediately, starting from the narrow end, and with the greaseproof (waxed) paper inside. Set aside to cool completely.

To make the chocolate filling, put the sugar, milk and chocolate into a saucepan and bring almost to boiling point, then simmer until the chocolate has melted. Blend the egg yolks in a bowl, then gradually stir in the chocolate mixture. Return to the saucepan and cook gently, stirring constantly, until this custard has thickened. Do not allow to boil or it will curdle. Once the custard is thick, remove from the heat and set aside to cool to room temperature.

Soften the butter and blend in the cooled chocolate custard. If the custard is too warm it will melt the butter, so be sure it has cooled sufficiently. Leave the filling in a cold place to thicken.

Carefully unroll the Swiss (jelly) roll and remove the paper. Spread the inside with half of the filling and roll up the cake again. Place the roll on a small tray. Spread the remaining buttercream all over the sides and top and decorate with chocolate curls. (These are made by scraping a slightly warmed block of chocolate with a potato peeler.)

To freeze: open freeze, then place in a polythene (plastic) bag, seal, label and return to the freezer.

To thaw and serve: remove from the bag, place on a serving dish and leave to thaw at room temperature for 4 hours.

AMERICAN
Sponge cake roll
½ cup self-rising flour
¼ cup cocoa powder
¼ teaspoon salt
3 eggs
⅜ cup superfine sugar
1 tablespoon hot water
Chocolate buttercream filling
¼ cup superfine sugar
⅝ cup milk
2 oz. (2 squares) semi-sweet chocolate
2 egg yolks
¾ cup unsalted butter
chocolate curls to decorate

Chilled Chocolate Layered Dessert

METRIC/IMPERIAL
4 rounded tablespoons
 drinking chocolate powder
2½ tablespoons instant coffee
 powder
100 g./4 oz. fresh white
 breadcrumbs
100 g./4 oz. Demerara sugar
125 ml./¼ pint double cream
125 ml./¼ pint single cream
chocolate flake bar

Mix together the drinking chocolate, coffee powder, breadcrumbs and sugar. Put the double (heavy) and single (light) cream in another bowl and whisk together until thick. Starting with the chocolate mixture, layer with the cream in a serving dish. (If glass, be sure to use strong moulded glass or ovenproof glass.) Finish with a layer of cream.
To freeze: cover with a lid of foil, label and freeze.
To thaw and serve: leave to thaw overnight in the refrigerator. Smooth over the top layer of cream if it has cracked while thawing. Crush the chocolate flake bar and sprinkle on top.

Serves 6 to 8.

AMERICAN
4 rounded tablespoons
 drinking chocolate powder
2½ tablespoons instant coffee
 powder
2 cups fresh white
 breadcrumbs
⅔ cup light brown sugar
⅝ cup heavy cream
⅝ cup light cream
chocolate flake candy bar

Ginger Biscuit Cookie Roll

METRIC/IMPERIAL
250 ml./½ pint double cream
200 g./8 oz. ginger biscuits
crystallized or stem ginger for
 decoration

Whisk half the cream until it is thick and fairly stiff. Use the cream to sandwich together the biscuits (cookies) to make a long roll.
To freeze: wrap in foil, seal, label and freeze.
To thaw and serve: unwrap, place on a serving dish and leave to thaw at room temperature for 2 hours. Whisk the remaining cream until thick and use to cover the roll completely. Decorate with small pieces of ginger.

Serves 4.

AMERICAN
1¼ cups heavy cream
8 oz. ginger snaps
crystallized or stem ginger for
 decoration

Mocha Pots

METRIC/IMPERIAL
6 eggs, separated
25 g./ 1oz. butter
150 g./6 oz. plain chocolate
1½ tablespoons rum
3 tablespoons coffee essence
3 tablespoons double cream

Put the egg yolks, butter and chocolate in a heatproof bowl placed over a pan of hot water. Cook gently, stirring occasionally, until the chocolate has melted. Remove from the heat and beat in the rum and coffee essence.

Whisk the egg whites until stiff and fold into the coffee mixture. Pour into eight small ramekin dishes or pots and leave in a cool place until set.
To freeze: open freeze, then cover the tops with foil, over-wrap in a polythene (plastic) bag, seal, label and return to the freezer.
To thaw and serve: unwrap and leave to thaw at room temperature for 1 hour. Whisk the cream until thick and use to decorate each pot. Serve with crisp sweet biscuits (cookies).

Serves 8.

AMERICAN
6 eggs, separated
2 tablespoons butter
6 oz. (6 squares) semi-sweet
 chocolate
1½ tablespoons rum
3 tablespoons coffee essence
3 tablespoons heavy cream

(Right) Apple Jalousie

~Summer Pudding~

METRIC/IMPERIAL

1¼ large sliced loaves of white bread (about 25 slices), crusts removed
1½ kg./3 lb. rhubarb, cut into pieces
1 kg./2 lb. blackcurrants
½ kg./1 lb. blackberries
1 kg./2 lb. sugar
250 ml./½ pint water
1 kg./1¾ lb. strawberries
½ kg./1 lb. raspberries

AMERICAN

1¼ large sliced loaves of white bread (about 25 slices), crusts removed
3 lb. rhubarb, cut into pieces
2 lb. blackcurrants
1 lb. blackberries
2 lb. sugar
1¼ cups water
1¾ lb. strawberries
1 lb. raspberries

If using fruits which you have previously frozen, allow to thaw slowly before you start. Slimmers can use low calorie bread.

Put five slices of bread aside for the tops of the puddings. Line the base and sides of five 1 l. (2 pint) round, fairly shallow dishes (such as foil dishes, soufflé dishes or cheap heavy glass dishes). If tall pudding basins are used, add a little extra bread to ensure they don't collapse when turned out.

Put the rhubarb, blackcurrants and blackberries in a saucepan with the sugar and water and bring to the boil. Simmer until barely tender, stirring. This will take only a few minutes. Add the strawberries and raspberries and cook for a further minute.

Divide the fruit mixture between the dishes. Put a slice of bread on top of each, bending over the top of the bread at the sides towards the centre. Put a saucer on top and press down a little until the juice rises to the top. Leave to soak until cold.
To freeze: cover, label and freeze.
To thaw and serve: leave to thaw at room temperature for 8 hours or overnight in the refrigerator. Turn out and serve with lots of cream.

Makes 5 puddings, each for 4 to 6 people.

~Fresh Fruit Salad~

METRIC/IMPERIAL

100 g./4 oz. caster sugar
8 tablespoons water
juice of ½ lemon
200 g./8 oz. large green grapes, peeled and pips removed
200 g./8 oz. eating apples, peeled, cored and sliced
2 oranges, peeled and segmented
1 small melon, peeled, seeded and cut into cubes
1 small pineapple, peeled, cored and cut into cubes
2 tablespoons orange-flavoured liqueur

AMERICAN

½ cup superfine sugar
8 tablespoons water
juice of ½ lemon
8 oz. large green grapes, peeled and pips removed
8 oz. eating apples, peeled, cored and sliced
2 oranges, peeled and segmented
1 small melon, peeled, seeded and cut into cubes
1 small pineapple, peeled, cored and cut into cubes
2 tablespoons orange-flavoured liqueur

Dissolve the sugar in the water over low heat. Cool, then stir in the lemon juice. Pour into a rigid container. Add all the fruit and mix well.
To freeze: cover and freeze. When frozen, transfer to a polythene (plastic) bag, seal, label and return to the freezer.
To thaw and serve: leave to thaw overnight in the refrigerator. Stir in the liqueur. If you like, add some individually frozen strawberries to the thawed fruit salad 30 minutes before serving.

Serves 8.

~Red Fruit Salad~

Use the same fruits as for Summer Pudding, with the same sugar syrup.
To freeze: divide between four rigid containers, cover, label and freeze.
To thaw and serve: leave to thaw at room temperature for 8 hours or overnight in the refrigerator. Stir in a little cherry brandy or brandy and serve with plenty of cream.

Makes 4 salads, each for 4 to 6 people.

~Tipsy Oranges~

METRIC/IMPERIAL
8 thin-skinned oranges
100 g./4 oz. caster sugar
4 tablespoons orange-
  flavoured liqueur

Peel the oranges, removing all the white pith. Divide the oranges into segments, removing as much of the membrane between each segment as possible. Put the segments into a rigid container and mix in the sugar. Leave for 1 hour.
To freeze: cover, label and freeze.
To thaw and serve: leave to thaw overnight in the refrigerator or for 4 hours at room temperature. Stir in the liqueur and serve with crisp thin biscuits (cookies) such as langues de chat.

Serves 6.

AMERICAN
8 thin-skinned oranges
½ cup superfine sugar
4 tablespoons orange-
  flavoured liqueur

~Blackcurrant Fool~

METRIC/IMPERIAL
½ kg./1 lb. blackcurrants
100 g./4 oz. sugar
4 tablespoons water
250 ml./½ pint double cream

Put the blackcurrants, sugar and water in a saucepan, cover and simmer gently for about 5 minutes or until just tender. Sieve the fruit and juice into a bowl and leave to cool.
   Whisk the cream until it is thick, then fold it into the fruit purée. Blend well. Turn into six small cream or yogurt cartons.
To freeze: cover each carton with a lid of foil, label and freeze.
To thaw and serve: leave to thaw at room temperature for 2 hours and turn into dishes for serving. Or turn out of the cartons and leave to thaw at room temperature for only 45 minutes to 1 hour and serve semi-frozen.
Note: other fruits such as gooseberries, rhubarb, blackberry and apple may be prepared in the same way. Or use sieved uncooked raspberries or strawberries sweetened with a little icing (confectioners') sugar.

Serves 6.

AMERICAN
1 lb. blackcurrants
½ cup sugar
4 tablespoons water
1¼ cups heavy cream

Cinnamon Apple Pancakes (Crêpes)

(right) Summer Pudding and Red Fruit Salad

~Cherry Shortcake~

METRIC/IMPERIAL
75 g./3 oz. butter
38 g./1½ oz. caster sugar
75 g./3 oz. flour
25 g./1 oz. custard powder
1 × ½ kg./1 lb. can cherry pie
    filling

A shortcake base is a good standby to have in the freezer because it takes very little last minute preparation and can be topped with your favourite pie filling. For a special occasion, add some kirsch to the filling and decorate with whipped cream.

Cream together the butter and sugar until the mixture is pale and fluffy. Sift in the flour and custard powder and mix well to a smooth dough. Roll out the dough on a greased baking sheet to a circle about 20 cm. (8 in.) in diameter. Prick well with a fork.
    Bake in a moderate oven, 180°C, 350°F, Gas Mark 4, for 20 to 30 minutes or until pale golden. Mark into four wedges with a knife, then leave to cool slightly on the baking sheet before transferring to a wire rack.
To freeze: cool, wrap in foil, label and freeze.
To thaw and serve: leave to thaw at room temperature for 2 hours, then unwrap and crisp in a moderate oven, 180°C, 350°F, Gas Mark 4, for 5 minutes. Pile the cherry filling on top.

Serves 4.

AMERICAN
⅜ cup butter
3 tablespoons superfine sugar
¾ cup flour
¼ cup custard powder
1 × 1 lb. can cherry pie filling

~Strawberry and Orange Delight~

METRIC/IMPERIAL
3 large oranges
75 g./3 oz. icing sugar
¾ kg./1½ lb. frozen
    strawberries

Peel the oranges, removing all the white pith. Divide the oranges into segments, removing as much of the membrane between each segment as possible. Put the segments into a shallow dish. Sift the sugar over the oranges and leave in a cool place for about 4 hours or until the sugar has dissolved completely.
To freeze: turn into a rigid container, cover, label and freeze.
To thaw and serve: put into a serving dish with the strawberries and leave to thaw at room temperature until the strawberries are just thawed. Mix lightly and serve with plenty of cream.

Serves 6 to 8.

AMERICAN
3 large oranges
½ cup confectioners' sugar
1½ lb. frozen strawberries

134

⏤Gooseberry Cream⏤

METRIC/IMPERIAL
1 kg./2 lb. frozen gooseberries
150 g./6 oz. sugar
4 tablespoons water
25 g./1 oz. powdered gelatine
250 ml./½ pint prepared
   custard
green food colouring
125 ml./¼ pint double cream
125 ml./¼ pint single cream

Put the gooseberries, sugar and water in a saucepan, cover and simmer gently until tender. Sieve the fruit and juice into a bowl and leave to cool.

Put the gelatine in a small heatproof bowl with 6 tablespoons cold water and place over a pan of simmering water. When the gelatine has dissolved, stir it into the gooseberry purée with the custard. Add a few drops of green food colouring if necessary. Leave in a cool place until the mixture is beginning to thicken slightly and set around the edges.

Whisk the double (heavy) and single (light) cream together until thick and fold into the gooseberry mixture. Turn into a serving dish.
To freeze: cover with a lid of foil and freeze until solid. Dip the dish into hand-hot water to unmould the cream, then put in a polythene (plastic) bag, seal, label, and return to the freezer.
To thaw and serve: return to the dish and leave to thaw for 6 hours in the refrigerator. If you like, decorate with whirls of whipped cream or mimosa balls and small pieces of candied angelica.

Serves 8.

AMERICAN
2 lb. frozen gooseberries
¾ cup sugar
4 tablespoons water
1 oz. powdered gelatin
1¼ cups prepared custard
green food colouring
⅝ cup heavy cream
⅝ cup light cream

⏤Chilled Orange Mousses⏤

METRIC/IMPERIAL
3 eggs, separated
grated rind and juice of
   2 oranges
100 g./4 oz. caster sugar
3 teaspoons powdered
   gelatine
3 tablespoons cold water
125 ml./¼ pint double cream
6 orange slices

Put the egg yolks, orange rind and juice and sugar in a heatproof bowl over a pan of hot water. Whisk the mixture briskly for 10 to 12 minutes or until it is thick and leaves a trail when the whisk is lifted out. Remove from the heat and continue to whisk for a few more minutes.

Put the gelatine and water in a small heatproof bowl. Place over the hot water and stir to dissolve, then stir into the egg yolk mixture. Leave in a cool place until just beginning to set.

Whisk the cream until thick and fold into the mixture. Whisk the egg whites until stiff and fold them into the mixture. Divide between six yogurt or cream cartons and leave in a cool place to set.
To freeze: cover each carton with a lid of foil, label and freeze.
To thaw and serve: turn out on to individual serving dishes and leave to thaw at room temperature for 45 minutes to 1 hour. Decorate each with an orange slice and serve with cream.

Serves 6.

AMERICAN
3 eggs, separated
grated rind and juice of
   2 oranges
½ cup superfine sugar
3 teaspoons powdered
   gelatin
3 tablespoons cold water
⅝ cup heavy cream
6 orange slices

Pineapple Mousse
(right) Mocha Pots

~Blackcurrant Mousse~

METRIC/IMPERIAL
1 packet blackcurrant-
  flavoured jelly
½ kg./1 lb. blackcurrants
3 tablespoons water
75 g./3 oz. sugar
3 eggs, separated

Dissolve the jelly (gelatin) in 125 ml. (¼ pint) or ⅝ cup boiling water. Make up to 250 ml. (½ pint) or 1¼ cups with cold water, and leave to become cold, thick and nearly set.

Put the blackcurrants, water and sugar in a saucepan, cover and simmer until tender. Sieve the fruit and juice into a bowl and stir in the jelly (gelatin).

Beat the egg yolks together and stir into the blackcurrant mixture. Whisk the egg whites until stiff and fold them into the mixture. Turn into a serving dish. (If glass, be sure it is strong moulded glass or ovenproof glass.)

To freeze: cover with a lid of foil, label and freeze.
To thaw and serve: leave to thaw in the refrigerator for 6 hours. Serve with whipped cream.

Serves 6.

AMERICAN
1 packet blackcurrant-
  flavoured powdered
  gelatin
1 lb. blackcurrants
3 tablespoons water
⅜ cup sugar
3 eggs, separated

~Blackberry Mousse~

METRIC/IMPERIAL
½ kg./1 lb. blackberries
4 tablespoons water
100 g./4 oz. sugar
12½ g./½ oz. powdered
  gelatine
1 × 150 ml./6 fl. oz. can
  evaporated milk, chilled
juice of ½ lemon

Put the blackberries, 2 tablespoons of the water and the sugar in a saucepan, cover and simmer until tender. Sieve the fruit and juice into a bowl and leave to cool.

Put the gelatine and remaining water in a small heatproof bowl and place over a pan of simmering water. Stir to dissolve the gelatine, then stir it into the blackberry mixture. Leave in a cool place until thick but not set.

Whisk the evaporated milk and lemon juice together until thickened. Fold the blackberry mixture into the whisked milk. Turn into a serving dish.

To freeze: freeze in the dish until solid, then dip in hand-hot water and unmould the mousse. Put it in a polythene (plastic) bag, seal, label and return to the freezer.
To thaw and serve: return the mousse to the dish and leave to thaw in the refrigerator for 6 hours.
Note: if you like a cream-based mousse, use 250 ml. (½ pint) double cream or 1¼ cups heavy cream, whipped, instead of the evaporated milk, and omit the lemon juice.

Serves 4.

AMERICAN
1 lb. blackberries
4 tablespoons water
½ cup sugar
½ oz. powdered gelatin
1 × 6 fl. oz. can evaporated
  milk, chilled
juice of ½ lemon

138

— Pineapple Mousse —

METRIC/IMPERIAL
3 eggs, separated
juice of 1 lemon
50 g./2 oz. caster sugar
12½ g./½ oz. powdered
gelatine
250 ml./½ pint canned
pineapple juice
125 ml./¼ pint double cream

Put the egg yolks, lemon juice and sugar in a heatproof bowl over a pan of simmering water and whisk until thick and pale. Remove from the heat and leave to cool, whisking occasionally.

Put the gelatine and 4 tablespoons of the pineapple juice in a small heatproof bowl and place over the simmering water. Stir to dissolve the gelatine, then add the remaining pineapple juice. Stir into the egg yolk mixture. Leave in a cool place until just beginning to set, stirring frequently.

Whisk the cream until it is thick and fold into the pineapple mixture. Whisk the egg whites until stiff and fold into the mixture. Turn into a serving dish.

To freeze: cover with a lid of foil, then freeze until solid. Dip the dish into hand-hot water and unmould the mousse. Put into a polythene (plastic) bag, seal, label and return to the freezer.

To thaw and serve: return to the dish and leave to thaw for 6 hours in the refrigerator. Decorate with whipped cream rosettes.

Note: if you would like pieces of crushed pineapple in the mousse, use a 250 g. (10 oz.) can of crushed pineapple or pineapple pieces.

Serves 6.

AMERICAN
3 eggs, separated
juice of 1 lemon
¼ cup superfine sugar
½ oz. powdered gelatin
1¼ cups canned pineapple
juice
⅝ cup heavy cream

— Raspberry Charlotte —

METRIC/IMPERIAL
1 × 375 g./15 oz. can
raspberries
12½ g./½ oz. powdered
gelatine
juice of ½ lemon
about 20 sponge finger
biscuits
3 eggs
75 g./3 oz. caster sugar
250 ml./½ pint double cream

Drain the raspberries and reserve the juice. Put 3 tablespoons of the juice in a small heatproof bowl with the gelatine and leave to soak for 5 minutes. Put the bowl over a pan of simmering water and stir to dissolve the gelatine. Add, with the lemon juice, to the rest of the raspberry juice.

Pour a ¾ cm. (¼ in.) layer of the juice mixture into a 17.5 cm. (7 in.) diameter china charlotte or soufflé dish. When the mixture has set, arrange sponge fingers around the side of the dish, with the sugar side towards the dish.

Sieve the raspberries and add the purée to the remaining juice mixture. Leave until the mixture thickens and is about to set at the edges.

Put the eggs and sugar in a heated bowl and whisk until the mixture is thick and foamy. Fold in the raspberry mixture. Whisk three-quarters of the cream until thick and fold into the mixture. Turn into the prepared dish. Keep the remaining cream for decoration.

To freeze: cover with a lid of foil, label and freeze. Use within 1 month. Place the dish in a part of the freezer where it will not be knocked and broken.

To thaw and serve: leave to thaw for 6 hours in the refrigerator. Trim the tops off the sponge fingers so that they are level with the raspberry mixture. Loosen the charlotte with a knife, then dip the dish into hand-hot water and unmould the charlotte. Decorate with the remaining cream, which has been whipped.

Serves 6 to 8.

AMERICAN
1 × 15 oz. can raspberries
½ oz. powdered gelatin
juice of ½ lemon
about 20 sponge finger
cookies
3 eggs
¾ cup superfine sugar
1¼ cups heavy cream

Chilled Raspberry Cheesecake
(right) Rich Dark Chocolate Cake

Griestorte with Raspberries

METRIC/IMPERIAL
3 eggs, separated
100 g./4 oz. caster sugar
½ teaspoon almond essence
50 g./2 oz. ground semolina
12½ g./½ oz. ground almonds
Filling
200 g./8 oz. frozen raspberries
125 ml./¼ pint double cream
50 g./2 oz. icing sugar

Put the egg yolks and sugar in a heatproof bowl over a pan of hot water and whisk until the mixture is pale and thick. Remove from the heat. Fold in the almond essence (extract), semolina (cream of wheat) and ground almonds. Whisk the egg whites until they form soft peaks, then fold them into the mixture.

Turn into a 20 cm. (8 in.) diameter cake tin which has been lined with greased greaseproof (waxed) paper and dusted with flour. Bake in a moderate oven, 180°C, 350°F, Gas Mark 4, for 30 minutes or until the cake is well risen and pale golden. Cool the cake on a wire rack.

To freeze: wrap in foil, or put in a container, seal, label and freeze.
To thaw and serve: leave to thaw, still in the foil or container, at room temperature for 2 hours. Thaw the raspberries. Split the cake in half. Whisk the cream until thick and fold in the raspberries and icing (confectioners') sugar. Use to sandwich the cake halves together. Sprinkle the top with icing (confectioners') sugar. Decorate with three large raspberries.

Serves 6.

AMERICAN
3 eggs, separated
½ cup caster sugar
½ teaspoon almond extract
⅓ cup cream of wheat
1½ tablespoons ground almonds
Filling
8 oz. frozen raspberries
⅝ cup heavy cream
⅓ cup confectioners' sugar

Chocolate Rum Truffles

METRIC/IMPERIAL
50 g./2 oz. seedless raisins, chopped
50 g./2 oz. glacé cherries, chopped
4 tablespoons rum
200 g./8 oz. sweet biscuits, crushed
200 g./8 oz. stale cake, crumbled
5 rounded tablespoons drinking chocolate powder
2 rounded tablespoons apricot jam, melted
about 75 g./3 oz. chocolate vermicelli

If you'd like more potent truffles, add more rum and leave overnight in the refrigerator before rolling into balls. This will give the mixture more time to absorb the liquid.

Put the raisins and cherries in a bowl and sprinkle with the rum. Leave for 2 hours.

Mix together the biscuits (cookies), cake crumbs, drinking chocolate and fruit and rum mixture. Add the melted jam and mix to a firm sticky dough. Chill for 1 hour.

Shape into small balls and coat in the vermicelli. Leave on a tray or flat plates to become firm.

To freeze: pack in a rigid container, cover, label and freeze.
To thaw and serve: place on a tray or plates and leave to thaw at room temperature for 30 minutes. Place in sweet cases.

Makes about 4 dozen truffles.

AMERICAN
⅓ cup seedless raisins, chopped
⅓ cup chopped glacé cherries
4 tablespoons rum
8 oz. sweet cookies, crushed
8 oz. stale cake, crumbled
5 rounded tablespoons drinking chocolate powder
2 rounded tablespoons aprico jam, melted
about ½ cup chocolate vermicelli

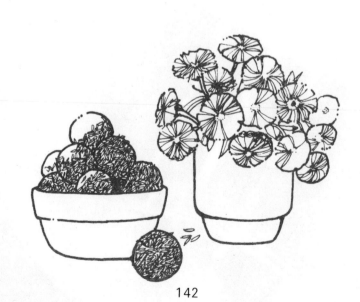

— Special Cheesecake —

METRIC/IMPERIAL
Pastry
75 g./3 oz. flour
2 tablespoons icing sugar
38 g./1½ oz. butter
1 egg yolk
2 teaspoons water
Filling
⅞ kg./1¾ lb. cream cheese
225 g./9 oz. caster sugar
2 tablespoons flour
finely grated rind of 1 lemon
4 eggs
1 egg yolk
125 ml./¼ pint double cream
Topping
1 × 375 g./15 oz. can
   pineapple pieces
1½ teaspoons arrowroot

To make the pastry, sift the flour and icing (confectioners') sugar into a bowl and add the butter. Cut it into small pieces, then rub the fat into the flour until the mixture resembles breadcrumbs. Mix the egg yolk and water together. Make a well in the centre of the flour mixture and add the egg yolk mixture. Stir it in using a fork. Turn out on to a floured board and knead lightly. Chill in the refrigerator for 1 hour.

Roll out the dough and use to line the bottom of a 20 cm. (8 in.) loose-bottomed cake tin. Prick well. Bake in a moderately hot oven, 200°C, 400°F, Gas Mark 6, for 15 to 20 minutes or until crisp and brown. Remove from the oven.

Line the sides of the tin with greased greaseproof (waxed) paper.

Mix together the cream cheese and sugar. Beat in the flour and lemon rind. Beat in the eggs and egg yolk one at a time. Stir in the cream. Pour into the prepared tin and bake in a moderately hot oven, 200°C, 400°F, Gas Mark 6, for 15 minutes. Reduce the oven temperature to very cool, 100°C, 200°F, Gas Mark ¼, and bake for 2 hours. Turn off the oven and leave the cheesecake inside until it has cooled completely.

Remove from the tin and take off the paper. Leave for 24 hours.
To freeze: freeze until firm then wrap in foil, seal, label and return to the freezer.
To thaw and serve: unwrap and leave to thaw at room temperature for 7 to 8 hours. Drain the pineapple and reserve the juice. Blend 2 tablespoons of the juice with the arrowroot and add to the remaining juice in a saucepan. Bring to the boil, stirring, to thicken and add the pineapple. Leave to cool, then spoon over the cheesecake.

Serves 12.

AMERICAN
Pastry
¾ cup flour
2 tablespoons confectioners'
   sugar
3 tablespoons butter
1 egg yolk
2 teaspoons water
Filling
1¾ lb. cream cheese
1 cup plus 2 tablespoons
   superfine sugar
2 tablespoons flour
finely grated rind of 1 lemon
4 eggs
1 egg yolk
⅝ cup heavy cream
Topping
1 × 15 oz. can pineapple
   pieces
1½ teaspoons arrowroot

— Chilled Raspberry Cheesecake —

METRIC/IMPERIAL
1 packet lemon-flavoured
   jelly
150 g./6 oz. digestive biscuits,
   crushed
25 g./1 oz. Demerara sugar
75 g./3 oz. butter, melted
125 ml./¼ pint double cream
300 g./12 oz. rich cream
   cheese
juice of 2 lemons
100 g./4 oz. caster sugar
Topping
4 tablespoons redcurrant jelly
200 g./8 oz. raspberries,
   frozen or fresh

Dissolve the jelly (gelatin) in 125 ml. (¼ pint) or ⅝ cup boiling water. Make up to 250 ml. (½ pint) or 1¼ cups with cold water, and leave to become cold, thick and nearly set.

Mix together the biscuits (crackers), Demerara (brown) sugar and melted butter and use to line the bottom of a 20 to 22.5 cm. (8 to 9 in.) diameter spring mould.

Whisk the cream until thick. Mash the cream cheese, then gradually beat in the thickened jelly (gelatin), lemon juice, cream and caster (superfine) sugar. Turn into the prepared mould.
To freeze: cover with a lid of foil, label and freeze.
To thaw and serve: leave to thaw overnight in the refrigerator. Thirty minutes before serving, arrange the raspberries around the edge of the cheesecake. Melt the redcurrant jelly over low heat and spoon over the cheesecake. If necessary, thin the jelly with a little water.

Serves 6.

AMERICAN
1 packet lemon-flavoured
   powdered gelatin
6 oz. graham crackers,
   crushed
3 tablespoons light brown
   sugar
⅜ cup butter, melted
⅝ cup heavy cream
12 oz. rich cream cheese
juice of 2 lemons
½ cup superfine sugar
Topping
4 tablespoons redcurrant jelly
8 oz. raspberries, frozen or
   fresh

(Overleaf) Wheatmeal Bread

Cakes and baking

~Demerara Fruit Cake~

METRIC/IMPERIAL
200 g./8 oz. self-raising flour, sifted
½ teaspoon salt
50 g./2 oz. glacé cherries, quartered
150 g./6 oz. butter, softened
150 g./6 oz. soft brown sugar
3 eggs
2 tablespoons milk
200 g./8 oz. seedless raisins
150 g./6 oz. sultanas
1 tablespoon golden syrup
25 g./1 oz. Demerara sugar

Sift the flour and salt into a bowl. Add all the remaining ingredients except the Demerara (light brown) sugar. Mix thoroughly together. Turn into a 1 kg. (2 lb.) loaf tin which has been lined with greased greaseproof (waxed) paper. Sprinkle the top with the Demerara (light brown) sugar. Bake in a cool oven, 150°C, 300°F, Gas Mark 2, for 2 hours or until a skewer inserted in the centre comes out clean. Cool in the tin for 10 minutes, then turn out on to a wire rack to cool completely.
To freeze: wrap in foil, label and freeze.
To thaw and serve: unwrap and leave to thaw at room temperature for 4 hours.

Makes 1 cake.

AMERICAN
2 cups self-rising flour
½ teaspoon salt
⅓ cup glacé cherries, quartered
¾ cup butter, softened
1 cup dark brown sugar
3 eggs
2 tablespoons milk
1⅓ cups seedless raisins
1 cup golden raisins
1 tablespoon light corn syrup
2½ tablespoons light brown sugar

~Special Fruit Cake~

METRIC/IMPERIAL
175 g./7 oz. self-raising flour
pinch of salt
100 g./4 oz. glacé cherries, halved
1 × ½ kg./1 lb. can pineapple chunks or rings, drained and finely chopped
125 g./5 oz. butter
112½ g./4½ oz. caster sugar
2 large eggs, beaten
2 tablespoons brandy or milk
300 g. (12 oz. mixed dried fruit

Sift the flour and salt together. Roll three-quarters of the cherries and all the pineapple in a little flour to coat them. Cut the remainder into small pieces and set aside for the topping.
Cream the butter and sugar together until the mixture is pale and fluffy. Blend in the eggs, adding a tablespoon of flour with the last amount of egg. Fold in the remaining flour with the brandy or milk, mixed dried fruit, pineapple and cherry halves.
Turn into a 1½ kg. (3 lb.) loaf tin which has been lined with greased greaseproof (waxed) paper. Arrange the reserved cherries on top. Bake in a warm oven, 170°C, 325°F, Gas Mark 3, for about 2 hours or until a skewer inserted into the centre comes out clean. Leave to cool in the tin, then remove the paper.
To freeze: wrap in foil, label and freeze.
To thaw and serve: leave to thaw at room temperature for 4 to 5 hours.

Makes 1 cake.

AMERICAN
1¾ cups self-rising flour
pinch of salt
⅔ cup glacé cherries, halved
1 × 1 lb. can pineapple chunks or rings, drained and finely chopped
⅝ cup butter
½ cup plus 1 tablespoon superfine sugar
2 large eggs, beaten
2 tablespoons brandy or milk
2 cups mixed dried fruit

~Cherry Cake~

METRIC/IMPERIAL
75 g./3 oz. self-raising flour
75 g./3 oz. plain flour
pinch of salt
200 g./8 oz. glacé cherries, halved
150 g./6 oz. butter or margarine
150 g./6 oz. caster sugar
grated rind of 1 lemon
3 eggs, beaten
75 g./3 oz. ground almonds
milk to mix if necessary

Sift the flours and salt together. Roll the cherries in a little flour to coat them. Cream the butter or margarine with the sugar and lemon rind until the mixture is pale and fluffy. Blend in the eggs, adding a tablespoon of flour with the last amount of egg. Fold in the remaining flour with the cherries and almonds. Mix well to a very stiff dropping consistency, adding a little milk if necessary.
Turn into a ½ kg. (1 lb.) loaf tin which has been greased and lined with greased greaseproof (waxed) paper. Smooth the surface. Bake in a moderate oven, 180°C, 350°F, Gas Mark 4, for 1¼ hours. Leave to cool for 5 minutes, then turn out, peel off the paper and cool on a wire rack.
To freeze: wrap in foil, seal, label and freeze. Use within 3 months.
To thaw and serve: leave to thaw overnight in the refrigerator or for 4 hours at room temperature.

Makes 1 cake.

AMERICAN
¾ cup self-rising flour
¾ cup all-purpose flour
pinch of salt
1⅓ cups glacé cherries, halved
¾ cup butter or margarine
¾ cup superfine sugar
grated rind of 1 lemon
3 eggs, beaten
½ cup ground almonds
milk to mix if necessary

～Rich Dark Chocolate Cake～

METRIC/IMPERIAL
275 g./11 oz. caster sugar
6 tablespoons water
75 g./3 oz. cocoa powder
150 ml./6 fl. oz. milk
200 g./8 oz. butter
4 eggs, separated
200 g./8 oz. self-raising flour
2 teaspoons baking powder
125 ml./¼ pint double cream
125 ml./¼ pint single cream

AMERICAN
1⅝ cups superfine sugar
6 tablespoons water
¾ cup cocoa powder
¾ cup milk
1 cup butter
4 eggs, separated
2 cups self-rising flour
2 teaspoons baking powder
⅝ cup heavy cream
⅝ cup light cream

Put 75 g. (3 oz.) or ⅜ cup of the sugar in a saucepan with the water and cocoa and mix to a thick paste. Cook gently until the mixture is thick and shiny. Stir in the milk and leave to cool.

Cream the butter with the remaining sugar until the mixture is pale and fluffy. Beat in the egg yolks with the chocolate mixture. Sift together the flour and baking powder and fold into the mixture. Whisk the egg whites until stiff, then fold into the mixture.

Divide the mixture between two sandwich (layer) cake tins, each about 20 cm. (8 in.) in diameter and 5 cm. (2 in.) deep, which have been lined with greased greaseproof (waxed) paper. Bake in a moderate oven, 180°C, 350°F, Gas Mark 4, for about 40 minutes or until the cake springs back when lightly pressed with a fingertip. Turn the cakes out, peel off the paper and cool on a wire rack.

Whisk the double (heavy) and single (light) cream together until thick. Split each cake into two layers and use the cream to sandwich them together.
To freeze: wrap each cake in foil, label and freeze.
To thaw and serve: leave to thaw for 5 hours at room temperature. Just before serving, sprinkle with icing (confectioners') sugar.

Makes 2 cakes.

～Chocolate and Orange Cake～

METRIC/IMPERIAL
150 g./6 oz. margarine
150 g./6 oz. caster sugar
150 ml./6 fl. oz. golden syrup
2 eggs
50 g./2 oz. ground almonds
grated rind and juice of 1 orange
150 g./6 oz. flour
50 g./2 oz. cocoa powder
¼ teaspoon bicarbonate of soda
125 ml./¼ pint milk
Icing
75 g./3 oz. butter
150 g./6 oz. icing sugar

AMERICAN
¾ cup margarine
¾ cup superfine sugar
¾ cup light corn syrup
2 eggs
⅓ cup ground almonds
grated rind and juice of 1 orange
1½ cups flour
⅓ cup cocoa powder
¼ teaspoon baking soda
⅝ cup milk
Icing
⅜ cup butter
1 cup confectioners' sugar

Cream the margarine and sugar together until the mixture is light and fluffy. Gradually beat in the syrup and eggs. Stir in the ground almonds and orange rind. Sift together the flour, cocoa and soda and fold into the mixture with the milk. Turn into a cake or roasting tin, 27.5 by 17.5 cm. (11 by 7 in.), which has been lined with greased greaseproof (waxed) paper. Bake in a warm oven, 170°C, 325°F, Gas Mark 3, for 1 to 1¼ hours or until a skewer inserted into the centre comes out clean. Turn out, remove the paper and cool on a wire rack.

For the icing, cream the butter and icing (confectioners') sugar together until the mixture is pale and fluffy. Beat in enough of the orange juice to flavour. Spread the icing over the top of the cake and mark with a fork.
To freeze: open freeze, then place in a polythene (plastic) bag, seal, label and return to the freezer.
To thaw and serve: leave to thaw at room temperature for 3 to 4 hours.

Makes 1 cake.

─Chocolate Fudge Cake─

METRIC/IMPERIAL
100 g./4 oz. self-raising flour
¼ teaspoon salt
38 g./1½ oz. cocoa powder
100 g./4 oz. butter
100 g./4 oz. soft brown sugar
2 eggs, beaten
1 tablespoon milk
Chocolate fudge icing
38 g./1½ oz. butter
25 g./1 oz. cocoa powder
3 tablespoons milk
100 g./4 oz. icing sugar, sifted

Sift together the flour, salt and cocoa. Cream the butter and sugar together until the mixture is pale and fluffy. Blend in the eggs, adding a tablespoon of the flour mixture with the last amount of egg. Fold in the remaining flour mixture with the milk and mix well. Turn into a 20 cm. (8 in.) diameter sandwich (layer) cake tin which has been lined with greased aluminium foil. Bake in a fairly hot oven, 190°C, 375°F, Gas Mark 5, for 30 minutes or until the cake springs back when lightly pressed with a fingertip. Leave to cool in the tin.

For the icing, melt the butter and stir in the cocoa. Cook over low heat for 1 minute, stirring. Stir in the milk and icing (confectioners') sugar and mix well. Spread the icing over the cake in the tin and leave to set.

To freeze: open freeze, then place on a polythene (plastic) bag, seal, label and return to the freezer.

To thaw and serve: unwrap, place on a plate and leave to thaw at room temperature for 3 to 4 hours.

Makes 1 cake.

AMERICAN
1 cup self-rising flour
¼ teaspoon salt
⅜ cup cocoa powder
½ cup butter
⅔ cup dark brown sugar
2 eggs, beaten
1 tablespoon milk
Chocolate fudge icing
3 tablespoons butter
¼ cup cocoa powder
3 tablespoons milk
⅔ cup confectioners' sugar, sifted

─Fruit Malt Loaf─

METRIC/IMPERIAL
150 g./6 oz. self-raising flour
2 tablespoons malt drink
25 g./1 oz. caster sugar
75 g./3 oz. mixed dried fruit
2 tablespoons golden syrup
125 ml./¼ pint milk

This is a good inexpensive family loaf.

Put all the ingredients in a bowl and mix well together to form a thick batter. Turn into a well-greased ½ kg. (1 lb.) loaf tin. Bake in a moderate oven, 180°C, 350°F, Gas Mark 4, for 50 to 60 minutes or until a skewer inserted into the centre comes out clean. Turn out on to a wire rack to cool.

To freeze: wrap in foil, label and freeze.

To thaw and serve: leave to thaw at room temperature for 4 hours and serve sliced with butter.

Makes 1 loaf.

AMERICAN
1½ cups self-rising flour
2 tablespoons malt drink
2 tablespoons superfine sugar
½ cup mixed dried fruit
2 tablespoons light corn syrup
⅝ cup milk

─Banana Fruit Loaf─

METRIC/IMPERIAL
200 g./8 oz. self-raising flour
½ teaspoon salt
½ teaspoon ground mixed spice
50 g./2 oz. glacé cherries, quartered
50 g./2 oz. walnuts, chopped
25 g./1 oz. chopped mixed candied peel
100 g./4 oz. butter
100 g./4 oz. soft brown or caster sugar
2 eggs, beaten
1 tablespoon clear honey
½ kg./1 lb. ripe bananas, peeled and mashed
100 g./4 oz. sultanas

Bananas freeze well in a cake and add to the moisture.

Sift the flour, salt and spice into a bowl. Add the cherries, walnuts and peel. Cream the butter and sugar together until the mixture is pale and fluffy. Blend in the eggs, then the honey. Add the mashed bananas, sultanas (raisins) and the flour mixture and mix well together.

Turn into a well-greased 1 kg. (2 lb.) loaf tin. Bake in a moderate oven, 180°C, 350°F, Gas Mark 4, for 1 hour, then reduce the oven temperature to cool, 150°C, 300°F, Gas Mark 2, and bake for a further 30 minutes or until a skewer inserted into the centre comes out clean. Turn out on to a wire rack to cool.

To freeze: wrap in foil, label and freeze.

To thaw and serve: unwrap and leave to thaw at room temperature for 4 hours. Serve sliced with butter.

Makes 1 loaf.

AMERICAN
2 cups self-rising flour
½ teaspoon salt
½ teaspoon ground mixed spice
⅓ cup glacé cherries, quartered
⅓ cup chopped walnuts
2½ tablespoons chopped mixed candied peel
½ cup butter
½ cup dark brown or superfine sugar
2 eggs, beaten
1 tablespoon clear honey
1 lb. ripe bananas, peeled and mashed
⅔ cup golden raisins

Victoria Sandwich

METRIC/IMPERIAL
100 g./4 oz. butter
100 g./4 oz. caster sugar
2 eggs, beaten
100 g./4 oz. self-raising flour
3 tablespoons jam

This is a good 'basic' which freezes well. It can be frozen filled or unfilled.

Cream the butter and sugar together until the mixture is pale and fluffy. Blend in the eggs, adding a tablespoon of flour with the last amount of egg. Sift in the remaining flour and fold it in. Turn into two 17.5 cm. (7 in.) diameter sandwich (layer) cake tins which have been lined with greased greaseproof (waxed) paper.

Bake in a fairly hot oven, 190°C, 375°F, Gas Mark 5, for 20 to 25 minutes or until the cakes spring back when lightly pressed with a fingertip. Turn out on to a wire rack to cool. Sandwich the cooled cakes together with the jam.

To freeze: wrap in foil, label and freeze.

To thaw and serve: leave to thaw at room temperature for 4 to 5 hours. Just before serving sprinkle with icing (confectioners') sugar.

Variations

Orange or lemon flavour: add the grated rind of 1 orange or lemon to the creamed mixture.

Coffee flavour: dissolve 1 heaped teaspoon instant coffee powder in the beaten eggs before adding.

Chocolate flavour: replace 25 g./1 oz. or $\frac{1}{4}$ cup flour with 25 g./1 oz. or $\frac{1}{4}$ cup cocoa powder.

Walnut flavour: add 50 g./2 oz. or $\frac{1}{3}$ cup chopped walnuts with the flour.

Makes 1 cake.

AMERICAN
$\frac{1}{2}$ cup butter
$\frac{1}{2}$ cup superfine sugar
2 eggs, beaten
1 cup self-rising flour
3 tablespoons jam

Bara Brith

METRIC/IMPERIAL
200 ml./8 fl. oz. water, hand-hot
1 teaspoon caster sugar
3 teaspoons dried yeast
$\frac{1}{2}$ kg./1 lb. flour
1 teaspoon salt
1 teaspoon ground mixed spice
75 g./3 oz. butter
1 egg
50 g./2 oz. Demerara sugar
$\frac{1}{2}$ kg./1 lb. mixed dried fruit
2 teaspoons clear honey

Put the water and sugar into a small bowl and sprinkle over the yeast. Leave in a warm place for about 10 minutes or until the mixture has become frothy.

Sift the flour, salt and spice into a bowl. Add the butter and cut it into small pieces, then rub it into the flour until the mixture resembles breadcrumbs. Stir in the yeast mixture and egg and mix well. Turn on to a floured board and knead thoroughly.

Place the dough in a lightly oiled polythene (plastic) bag and leave to rise in a warm place until doubled in bulk. This will take about 1$\frac{1}{4}$ hours. Turn on to a floured board and knead in the Demerara (brown) sugar and dried fruit. Divide the dough in half and shape into loaves to fit into two $\frac{1}{2}$ kg. (1 lb.) loaf tins. Put the dough in the tins, cover with an oiled polythene (plastic) bag and leave to rise until the dough is 2.5 cm. (1 in.) above the rim of the tin.

Remove the bag and bake in a moderate oven, 180°C, 350°F, Gas Mark 4, for 50 to 60 minutes or until golden brown. Brush the tops of the loaves with honey and leave to cool on a wire rack.

To freeze: wrap in foil, label and freeze.

To thaw and serve: wrap and leave to thaw at room temperature for 4 hours.

Makes 2 loaves.

AMERICAN
1 cup water, hand-hot
1 teaspoon superfine sugar
3 teaspoons dried yeast
1 lb. (4 cups) flour
1 teaspoon salt
1 teaspoon ground mixed spice
$\frac{3}{8}$ cup butter
1 egg
$\frac{1}{3}$ cup light brown sugar
1 lb. (2$\frac{2}{3}$ cups) mixed dried fruit
2 teaspoons clear honey

⁓Butter Icing⁓

METRIC/IMPERIAL
50 g./2 oz. butter
100 g./4 oz. icing sugar
2 drops vanilla essence
a little warm water

This is enough icing to fill a 17.5 cm. (7 in.) sandwich (layer) cake such as a Victoria Sandwich.

Cream the butter until it is softened. Gradually sift in the icing (confectioners') sugar and beat well. Add the vanilla and a little warm water and beat until smooth.

Variations
Orange or lemon flavour: add 1 teaspoon grated orange or lemon rind and about 1 tablespoon orange or lemon juice instead of the water and vanilla.
Coffee flavour: add 1 teaspoon instant coffee powder, which has been dissolved in 2 teaspoons boiling water and cooled, or 1 tablespoon coffee essence.
Chocolate flavour: add 1 teaspoon cocoa powder which has been dissolved in 2 teaspoons boiling water and cooled.

AMERICAN
¼ cup butter
⅔ cup confectioners' sugar
2 drops vanilla extract
a little warm water

⁓Whisked Sponge Cake⁓

METRIC/IMPERIAL
3 eggs
75 g./3 oz. caster sugar
75 g./3 oz. self-raising flour
3 tablespoons jam
whipped cream

Fatless sponges freeze exceptionally well. If you prefer, fill with fruit or jam and whipped cream after thawing.

Put the eggs and sugar in a heatproof bowl placed over a pan of hot water and whisk until the mixture is thick, white and creamy, and the whisk leaves a trail when lifted out. Remove from the heat and whisk for a further 2 minutes. Sift in the flour and carefully fold it in.

Turn into two 17.5 cm. (7 in.) diameter sandwich (layer) cake tins which have been lined with greased greaseproof (waxed) paper. Bake in a fairly hot oven, 190°C, 375°F, Gas Mark 5, for 20 minutes or until the cakes spring back when lightly pressed with a fingertip. Turn out on to a wire rack to cool. Sandwich the cooled cakes together with the jam and cream.
To freeze: wrap in foil and over-wrap in a polythene (plastic) bag, seal, label and freeze.
To thaw and serve: leave to thaw overnight in the refrigerator or for 4 hours at room temperature, unwrap and sprinkle with sugar.

Makes 1 cake.

AMERICAN
3 eggs
⅜ cup superfine sugar
¾ cup self-rising flour
3 tablespoons jam
whipped cream

Lemon Swiss (Jelly) Roll

METRIC/IMPERIAL

3 large eggs, at room
    temperature
75 g./3 oz. caster sugar
75 g./3 oz. self-raising flour
lemon curd, preferably
    homemade, to fill

AMERICAN

3 large eggs, at room
    temperature
¾ cup superfine sugar
¾ cup self-rising flour
lemon curd, preferably
    homemade, to fill

Be sure to measure the flour carefully because too much makes the cake crack when it is being rolled up.

Put the eggs and sugar into a bowl and whisk until the mixture is thick, pale and frothy. Sift in the flour and fold it in. Turn into a Swiss (jelly) roll tin, 22.5 by 30 cm. (9 by 12 in.), which has been lined with greased greaseproof (waxed) paper. Smooth the top. Bake in a fairly hot oven, 190°C, 375°F, Gas Mark 5, for 15 minutes, or until the cake is just firm to the touch.

Turn the sponge cake out on to a piece of greaseproof (waxed) paper which has been sprinkled with sugar. Trim the edges of the cake to make a neat rectangle. Spread generously with lemon curd, then roll up the cake. Leave to cool on a wire rack.

To freeze: open freeze on a small tray, then wrap in foil, label and return to the freezer.

To thaw and serve: loosen the foil and leave to thaw at room temperature for 3 to 4 hours. Unwrap just before serving.

Makes 1 cake.

Chocolate Eclairs

METRIC/IMPERIAL

Choux pastry
50 g./2 oz. butter
125 ml./¼ pint mixed milk
    and water
63 g./2½ oz. flour, sifted
2 eggs
Filling and icing
125 ml./¼ pint single cream
125 ml./¼ pint double cream
200 g./8 oz. icing sugar
1 tablespoon cocoa powder
1 tablespoon rum
1 to 2 tablespoons warm
    water

AMERICAN

Choux pastry
¼ cup butter
⅝ cup mixed milk and water
½ cup plus 2 tablespoons
    flour, sifted
2 eggs
Filling and icing
⅝ cup light cream
⅝ cup heavy cream
1⅓ cups confectioners' sugar
1 tablespoon cocoa powder
1 tablespoon rum
1 to 2 tablespoons warm
    water

Put the butter and milk and water mixture in a saucepan and bring to the boil, stirring occasionally. Remove the pan from the heat. Add the flour all at once and beat until the mixture forms a ball. Gradually beat in the eggs to make a smooth shiny paste. Place the mixture in a large piping bag fitted with a 1.25 cm. (½ in.) plain nozzle. Pipe 12 to 14 eclairs, 5 cm. (2 in.) long, on to a greased baking sheet. Bake in a moderately hot oven, 200°C, 400°F, Gas Mark 6, for 20 minutes or until well risen and golden brown.

Split one side of each eclair so that the steam can escape. Leave to cool on a wire rack.

To freeze: pack in a polythene (plastic) bag or foil, seal, label and freeze. Use within 6 months.

To thaw and serve: leave to thaw at room temperature for 1 hour, then unwrap and refresh in a moderate oven, 180°C, 350°F, Gas Mark 4, for 5 minutes. Or place frozen in the oven and refresh for 10 minutes. Cool before filling.

To make the filling, whisk the single (light) and double (heavy) cream together until thick. Use to fill each eclair. Sift the icing (confectioners') sugar and cocoa into a bowl and stir in the rum with enough warm water to make a thick icing. Spear each eclair with a fork and dip the tops in the icing. Leave to set and serve the same day.

Makes 12 to 14 eclairs.

METRIC/IMPERIAL
5 tablespoons water,
    hand-hot
4 teaspoons caster sugar
2 teaspoons dried yeast
200 g./8 oz. flour
pinch of salt
25 g./1 oz. lard
1 egg, beaten
125 g./5 oz. butter
1 egg yolk mixed with 1
    tablespoon cold water for
    glaze
Almond paste
50 g./2 oz. ground almonds
50 g./2 oz. caster sugar
few drops of almond essence
egg white
Topping
100 g./4 oz. icing sugar
flaked almonds, lightly
    toasted
glacé cherries, cut into small
    pieces

These crisp, buttery, flaky-layered confections do take time — about 2 hours from measuring the ingredients to decorating the finished pastries — but if you follow the step-by-step instructions, you'll be surprised what fun they are to make. Should there be any pastries left over, reheat them the next day and serve warm.

Put the water and 1 teaspoon sugar into a small bowl and sprinkle over the yeast. Leave in a warm place for about 10 minutes or until the mixture has become frothy.

Sift the flour and salt into a bowl. Add the lard and cut it into small pieces, then rub the lard into the flour until the mixture resembles breadcrumbs. Add the egg, yeast mixture and the remaining sugar and mix to a soft dough with a fork and then your hands. If the dough is sticky, add an extra tablespoon of flour.

Turn on to a lightly floured board and knead lightly for about 5 minutes or until the dough is smooth. Place in a lightly oiled polythene (plastic) bag and leave to rest in the refrigerator or another cool place for 10 minutes.

Cream the butter until it is softened. Roll out the dough to form a 25 cm. (10 in.) square. Spread the butter in a rectangle in the centre of the dough but do not spread it nearer than 1.25 cm. (½ in.) of the edges at the top and bottom, otherwise the butter will ooze out when the dough is handled.

Fold the two sides of the dough into the centre so that they just overlap in the middle. Seal the bottom and top edges by pressing them with a rolling pin.

Roll out the dough to an oblong strip about three times as long as it is wide — about 12.5 by 37.5 cm (5 by 15 in.). Fold the bottom third towards the middle and then bring the top third over to cover it. Make a mark with a knuckle in the dough to remind you that it has had one rolling. Put the dough into a polythene (plastic) bag and leave it to rest in the refrigerator for about 10 minutes.

Remove the dough from the bag and place it on the board so that the open edge is on your left. Roll and fold the dough as before. Make two marks with a knuckle. Return to the bag and chill again.

Repeat the rolling, folding and chilling process a third time. While the dough is chilling, make the almond paste. Mix together the ground almonds, sugar and almond essence (extract) with just enough egg white to bind the ingredients.

Divide the dough in half and shape the pastries as follows. *Crescents:* roll out half the dough to form a 22.5 cm. (9 in.) diameter circle. Divide the circle into eight sections. Cut a small lengthwise slit about 1.25 cm. (½ in.) long near the pointed end of

AMERICAN
5 tablespoons water,
    hand-hot
4 teaspoons superfine sugar
2 teaspoons dried yeast
2 cups flour
pinch of salt
2 tablespoons lard
1 egg, beaten
⅝ cup butter
1 egg yolk mixed with 1
    tablespoon cold water for
    glaze
Almond paste
⅓ cup ground almonds
¼ cup superfine sugar
few drops of almond extract
egg white
Topping
⅔ cup confectioners' sugar
flaked almonds, lightly
    toasted
glacé cherries, cut into small
    pieces

each section. Place a small amount of almond paste at the wide end of each and roll them up from this end towards the point. Bend slightly into a crescent shape.

Stars: roll out half the remaining dough to form a 15 cm. (6 in.) square. Cut the square into quarters. Place a small amount of almond paste in the centre of each small square. To shape one small square, make cuts from the corners almost to the centre, then lift the left-hand corner of the bottom triangle into the centre to cover part of the almond paste. Repeat with the other three triangles to form a star. Shape the remaining three squares the same way.

Kites: roll out the remaining dough very thinly to form a 20 cm. (8 in.) square. Cut the square into quarters. Place a small amount of almond paste in the centre of each small square. To shape one small square, bring two opposite corner points into the centre and overlap them over the almond paste. Shape the remaining three squares in the same way.

Place the pastries on two greased baking sheets, allowing room between them to spread. Brush the pastries with the egg glaze. Cover with a polythene (plastic) bag and leave in a warm place to prove for about 15 to 20 minutes, or until they look puffy. Warm room temperature is suitable; in too warm a place the butter will melt out of them.

Brush again with the egg glaze and bake in a very hot oven, 220°C, 425°F, Gas Mark 7, for 12 to 15 minutes, or until they are golden brown. Transfer to a wire rack to cool.

To freeze: wrap in a single layer in a polythene (plastic) bag or foil or place in a rigid foil container, seal, label and freeze. Use within 1 month.

To thaw and serve: loosen wrap and leave to thaw at room temperature for 1½ hours. Unwrap and refresh in a moderate oven, 180°C, 350°F, Gas Mark 4, for 5 minutes.

For the topping, blend the icing (confectioners') sugar with enough water to make a rather runny icing. Spoon this over the pastries while they are still warm. Sprinkle some with almonds and decorate the rest with cherry pieces.

Makes 16 pastries.

⌁ Butter Shortbread ⌁

METRIC/IMPERIAL
200 g./8 oz. flour
50 g./2 oz. cornflour
50 g./2 oz. custard powder
200 g./8 oz. butter
100 g./4 oz. caster sugar

AMERICAN
2 cups flour
½ cup cornstarch
½ cup custard powder
1 cup butter
½ cup superfine sugar

Sift together the flour, cornflour (cornstarch) and custard powder. Cream the butter and sugar together until the mixture is pale and fluffy. Blend in the sifted ingredients a tablespoon at a time. Knead the mixture together.

Divide the mixture in half and place each piece in a Swiss (jelly) roll tin. 17.5 by 27.5 (7 by 11 in.). Roll or press each piece out with the flat of your hand. Prick well with a fork. Chill for 15 minutes.

Bake the shortbread in a warm oven, 170°C, 325°F, Gas Mark 3, for 35 minutes or until pale golden brown. Sprinkle with sugar. Cool for a few minutes, then mark each shortbread into 12 fingers. Cool in the tins for 30 minutes, then transfer to a wire rack to cool completely.

To freeze: wrap in foil, label and freeze.

To thaw and serve: leave to thaw at room temperature for 2 to 3 hours.

Makes 24 shortbread fingers.

— Dutch Crisp Biscuits (Cookies) —

METRIC/IMPERIAL
12½ g./½ oz. custard powder
150 g./6 oz. flour
125 g./5 oz. butter
75 g./3 oz. caster sugar
1 egg yolk

Sift together the custard powder and flour. Cream the butter and sugar together until the mixture is pale and fluffy. Beat in the egg yolk and stir in the flour mixture. Put into a piping bag fitted with a large rose nozzle. Pipe the mixture on to a greased baking sheet in three zig-zag patterns about 4.5 cm. (1¾ in.) wide and 25 cm. (10 in.) long. Chill for 30 minutes.

Bake in a moderate oven, 180°C, 350°F, Gas Mark 4, for 15 to 20 minutes or until pale golden brown at the edges. While still warm cut each zig-zag into six pieces. Leave to cool on a wire rack.
To freeze: wrap in foil, label and freeze.
To thaw and serve: unwrap and leave to thaw at room temperature for 30 minutes.

Makes 18 biscuits (cookies).

AMERICAN
2 tablespoons custard powder
1½ cups flour
⅝ cup butter
⅜ cup superfine sugar
1 egg yolk

— Macaroons —

METRIC/IMPERIAL
whites of 2 large eggs
100 g./4 oz. ground almonds
150 g./6 oz. caster sugar
25 g./1 oz. ground rice
few drops of almond essence
8 blanched almonds, halved

If you cannot get rice paper, use nonstick silicone paper instead. It is ideal for biscuits (cookies) and cakes with a high sugar content like macaroons and meringues, and the paper may be used several times.

Place about 1 teaspoonful of the egg white on one side in a small bowl. Whisk the remaining egg whites until they form soft peaks. Fold in the ground almonds, sugar, ground rice and almond essence (extract). Put heaped teaspoonsful of the mixture on to two baking sheets lined with rice paper (or nonstick silicone paper) and smooth them out with the back of the spoon to form circles. Do not flatten too much. Place half a blanched almond in the centre of each and brush the tops with the reserved egg white.

Bake in a cool oven, 150°C, 300°F, Gas Mark 2, for 25 minutes or until the macaroons are pale golden. Leave to cool slightly before removing from the baking sheets. If rice paper has been used, remove any excess paper from around the edge of the macaroons. Leave to cool completely.
To freeze: place in a polythene (plastic) bag, seal, label and freeze.
To thaw and serve: leave to thaw at room temperature for 30 minutes.

Makes 16 macaroons.

AMERICAN
whites of 2 large eggs
⅔ cup ground almonds
¾ cup superfine sugar
2 tablespoons ground rice
few drops of almond extract
8 blanched almonds, halved

~Ginger Fairings~

METRIC/IMPERIAL
150 g./6 oz. self-raising flour
1 teaspoon ground ginger
pinch of bicarbonate of soda
75 g./3 oz. margarine
75 g./3 oz. caster sugar
1 tablespoon golden syrup

These crisp spicy biscuits (cookies) are best frozen as dough balls and then baked after thawing. If you prefer to bake them before freezing, they will need to thaw for 30 minutes at room temperature.

Sift together the flour, ginger and soda. Put the margarine, sugar and syrup in a saucepan and heat gently until the margarine has melted. Stir in the flour mixture. Shape into 24 small balls.
To freeze: open freeze, then put in a polythene (plastic) bag, seal, label and return to the freezer.
To thaw and serve: unwrap and leave to thaw at room temperature for 1 to 1½ hours. Place on an ungreased baking sheet and press each ball down firmly with a fork. Bake in a moderate oven, 180°C, 350°F, Gas Mark 4, for 12 to 15 minutes or until golden. Leave to cool on a wire rack.

Makes 24 biscuits (cookies).

AMERICAN
1½ cups self-rising flour
1 teaspoon ground ginger
pinch of baking soda
⅜ cup margarine
⅜ cup superfine sugar
1 tablespoon light corn syrup

~Lancashire Lemon Fingers~

METRIC/IMPERIAL
150 g./6 oz. self-raising flour, sifted
150 g./6 oz. caster sugar
150 g./6 oz. butter, softened
2 eggs
grated rind and juice of 1 lemon
100 g./4 oz. granulated sugar

These are so good that unless you make twice this amount they may never get as far as the freezer.

Put the flour, caster (superfine) sugar, butter, eggs and lemon rind in a bowl and beat together until well blended. Spread the mixture in a 30 by 20 cm. (12 by 8 in.) sandwich (layer) cake tin which has been lined with greased greaseproof (waxed) paper. Bake in a moderate oven, 180°C, 350°F, Gas Mark 4, for 15 minutes or until pale golden brown.
Mix together the lemon juice and granulated sugar. Spread over the cake while it is still warm. Leave to cool in the tin, then turn out and cut into 24 fingers.
To freeze: open freeze, then pack in a polythene (plastic) bag, seal, label and return to the freezer.
To thaw and serve: remove from the bag and leave to thaw at room temperature for 45 minutes.

Makes 24 fingers.

AMERICAN
1½ cups self-rising flour, sifted
¾ cup superfine sugar
¾ cup butter, softened
2 eggs
grated rind and juice of 1 lemon
½ cup granulated sugar

~Wholemeal Scones~

METRIC/IMPERIAL
100 g./4 oz. plain flour, sifted
100 g./4 oz. wholemeal flour
1 teaspoon baking powder
50 g./2 oz. butter
125 ml./¼ pint milk

For savoury scones add ½ teaspoon salt and for sweet scones add 2 tablespoons caster (superfine) sugar.

Put the flours, baking powder and salt or sugar into a bowl. Add the butter and cut it into small pieces, then rub it into the flour until the mixture resembles breadcrumbs. Stir in enough milk to make a firm dough.
Roll out the dough on a lightly floured board, then cut into circles about 3.75 cm. (1½ in.) in diameter. Place the circles on a baking sheet and brush with a little milk. Bake in a hot oven, 220°C, 425°F, Gas Mark 7, for 10 to 15 minutes or until the scones are well risen and golden brown. Cool on a wire rack.
To freeze: put in polythene (plastic) bags, seal, label and freeze.
To thaw and serve: remove from the bags and reheat in a moderate oven, 180°C, 350°F, Gas Mark 4 for 15 minutes. Serve split and buttered.

Makes about 15 scones.

AMERICAN
1 cup all-purpose flour, sifted
1 cup wholewheat flour
1 teaspoon baking powder
¼ cup butter
⅝ cup milk

— Drop Scones —

METRIC/IMPERIAL
200 g./8 oz. flour
pinch of salt
2 tablespoons caster sugar
1 teaspoon bicarbonate of
   soda
1½ teaspoons cream of tartar
1 egg
milk to mix
lard for frying

Sift the flour, salt, sugar, soda and cream of tartar into a bowl.
Make a well in the centre and add the egg. Beat well to a smooth
batter, adding enough milk to give the consistency of thick cream.
To freeze: pour into a rigid container, seal, label and freeze.
Use within 3 months.
To thaw and serve: leave to thaw overnight in the refrigerator or for
4 hours at room temperature. Whisk, leave to stand for 30 minutes
and whisk again.

   Lightly grease a hot frying-pan or griddle with a little lard. Drop
tablespoonsful of the batter on to the hot pan and cook until
bubbles appear on the surface. Turn the scones over and cook the
other sides until set. Remove from the pan and place on a towel.
Cover and make the remaining scones in the same way. Serve
thickly buttered.

Makes 30 to 35 scones.

AMERICAN
2 cups flour
pinch of salt
2 tablespoons superfine
   sugar
1 teaspoon baking soda
1½ teaspoons cream of tartar
1 egg
milk to mix
lard for frying

— Wheatmeal Bread —

METRIC/IMPERIAL
375 ml./¾ pint water,
   hand-hot
3 teaspoons sugar
12½ g./½ oz. dried yeast
300 g./12 oz. strong plain
   flour, sifted
300 g./12 oz. wholewheat
   flour
2 to 3 teaspoons salt
1 tablespoon salad oil
cracked wheat

Put the water and 1 teaspoon sugar in a small bowl and sprinkle
over the yeast. Leave in a warm place for about 10 minutes or until
the mixture has become frothy.

   Put all the remaining ingredients, except the cracked wheat, in a
bowl and add the yeast mixture. Mix with a fork, then knead until
smooth and no longer sticky. This will take about 10 minutes.

   Put the dough in an oiled polythene (plastic) bag and leave to
rise until doubled in bulk. This will take about 1 hour at room
temperature and overnight in the refrigerator. Knead the dough
back to its original bulk. Divide the dough in half.

   Shape one half into a ball and place it in a well-greased and
pre-baked 12.5 cm. (5 in.) diameter flower pot. (Do not use a plastic
flower pot.) Shape the second piece of dough into a loaf and put
on a baking sheet or in a ½ kg. (1 lb.) loaf tin.

   Cover with an oiled polythene (plastic) bag and put to rise in a
warm place until doubled in bulk or the dough has risen to the top of
the tin. Remove the bag. Brush the tops of the loaves with a little
salted water and sprinkle with the cracked wheat.

   Bake in a very hot oven, 230°C, 450°F, Gas Mark 8, for 30 to
40 minutes or until the loaves are evenly browned and sound
hollow when tapped on the bottom. Leave to cool on a wire rack.
To freeze: wrap in a double thickness of foil or in a polythene
(plastic) bag, seal, label and freeze. If bread is likely to be required
quickly, always wrap it in foil so that it can be placed frozen in the
oven to thaw and refresh. Use within 6 to 8 weeks.
To thaw and serve: leave to thaw for 3 to 4 hours at room
temperature or overnight in the refrigerator. Or place frozen,
wrapped in foil, in a moderately hot oven, 200°C, 400°F, Gas Mark
5, and heat for 45 minutes.

Makes 2 loaves.

AMERICAN
2 cups water, hand-hot
3 teaspoons sugar
½ oz. dried yeast
3 cups strong all-purpose
   flour, sifted
3 cups wholewheat flour
2 to 3 teaspoons salt
1 tablespoon salad oil
cracked wheat

—Seville Orange and Apricot Marmalade—

METRIC/IMPERIAL
½ kg./1¼ lb. frozen Seville
  oranges
1 l./2 pints water
1 × 375 g./15 oz. can apricots
juice of 1 large lemon
1 kg./2½ lb. sugar

Put the oranges in a large pan with the water. Bring to the boil, cover and simmer gently for about 2 hours or until the skin of the oranges is tender. Test by piercing the skin with a pin – if it goes in easily the oranges are ready.

Lift out the fruit, cut in half and remove the pips. Put the pips in a piece of muslin (cheesecloth) and tie to form a bag. Slice the oranges and return to the pan with the bag of pips. Bring to the boil and boil rapidly, uncovered, until the liquid has reduced by about one-third. Discard the bag of pips.

Chop the apricots and add to the pan with the apricot juice, lemon juice and sugar. Stir to dissolve the sugar, then boil rapidly for about 15 minutes or until setting point is reached (110°C, 220°F on a sugar thermometer). Test by spooning a small amount on to a saucer; when cool the skin that forms will wrinkle when pushed with a finger.

Pour into hot, clean, dry jars. Cover and label.

Makes about 2 kg. (4½ lb.).

AMERICAN
1¼ lb. frozen Seville oranges
5 cups water
1 × 15 oz. can apricots
juice of 1 large lemon
2½ lb. (5 cups) sugar

A note on measurements

Where terms differ for different countries, the British term is followed by the equivalent in parentheses. For example: courgettes (zucchini).

All recipe ingredients are given in two columns, one for Metric/Imperial weight conversions and the other for American cup and spoon measures. In the information text, the Metric measurement is followed by the Imperial conversion and then the American equivalent. For example: 2 l. (4 pints) or 5 pints indicates 2 Metric litres, 4 Imperial pints, 5 American pints. Where a cup is referred to it is an American cup.

— Index —

Acknowledgments   All photographs are by Melvin Grey. Food prepared for photography by Shirley Nightingale.
Drawings on pages 1, 4, 5, 6, 17, 23, 31, 51, 55, 71, 105, 113, 118, 145 are by Linda Flower. All other drawings are by Mary Tomlin.
We would like to thank Elizabeth David for the use of the soup tureen in the photograph on the jacket; Gered for the china on pages 3, 99 and 129; and David Mellor for ovenware featured on pages 72, 73, 106 and 110.